"Fast food was offered to Black Americans as the solution for a variety of social ills—but the history that [Marcia] Chatelain lays out proves that it could never fully rise to that task."   —Camille Squires, *Mother Jones*

"A book of big, sweeping ideas that goes far in portraying fast-food restaurants as yet another burden on black America. . . . The book's examination of McDonald's marketing efforts offers an illuminating look at the fraught interplay between corporations and civil rights leaders during that era."
—Michael A. Fletcher, *Washington Post*

"This isn't just a story of exploitation or, conversely, empowerment; it's a cautionary tale about relying on the private sector to provide what the public needs, and how promises of real economic development invariably come up short. . . . [Marcia Chatelain's] sense of perspective gives this important book an empathetic core as well as analytical breadth, as she draws a crucial distinction between individual actors, who often get subjected to so much scrutiny and second-guessing, and larger systems, which rarely get subjected to enough."   —Jennifer Szalai, *New York Times*

"One of my strongest takeaways [from *Franchise*] is that the very paradigms of 'choice' and individual responsibility in how we eat are just as flawed as those ideas are in other arenas, like reproductive rights. You don't make the decision to eat that hamburger—or to have fast food every day—in isolation."
—Cynthia Greenlee, *Vox*

"As I learned recently from Marcia Chatelain's new book, *Franchise: The Golden Arches in Black America*, the preponderance of Golden Arches in locations like my poor, redlined, black neighborhood was hardly some accident. Chatelain . . . outlines a forgotten history of the fast-food behemoth's rapid expansion into black America in the post-civil rights world."
—Gene Demby, NPR's *Code Switch*

"Terrific . . . incredibly timely."
—Jason Kelly, *Bloomberg Businessweek* podcast

"[A] stellar, deeply researched new book. . . . I will never look at McDonald's in the same way after reading *Franchise*."   —Patrick J. Sauer, *Marker*

ALSO BY MARCIA CHATELAIN

South Side Girls:
Growing Up in the Great Migration

Franchise

The Golden Arches in Black America

MARCIA CHATELAIN

LIVERIGHT PUBLISHING CORPORATION
A Division of W. W. Norton & Company
Independent Publishers Since 1923

For information about permission to reproduce selections from this book,
write to Permissions, Liveright Publishing Corporation, a division of
W. W. Norton & Company, Inc., 500 Fifth Avenue, New York, NY 10110

For information about special discounts for bulk purchases, please contact
W. W. Norton Special Sales at specialsales@wwnorton.com or 800-233-4830

Manufacturing by LSC Communications, Harrisonburg
Book design by JAMdesign
Production manager: Julia Druskin

The Library of Congress has cataloged a previous edition as follows:

Names: Chatelain, Marcia, 1979– author.
Title: Franchise : the golden arches in black America / Marcia Chatelain.
Description: First Edition. | New York : Liveright Publishing Corporation, 2020. | Includes
bibliographical references and index.
Identifiers: LCCN 2019030794 | ISBN 9781631493942 (hardcover) |
ISBN 9781631493959 (epub)
Subjects: LCSH: Fast food restaurants—United States. | Franchises (Retail trade)—United
States. | McDonald's Corporation. | Business enterprises—Purchasing—United States. |
African Americans—Civil rights. | Race discrimination—United States. |
African Americans—Economic conditions.
Classification: LCC TX945.3 .C46 2020 | DDC 338.70973—dc23
LC record available at https://lccn.loc.gov/2019030794

ISBN 978-1-63149-870-1 pbk.

Liveright Publishing Corporation, 500 Fifth Avenue, New York, N.Y. 10110
www.wwnorton.com

W. W. Norton & Company Ltd., 15 Carlisle Street, London W1D 3BS

2 3 4 5 6 7 8 9 0

For Mark Yapelli and his mother, Elaine Desow Yapelli

CONTENTS

PREFACE TO THE PAPERBACK EDITION

Black and so excellent,
Black and so excellent
Melanated, we shine, SHINE
So excellent and divine, DIVINE
And yea we golden, golden, golden, WE GOLDEN

In the spring of 2019, McDonald's commissioned performing artist Moses Stone to write an anthem celebrating the launch of its "Black and Positively Golden" campaign, its first major advertising drive in nearly twenty years intended to appeal to African Americans. As part of the campaign, McDonald's held a star-studded event at a South Los Angeles YWCA to fete their black customers in twenty-first century style. The McRig, McDonald's version of a food truck, supplied partygoers with their favorite menu items. Revelers were encouraged to follow the campaign's Instagram account, @wearegolden. The event highlighted a new program of sponsored entrepreneurship classes for women in select markets. In a press release announcing the multimillion dollar campaign, McDonald's called Black and Positively Golden a "movement designed to uplift communities and shine a brilliant light on Black excellence through empowerment, entrepreneurship and education."[1] A little more than a year after the debut of Black and Positively Golden, McDonald's would find itself contending with a much more powerful and critical movement than the fight to sell more hamburgers—the Black Lives Matter Movement.

In the late spring and summer of 2020—while the nation was in the grips of a global pandemic that forced many to stay inside their homes—activists, clergy, and everyday people took to the streets and launched a wave of direct action protest in all fifty states. After bystanders and body cameras captured a series of killings of African Americans by police, most notably of George Floyd in Minneapolis, urgent calls for justice eclipsed news coverage of the novel coronavirus and its devastating impacts on health and wealth in America and around the world. Protests, property damage, and confrontations with police dominated headlines and broadcasts. Almost immediately, corporations and institutions that were silent when the BLM emerged in 2013 determined that, this time, they supported and stood in solidarity with the marchers.

In a statement that struck a much different chord than Stone's gilded rhymes that declared blacks "came a long way, now we on top," McDonald's posted a simple video with no music, just a series of words appearing in a muted gold, red, and black palette, to its social media channels. The announcement began with a litany of the slain: Trayvon Martin. Michael Brown. Alton Sterling. Botham Jean. Atatiana Jefferson. Ahmaud Arbery. George Floyd. The video assured viewers that black people are seen by McDonald's, whether they are "customers," "crew members," or "franchisees," and explained that the company would be making donations to the National Urban League and the NAACP. The video concluded: "Black lives matter."

Other fast food companies took to social media to share their messages of support as well. Burger King offered that "when it comes to people's lives, there's only one way to have it. without discrimination." Popeyes revised an original statement that the chicken chain was "nothing without Black lives," proclaiming, on their second try, that they intended to use their "platform to support this movement." Wendy's acknowledged that "a lot people are hurting because of blatant racism," nine days before Atlanta police officers killed 27-year-old Rayshard Brooks outside one of its franchises. The next day, arsonists torched it.

The fast food industry, for the most part, has previously avoided wading into racial politics. But McDonald's has been down this road before. Since its first foray into black communities in 1968, that famous year of racial protests and uprisings, McDonald's has played a complex, if largely unknown, role in both helping and holding back progress in black America. In McDonald's own telling, the company was at the vanguard of progressive business action after Martin Luther King Jr.'s assassination, and it was an ally during the spring when Los Angeles was ablaze after the police officers who beat Rodney King were acquitted in 1992. The truth is less rosy. In the first half of 2020— when its black employees risked their lives to go to work amid the pandemic, and by which point the number of black franchisees had declined by a third since 2008—McDonald's was continuing a long tradition of obscuring its complicated relationship to black America. As it had so many times before, it said the right words, but took little action.

From the moment that black America was forced to pursue Martin Luther King Jr.'s beloved community without him, to the struggle to make black lives matter, the Golden Arches has been part of the story of race in this country, in ways that go far beyond corporate advertising campaigns or statements. As this book strives to show, McDonald's has helped determine—for better and for worse—where we live, what we eat, and how we fight for justice.

Marcia Chatelain
June 2020

INTRODUCTION

From Sit-In to Drive-Thru

Police and National Guard forces swarmed the McDonald's on Florissant Avenue in Ferguson, Missouri, about one week after police officer Darren Wilson killed Michael Brown, an unarmed teenager, on August 9, 2014. Photo by Scott Olson / Getty Images.

"Hands up . . ."

"Don't shoot!"

Across the streets of Ferguson, Missouri, protesters and mourners shouted the call-and-response dirge in memory of Michael Brown Jr. On August 9, 2014, police officer Darren Wilson shot and killed the teenager while he was walking through an apartment complex with a friend. After six of Wilson's bullets struck the recent high school graduate, his body remained uncollected and uncovered for nearly four hours. Residents captured the morbid scene—with their cellphones and their memories—and shared them across social media. Brown's death and all it represented—police violence and disregard, racism, and poverty—catalyzed the nascent Movement for Black Lives and sparked a global conversation about American justice. By the next evening, seasoned and first-time protesters joined Ferguson residents on the town's main drag, Florissant Avenue. Some carried signs demanding JUSTICE FOR MICHAEL BROWN! Others linked arms with clergy members, belting out civil-rights-era freedom songs. Savvy political leaders and grief-stricken family members sat for interviews with the reporters who traveled to Missouri searching for new angles on the story. A small group of provocateurs brought Molotov cocktails, glass bottles, and matches to the streets. All of these people were met by local and county police, and later the Missouri National Guard, armed with tear gas, rubber bullets, and tanks. The gear was courtesy of the U.S. Department of Defense's 1033 Program, which outfits domestic police forces with weapons unused in Afghanistan and Iraq.[1]

For weeks, traditional news outlets and amateur digital storytellers broadcast updates on the uprising that disrupted life in the town of 21,000. Ferguson's landmarks became familiar scenes for the millions who followed the crisis on their televisions and smartphones. Newscasters appeared live in front of the QuikTrip gas station that was burned down the day after Brown's death. Facebook and Twitter curated the images of makeshift memorials to Brown in the center and on the edges of Canfield Road where he died. But, of all the places that represented Ferguson in the public eye that summer, the McDonald's restaurant at 9131 West Florissant best symbolized the interplay between racial justice and the marketplace in America, past and present.[2]

The Florissant Avenue McDonald's was both an escape from the uprising and one of its targets. On some days, the McDonald's was a beacon. Reporters found live electrical outlets to charge their computers and Wi-Fi to send emails to their editors. Demonstrators took breaks from marching and ordered cold drinks as the daytime temperature hovered around 80 degrees. Police officers, overheated by their uniforms of domestic war, found air-conditioned relief as they awaited shift changes. In the parking lot, television camera crews arranged tripods. Organizers distributed leaflets. At the counter, cashiers managed their regular duties while also attending to an increase in requests for bottles of milk, used to relieve the sting from the chemicals launched into the late summer sky. The manager kept a television tuned to the news and watched alongside patrons when President Barack Obama addressed the nation about "the passions and the anger" that had been ignited in Ferguson. The McDonald's was a center of that passion and anger too. One night, two journalists were arrested for trespassing after they questioned why they were being asked to leave an ostensibly open restaurant.[3] On the night of August 17, a crowd broke the front window of the McDonald's; some say they were fleeing another tear gas attack and needed more milk. Others wrote them off as looters. Eventually, calm was restored in Ferguson, and in the recap of what happened in the St. Louis exurb, the Florissant McDonald's was portrayed as a bright spot and an anchor for the community.

The Ferguson moment was not the first time that McDonald's played a major role in a racial crisis. In fact, the Florissant Avenue McDonald's—as a franchise location owned and operated by an African American businessman—is the descendant of a somewhat bizarre but incredibly powerful marriage between a fast-food behemoth and the fight for civil rights. After the assassination of Martin Luther King Jr. in 1968 and the ensuing urban upheavals, the movement for racial justice pivoted its focus toward black business ownership. Hamburger, fried chicken, and taco chains eagerly met the gaze of those interested in using business development as a strategy to quell unrest, and introduced fast-food franchising to inner-city black communities. This book tells the hidden history of the intertwined relationship between the struggle for civil rights and the expansion of the fast-food industry.

The United States is the birthplace of some of the world's most successful fast-food brands, as well as the home of its most enthusiastic eaters. On any given day, an estimated one-third of all American adults is eating something at a fast-food restaurant.[4] Millions of people start their mornings with paper-wrapped English muffin breakfast sandwiches, order burritos hastily secured in foil

for lunch, and end their evenings with extravalue dinners consumed in cars. People of all ages and backgrounds enjoy fast food,
but it does not mean the same thing to all people. For African
Americans, the history of the development of the fast-food industry and its presence in their communities reveals the complicated
ways that race is lived in America. Racism constrains choices and
limits opportunities, from how much you earn to how long you
live. Race also informs where you can sit comfortably and what
foods are available to you. Even after segregation was legally dis-
solved by the Civil Rights Act of 1964, African Americans were
still left with a low ceiling hovering over their social and economic
mobility. The restrictions that emerge because of race and class
would place African Americans in a close relationship with an
industry built on the idea that food could be delivered cheaply,
uniformly, and without consideration of a person's social station.
Fast food is a prism for understanding race, shifts in the movement for civil rights, the dissemination of black culture, and racial
capitalism—the deep connections between the development of
modern capitalism and racist subjugation and oppression—since
the 1960s.[5] Before fast food became a quotidian fixture of American life in shopping malls, schools, airports, and rest stops, it was
an object of curiosity, fascination, and even hope for many black
communities.

Today, fast-food restaurants are hyperconcentrated in the places
that are the poorest and most racially segregated.[6] Due to its saturation in black America, fast food is often identified as the culprit
among the research on high rates of obesity, diabetes, and hyper-
tension among blacks. Since the early 2000s, studies have focused
on the relationship between access to healthy foods and the nutrition color line. Researchers have warned that a black child born in
the year 2000 has a 53% chance of developing type 2 diabetes; the
likelihood of a white child developing the potentially fatal disease
is less than 30%.[7] In 2015, nearly 75% of African-American adults
and 33% of black adolescents were considered overweight or obese.
Blacks were 1.4 times more likely than their white counterparts to

be obese.[8] Economic inequality exacerbates health inequality, and poor and working-class black families often lack access to quality preventative health care. In the year that Ferguson entered the national consciousness, the average white family had the equivalent of one month's income in liquid savings, while a black family could rely on only five days of pay.[9]

In addition to the well-circulated results of health studies, scrutiny of the fast-food industry has come from journalists, documentarians, and even customers. The publication of Eric Schlosser's *Fast Food Nation: The Dark Side of the All-American Meal* in 2001 and the release of the Academy Award–nominated documentary *Super Size Me* four years later helped raise awareness about the fast food industry's impact on the health of people of color.[10] In 2002, two teenagers from the Bronx filed a lawsuit against McDonald's for causing their obesity and diabetes. By 2010, when former First Lady Michelle Obama introduced her Let's Move! initiative to promote improved child nutrition and healthier school lunches, the nation was well versed in the vocabulary of healthy eating: "whole grains," "low fat," and "organic." Racialized health disparities—as well as the dearth of grocery stores in poor communities of color—have inspired a food justice and nutrition education movement. Farmers' markets now occupy empty city lots. Nutritionists visit inner-city schools to teach children the difference between mustard greens and kale. Public service announcements interrupt family-friendly television programs to remind parents to encourage good eating habits at home. The message is clear, but the problems persist.

While health warriors laudably fight an army of trans fats, kids' meals, and splashy advertisements, few have considered how exactly fast food became a staple of black diets. Many of the critiques and responses to the impact of fast food on communities of color focus solely on food and not the infrastructure that surrounds food systems. In a response to the failed lawsuit filed by the Bronx teenagers, the *New York Times* editorial page rehearsed an argument that is often expressed in conversations about race and health. "That Americans are getting heavier is especially hard to deny the day after Thanksgiving. But America's weight problem has less to do with holiday binges than with everyday choices and circumstances. That's especially true for children, who are gaining weight in epidemic numbers, particularly in minority communities." The editorial concluded that while more data on child obesity are needed, for the time being, children should be encouraged to become more physically active. "In many low-income minority neighborhoods, fried carryout is a cinch to find, but affordable fresh produce and nutritious food are not. Those same neighborhoods often lack many safe public places to play and exercise."[11] At best, these kinds of reflections are simply shortsighted and affirm what we already know about the importance of healthy food and exercise for all people. Unfortunately, this type of analysis ignores history. It presupposes that people of color have a natural affinity for fast food. What are the "everyday choices and circumstances" for black Americans? Why is "fried carryout" so easy to get? Why is "fresh produce" a rarity? What failures have created cities with few "safe public places to play and exercise"? Instead of simply evaluating the fact that so many African Americans patronize fast food today, it is far more instructive to consider what has undergirded the symbiotic relationship between African-American communities and the fast food industry.[12]

For too long, research on race and fast food has placed the onus solely on black palates and parents for the dismal state of black health. Without an understanding of how we got here, the food justice movement will never move beyond the idea of individual choice and continue to ignore structural disequilibrium. Knowing the caloric content and fat grams in a cheeseburger from Krystal is important. Educating the public on how much of the recommended daily allowance of sodium is exceeded by an order of Burger King onion rings is helpful. Promoting healthy lifestyles can improve lives. But understanding how shifts in the priorities of the mid-century civil rights struggle, changes in federal policy on business and urban development, and the boom years of fast food converged in the lives of black America is equally critical.

* * *

Fast food restaurants were, and are, able to expand quickly because of the franchising model, which draws upon an old business practice and adapts it for a modern world. Most business scholars believe that the roots of franchising can be traced to the Catholic Church in the Middle Ages, when tax collectors were allowed to keep a portion of revenues retrieved from citizens. Fast forward several hundred years to the late nineteenth century, when the current practice of franchising began with Coca-Cola. First made in 1888, Coca-Cola (the franchisor) licensed businesses (franchisees) to mix, bottle, and sell their refreshing sugary beverage in drugstores, and later restaurants, across the country. Environmental historian Bart Elmore has called this method Coca-Cola capitalism, in which a company relies on a massive "outsourcing strategy to build a mass marketing giant." This form of commercial development allows corporations to pass on their liabilities to third-party suppliers, franchisees, and to some degree, local governments. Cities eager to attract businesses subsidize business growth through the preparation of land, by providing increased policing, and by offering tax breaks.[13] Franchising is big business in America because it may be the most American idea in the world. An individual with no formal training or education can become a business owner— maybe even a millionaire—with only an owner's manual and sheer will. Franchising was the channel for converting a couple of ice-cream parlors or a few hot dog outfits into multibillion-dollar businesses, with the power to influence supply chains, workers' wages, and global tastes.[14]

The fast food family tree reads like the book of Genesis, with businesses begetting other businesses in rapid succession. Although not the oldest member of the family, McDonald's looms as an ambitious offspring who managed to outpace and outshine its elders. Fast food's mainstay, the hamburger, was once considered a low-quality food product designed to nourish workers and the poor. Cash-strapped laborers could purchase these sandwiches from carts and stands in urban centers, near work sites and bustling downtowns. White Castle helped popularize, and perhaps dignify, the burger with signature "thin, one-inch-square patties," which came to be known as sliders.[15] In the pioneering era of fast food, corporate marriages reconfigured the blood lines that fueled the franchise race. In 1919, Lodi, California's A&W root beer entered the beverage franchising game, alongside Coca-Cola, and would later try its hand at burgers and other fare.[16] The partnership of Allen and Wright—the A and the W—inspired one of their franchisees, J. Willard Marriott, to strike out on his own and establish a national hotel chain.

Burgers paved the way for the expansion of other brands that started in small towns before setting up shop along highway exits or in newly built suburban plazas. The first national burger chain, Billy Ingram and Walt Anderson's White Castle—inspired by Chicago's iconic Water Tower building—was established in 1921. White Castle innovated many of the practices that would be revolutionized by McDonald's, including streamlining and centralizing their supplies in warehouses, creating assembly-line consistency across its locations, and defending its corporate identity. White Castle's commercial success and ability to convert a public once suspicious of ground beef into fans of the slider inspired copycats, including White Tower and Royal Castle. Royal Castle—an evil twin in the franchising origin story—eventually surpassed White Castle in numbers of location. White Castle is still with us today—and many iconic brands are protected—because of their pursuit of their imitators in court. The outcome of a 1937 Supreme Court case determined that White Tower couldn't copy the design, color scheme, and style of White Castle's offerings. They were also told they couldn't use the derivative slogan "Take Home a Bagful," as long as White Castle urged its customers to "Buy 'Em by the Sack."[17]

Royal Castle was later absorbed by a fried chicken concern promoted by performer Minnie Pearl and gospel standout Mahalia Jackson. Minnie Pearl's and Mahalia Jackson's Glori-Fried formed after their founders took note of the immense popularity of Kentucky Fried Chicken, established when Harland Sanders visited

Pete and Arline Harman in Utah; their bestselling chicken was "made Southern" in Louisville, Kentucky, with a move in 1954. Dave Thomas, an Army veteran in Ohio, worked for the real Colonel Sanders, before he joined two endeavors that were once eponymous and are now largely forgotten, Arthur Treacher's Fish & Chips and Burger Chef.[18] He finally found his stride with his own burger franchise, Wendy's, named for his daughter. In 1954, Ray Kroc entered business with Maurice and Richard McDonald, and he built the foundations of the world's most powerful burger. Glen Bell and Neal Baker, founders of Taco Bell, like the McDonald brothers, were from San Bernardino and turned to their interpretation of Mexican food after a failed attempt to compete with the McDonalds' burgers. Glen's Taco Bell begot Del Taco, which was opened by Ed Hackbarth, a former Taco Bell employee who loved eating at the original San Bernardino McDonald's location.[19] El Pollo Loco was later adopted by the Denny's family, and it produced a child that was one of the first nonfried chicken outlets in the country.[20]

West of San Bernardino, Harry and Esther Snyder sold their hamburgers and French fries in the town of Baldwin Park to workers, and they assured customers they could "get in and get out" quickly. The Snyders established In-N-Out Burger in 1948. They were encouraged to enter the business by their friends Carl and Margaret Karcher. The Karchers turned the hot dog stands they started in 1941 into a barbecue enterprise in 1945, which began offering hamburgers a year later. The family's Carl's Jr. international franchise would always share a special bond with the geographically bound In-N-Out, which never became a franchise.[21]

The founding generation worked hard, made wise decisions, and made the most of every opportunity. For many of the first families of fast food franchising, they were connected not only by place (many of them were Southern Californians), but they were also racially homogenous and privileged in their time. The people who established the franchises that are so easily identified by their logos, their slogans, and the distinct taste of their French fries over a competitors' were all white Americans whose whiteness worked in their favor. They were able to benefit from a host of financial and social pathways for their businesses to start, expand, rebound from setbacks, and remain within their family networks. Shortly after the federal government declared that their establishments would not be allowed to refuse customers on the basis of race in 1964, their progeny—the franchises—would slowly accept non-white members.

The relationship between franchisor and franchisee is like a distorted parent and child bond, in which the parent sets the rules and the child pays all the household bills. At its heart, franchising is based on expectations set by a parent company (Subway, Hilton Worldwide Holdings Inc., Roto-Rooter Plumbing and Water Cleanup) and an individual entity (Jane Doe, Bob Smith, Doe-Smith Enterprises) to operate an outlet of said business. Franchises do the same thing in different places; they yield fortunes birthed from uniformity. A Dunkin' Donuts store in Rhode Island and Illinois should have the same menu, save a few regional specificities (like the copious packets of sugar and half-and-half that Ocean Staters like in their "regular coffees"). The uniforms at the Chick-fil-A in Oklahoma City are the same ones worn in Manhattan, although the workers wearing the signature red-and-black ensembles most likely earn different wages. Save Alaska and Hawaii, you should be able to get nearly identical deals on Little Caesars pizza in Las Vegas as you would on Long Island. The success of the fast food franchise model has inspired other retail and service categories. Franchise newcomers like boutique exercise studios Orangetheory Fitness and SoulCycle, and speedy beauty service providers Drybar and Massage Envy, may have little in common with their chicken-frying franchise cousins. But they can be just as costly to invest in, requiring fees up to a million dollars or more, and they are governed by the same laws and regulations.

Franchisees can make good money, but the franchising system requires skill at navigating an unequal power relationship. After fees are paid—ranging from tens of thousands to millions of dollars—and documents are signed stating that a franchisee will do business in the ways that the headquarters have determined—

the dream can begin.[22] Jane and Bob must be prepared to assume the liabilities and risks of business ownership that the corporate heads of Taco Bueno in Farmers Branch, Texas, or Domino's in Ann Arbor Charter Township, Michigan, never have to consider. Jane and Bob deal with it all. They have to file a police report after a robbery during the lunchtime rush. They have to determine when to close if a hurricane is coming and then clean up after it hits. They need to know how to respond to upticks in the cost of flour, which leads to hamburger buns cutting deeper into the bottom line. If Jane and Bob are people of color, they are more likely to do business in a community with higher insurance costs or receive less attention from the parent company, despite earning the most profits in their chain's system.

*　*　*

Among the brands that have emerged in the fast food franchise world, none has eclipsed McDonald's in influence. With more than 14,000 restaurants in the United States, and another 23,000 locations in 100 countries, McDonald's has affected the ways Americans eat, play, and work. Journalists, business historians, economists, and cultural critics have all investigated and written about the chain, which was established as a franchise company in 1955. Yet, despite the wide body of Golden Arches scholarship, few acknowledge, let alone analyze, the way that McDonald's ingratiated itself to black America, and the ways that black America has been integral in McDonald's many feats. Due to its age, size, and footprint, McDonald's looms large in this history of fast food and race in America, and other fast food chains followed McDonald's path as they identified and cultivated a black consumer market and franchisee corps.

The roots of the contemporary conversation about race and fast food begin with the founding of McDonald's in the 1940s. When Maurice and Richard McDonald established their hamburger drive-in, they may have been unconcerned with the racial politics of their age. Yet segregation, racial restrictions on housing, discriminatory financial lending, and the growth of a highway system that decimated African-American communities allowed the men all the advantages necessary to establish a formidable business. The original McDonald's was able to survive through World War II and thrive in the postwar economic boom. The restaurant's accessible menu coupled with their family-friendly dining experience ensured their marketability and profitability. As the brothers' small business evolved into an industry-defining franchise, McDonald's was also shaping the country's definition of what historian Lizabeth Cohen calls a "consumer republic." Cohen argues that as consumption of goods and services rose in the 1950s, Americans began to see "their nation as the model for the world of a society committed to mass consumption and what were assumed to be its far-reaching benefits." These benefits extended beyond the department store or the local five-and-dime shop. In the consumer republic, Cohen asserts, the marketplace "also dictated most central dimensions of postwar society, including the political economy, as well as the political culture." [23]

African Americans, who were systematically denied citizenship in the consumer republic, used the marketplace to make claims for their rights. Since the dawn of the twentieth century, the National Association for the Advancement of Colored People, the Urban League, the Congress of Racial Equality, and the Southern Christian Leadership Conference all organized mass-movement campaigns to deny businesses their dollars if they operated on a segregated basis or failed to employ members of the communities that supported them. Activists targeted fast food chains, drugstore lunch counters, soda fountains, and diners, in a crusade to end separate but equal dining, especially in the South. Their strategies connected consumer power to citizenship rights and effectively expanded black access to the marketplace. Eventually, the focused and steady activism of great orators, skilled organizers, and the will of everyday people upended segregation. What was to come next? Legally, the state was no longer a party to excluding blacks from the schoolhouse or the snack bar. But equal opportunity and antipoverty legislation, no matter how strongly supported by a president or a Congress, could only do so much. Rather than agitating for more generous social spending or suggesting that elected leaders champion civil and economic rights more vociferously, a cadre of American leaders across the ideological spectrum determined that private business would be the answer to the unfinished business of securing equality for all.

As African-American consumers were gaining rights in the marketplace, the fast food franchise frenzy was underway. *Barron's* reported in the summer of 1969—five years after the federal government banned discrimination in public accommodations—that restaurant franchises rose from a "scant dozen or two in the postwar years to more than 150 by 1967."[24] Two years later, one hundred more franchise businesses were established, from Mr. Rib International to Tennessee Ernie Ford's Steak and Biscuits. An American born in 1945 came into a world with 3,500 fast food outlets; by the time he or she celebrated a thirtieth birthday, there were 44,000 places to pick up lunch on the go, and most of them were franchises.[25] When the sit-in protest—the ultimate symbol of nonviolent resistance to segregation and discrimination—faded out of public view, the march for civil rights changed course. After claiming major legislative victories but witnessing few gains in black economic security, activists sought other avenues to advocacy. Exhausted freedom fighters, who viewed boycotts and pickets as efficacious during the preceding decades, found themselves more and more interested in using the marketplace as a means of securing progress, not just access. As the 1970s approached, they began to run for elective office and to ascend the ranks of the private sector. In their new roles as politicians and business owners, they strategized how to convert their social gains into economic ones. They looked to black business ownership as a viable way forward.[26]

In the 1960s, after a century of protracted growth since the abolition of slavery, Martin Luther King Jr. identified economic justice—not business development—as his fuller, more vivid dream for the nation's future. His death cut short the possibility of a social revolution guided by the needs of the poor, and his absence forced his various successors to search for a strategy to bridge the widening chasm between blacks and whites. The violent and destructive reactions to King's assassination during the period after his death, dubbed the Holy Week Uprising, sparked a number of efforts to respond to the anger and grief of the poor communities that burned. Governors, city councils, and interracial commissions convened to discover what caused uprisings—and what would future ones. Both discussions tended to converge on the role of business. In report after report, "ghetto businesses" were cited as the reason why poor blacks in urban communities felt overcharged, exploited, and demeaned while shopping. Part of the answer would be a sort of Marshall Plan for black America; a cluster of programs that ensured an infusion of capital for small business development, the opening of new job-training centers, and assistance for youth who did not complete high school. These efforts concentrated on keeping black dollars within black communities and, more important, incorporating black business ownership into the federally funded list of solutions to an array of issues from poverty to marketplace discrimination to emotional despair. In the post-King years, businesses would not simply be targets of protest, they would become the vehicles for the economic prosperity that President Lyndon Johnson's War on Poverty could never deliver.[27]

The disparate ideas and earmarks for building black America after the King uprising all fit under the capacious umbrella of black capitalism. The notion that black liberation can come through black control of the means of production and access to consumption was not created in the late 1960s. Since the late nineteenth century, African-American business clubs, churches, and mutual aid societies have preached that blacks were wise to establish their own economic centers, if only to avoid the indignities of Jim Crow or as a way of proving their suitability to vote and participate in the larger democracy. Regardless of the motivations surrounding the endorsement of black capitalism, the concept enjoyed a revival in the late 1960s and 1970s, as the discourse of social welfare as a response to racism quieted. The new mandate toward marketplace solutions reasoned that capitalism could loosen the grip that racism had over the quality of black life.[28]

Black capitalism united seemingly incongruent organizations and people. President Richard Nixon, who perfected racial dog whistles and oversaw the covert destruction of Black Power organizations, was black capitalism's goodwill ambassador and benefactor. In lieu of supporting critical civil rights protections for fair housing and school desegregation, Nixon promoted legislation that provided business loans, economic development grants, and affirmative action provisions on federally contracted projects as a means of suppressing black rage and securing black endorsements.[29] From former civil rights activist Floyd McKissick to soul singer James Brown and football star Jim Brown, Nixon formed alliances with black notables who all agreed with him: more capitalism would mean less unrest in a nation divided by not only racism, but also war abroad and the demands of domestic feminism, economic justice, and environmental movements.[30]

With so much growth in the franchise sector, the federal government encouraged this type of venture for first-time business owners. Feds promoted franchising to budding black entrepreneurs who wanted to help revitalize neighborhoods ravaged by economic decline and the domestic rebellions of the 1960s that destroyed parts of Watts, Chicago, and Newark. Beginning with Nixon's support for black capitalism, the federal government would prop up and underwrite the expansion of fast food restaurants in black communities for decades. Regardless of political affiliation, the White House, through the Small Business Administration, would be a loyal partner in bringing fast food to black America.[31] This constellation of plans—coupled with the dizzying growth of the franchise—paved the way for the first black franchisees to enter into the thoroughfares of hollowed-out and burned-up black America. Equipped with federal loans and personal commitments to the urban centers in which they would open their little piece of hope, the franchise pioneers believed that business would save the day and the days to come for their people.

Shortly after the first African American took possession of his own franchise, the fast food restaurant—a symbol of American dependence on cheap mass-produced sustenance for economic efficiency—became a focal point of organized efforts to ride the wave of black capitalism. African Americans have never had an easy time breaking the color barrier in their respective fields, and franchising was no different. Herman Petty, the first African American to franchise a McDonald's restaurant, acquired the keys to a restaurant in one of the many Chicago neighborhoods shaken by the King uprising. Petty relied on a mix of franchise training and street smarts to turn around the location, and he went on to not only own additional restaurants, but also helped to establish the National Black McDonald's Operators Association (NBMOA). The NBMOA, formally established by black operators in 1972, was the first black franchise affinity group and soon became the black voice within the McDonald's corporation. As was the case in Petty's early years, the overwhelming majority of black franchisees operate businesses in majority black locations, and as fast food became the predominant retail food option in many communities, NBMOA outperformed their white counterparts. The rapid success of these locations sparked McDonald's and their competitors to concentrate on black diners, recruit more black franchisees, and commit to developing strategies to cultivate this consumer base.

Petty and other NBMOA founders reasoned that their restaurants' popularity was an outgrowth of the deliciousness of McDonald's burgers, as well as the sweet satisfaction found in supporting a black business. In the 1970s, African Americans gained more opportunities to not only buy black, but also vote black. In urban centers, where blacks had delivered electoral change through city councils and city halls, McDonald's entry into black communities was sometimes met with protest. In Cleveland, locals asserted that they should establish the rules of engagement with McDonald's, and they demanded opportunities for local black entrepreneurs to enter franchising because blacks were shoring up unprecedented profits for the corporation. Operation Black Unity (OBU) formed with the explicit purpose of challenging the presence of white franchisees in black communities and compelling the city's first black mayor, Carl Stokes, into action on the issue.

The standoff between residents of Cleveland's predominately black Hough community and McDonald's reveals the way that fast food was redefining the political culture of black consumer activism. While OBU appealed to Stokes, mainstream civil rights groups, and Black Power collectives to make their case against McDonald's, the limits of black capitalism were being exposed. Black franchise ownership could only do so much for a community that experienced overwhelming rates of poverty and unemployment. But the OBU protest forced McDonald's broadly, and black franchisees specifically, to develop practices and protocols for addressing black consumers who were critical of entities that profited so much from people with so little. In the short but quite dramatic saga of black Cleveland and McDonald's, it became clear that black capitalism not only created friendships of convenience among probusiness enthusiasts, but it also could easily tear apart these same comrades when they were forced to agree upon a definition of victory.

McDonald's survived what newspapers were calling a "burger battle" in Cleveland, but it was not done dealing with community resistance. Throughout the 1970s, the fast food industry had to contend with attacks on its business model, its labor policies, growing concern about its impact on the American diet, and its influence on small children. In black communities, the critiques of fast food rested in its poor citizenship practices and its lack of racial authenticity. Grassroots movements against fast food desired different things, but they were all united in their certainty that African Americans were exploited, manipulated, and taken for granted by the industry they supported. The solutions would range from negation to elimination to imitation. In Portland, Oregon, the local chapter of the political organization the Black Panther Party for Self-Defense demanded that their McDonald's be a good neighbor and support the Party's local efforts, especially their Free Breakfast for School Children program. In Atlanta, future Congressman Julian Bond joined a biracial business partnership to open a Dairy Queen franchise in the inner city. He believed that the enterprise would demonstrate the power of black capitalism. Black

Atlantans had little to say about soft serve treats and much to say about whether the business was authentically black. In Philadelphia, a multiracial coalition gathered to stop the building of a new McDonald's restaurant in the Ogontz neighborhood, a racially mixed, working-class neighborhood that held a long history of supporting school desegregation. They linked their concerns about McDonald's in their backyard to their lack of control over commercial development and the city's prioritization of business over social services. Enterprising African Americans noticed these conflicts, and they rightfully sensed that the black consumer market was often united by a desire to purchase from black businesses as an act of racial solidarity and pride. Black celebrities launched a number of "real" black businesses which catered to a desire to keep dollars in black hands and interest in low-cost franchising opportunities that appealed to individuals as well as community groups. Three short-lived celebrity-backed endeavors—Muhammad Ali's ChampBurger, Mahalia Jackson's Glori-Fried Chicken, and James Brown's Gold Platter Restaurants—exemplified this trend. These restaurants used the language of black capitalism to convince blacks that patronizing their respective establishments would be in the best interest of the black community at large. The conditions that imperiled each of these ideas highlight why this form of black wealth building belied its authenticity claims, and their lack of viability further exposed black capitalism's incompatibility with its own goals of black freedom.

Black Power burger joints and soul-styled chicken shacks did not survive the competition to conquer black America's appetite. This did not mean that the leaders of the fast food industry could ignore black customers entirely. After consumer studies and internal reports assured fast food companies that blacks led among their most frequent customers, they enlisted black franchisees, advertisers, and marketing specialists to grow this reliable base. Chicago-based market research firm ViewPoint, Inc., and advertising agency Burrell Communications facilitated this transition. ViewPoint's studies of black preferences for fast food and Burrell's targeted advertising campaigns worked in concert to keep fast food companies abreast of what black America wanted. In the race to capture black hearts and minds through targeted marketing and philanthropy, the fast food industry provided a platform for black culture and taste making. Regional and national advertising campaigns, as well as on-the-ground franchisee engagement, brought black dance, art, and history to audiences inside and outside of restaurants. From high-profile philanthropic partnerships with organizations like the United Negro College Fund and the underwriting of gospel music performances and black literary contests, black franchisees became leaders in their communities. The growth of black franchisee networks and direct appeals to black audiences uncovered the way that fast food satiated a hunger for representation and cultural validation.

By the 1980s, most fast food franchises had settled into the landscape of black and, increasingly, Latino neighborhoods. McDonald's continued to lead the way in developing franchisees of color and establishing trust among black eaters, but these gains were still subject to questions about equity and fairness, both outside and inside the corporation. A legal conflict between Charles Griffis, a black McDonald's franchisee in Los Angeles, and McDonald's headquarters uncovered that even among wealthy black operators, black capitalism only went so far in delivering equal access to profits. The dispute included accusations that McDonald's only assigned black franchisees to unstable neighborhoods that generated high profits, but required high overhead costs. McDonald's viewed Griffis as a faulty franchisee and reiterated a claim they first made in the late 1960s that expansion into the inner city was a socially progressive move. As the two sides argued their positions in the pages of major newspapers, the Los Angeles chapter of the NAACP was trying to mediate the conflict, with attention to how Griffis's grievance could translate into support for its own revamped black capitalism style initiatives. After the collapse of the Nixon administration and a retrenchment in funding for black businesses when Ronald Reagan assumed the Oval Office, the language of black capitalism had lost cachet. But the idea that business could "fix" black America did not perish in the 1980s. The

NAACP and its counterparts, including relative newcomer Operation PUSH (People United to Save Humanity), breathed new life into black capitalism under the guise of Fair Share programs, which settled boycotts and protests with agreements to invest in black America. The agreements required corporations to expand access to franchising contracts, therefore encouraging the introduction of more fast food outlets into already crowded black communities.

The dozens of franchise covenants that were inked and celebrated throughout the 1980s and early 1990s required companies to go beyond their traditional recruitment strategy, in which individuals used life savings and relatively small government loans to take possession of one or two stores at a time. Fair Share goals and timetables brought wealthy African Americans and asset-rich development groups into the fold, and many were granted multiunit, multiterritorial rights to expand into some of the most blighted communities in the country. The fast food industry entrusted its expansion to a number of business entities—some wildly successful, others stunningly reckless. Two black franchisees—Ted Holmes, founder of the now-defunct Chicken George chain, and La-Van Hawkins, a fallen franchise entrepreneur, illustrate the ways that black capitalism underdeveloped black America.

A few years after the Los Angeles NAACP toasted its Fair Share deals with McDonald's, Burger King, and other fast food chains, the organization returned to its core issue from the early twentieth century: racial violence. The acquittal of four police officers for the beating of taxi driver Rodney King ignited the 1992 Los Angeles uprising, which mirrored many of the elements of the response to Martin Luther King's assassination twenty-four years earlier. As was the case after King was slain, much of the postrecovery analysis of South Los Angeles focused on the property damage to businesses and the disaffection of black and brown consumers in neighborhoods where few black or brown people owned businesses. This time was a bit different in that a handful of franchisees of color testified to the power of their business's presence in the community, and they claimed little to no damage during an event that destroyed a billion dollars in property. Their anecdotes helped fuel another round of experimentation with using fast food as a tool of racial justice, and this iteration of federal support was christened black empowerment. Supported by a government's purse of Empowerment Zone programs throughout the 1990s and into the 2000s, fast food was able to more efficiently and economically capitalize on the burned- out lots that had been vacant since 1968, or were leveled in 1992.

The contemporary health crisis among black America—like all of our society's most pressing problems—has a history. By unmasking the process of how fast food "became black," we are able to appreciate the difficult decisions black America has had to make under the stress of racial trauma, political exclusion, and social alienation. This story is about how capitalism can unify cohorts to serve its interests, even as it disassembles communities. By locating the origins of the urban food crisis to the advent of the fast food franchise, we can become more aware of choices—who has them and who creates them. Ultimately, history encourages us to be more compassionate toward individuals navigating few choices, and history cautions us to be far more critical of the institutions and structures that have the power to take choices away.

CHAPTER ONE

Fast Food Civil Rights

After Ray Kroc purchased the McDonald's drive-in concept from founders Richard and Maurice McDonald, he concentrated on recruiting franchisees to open new restaurants in growing suburbs across the United States. Photo by Hulton Archive / Getty Images.

San Bernardino, California's stretch of Route 66 has seen better days.

The former "Mother Road" that connected Chicago to Los Angeles was born in 1926. Route 66 has been memorialized in movies, television, and song. Long since replaced by a network of superhighways, freeways, and toll roads, old Route 66 intersects cities and towns across a 2,448-mile expanse. Some Chambers of Commerce and city councils have allocated funds to ensure their Route 66 historical markers remain clean and old neon road signs illuminated. San Bernardino isn't so fortunate. Many of the indicators of its history as part of the "Main Street of America" have been largely neglected, a victim of the city's economic woes: a deflated housing market, a Chapter 9 bankruptcy in 2012, population loss, and shuttered buildings in the city's central business district. Amid the empty storefronts and vacant houses, one of the remnants of Route 66's golden years draws thousands of visitors to the corner of 14th and E Streets.[1]

On weekends, rental car sedans, motor coaches too large to fit in the parking lot, and muddied motorcycles converge outside of the Original McDonald's Site and Museum, a shrine to mid-century America, fast food, and the route itself. The Site and Museum is carefully named to distinguish it as the first-ever McDonald's, founded by two brothers in 1940. The museum is not affiliated with the behemoth franchise that rewrote its founding story to claim its birthplace as Des Plaines, Illinois, in 1955, after being acquired by franchise pioneer Ray Kroc. Although it is not the official McDonald's Museum sanctioned by the corporate giant based in Chicago, it is no less an overwhelmingly rich tribute to the brand, its founders, and the globalization of all-American tastes and sensibilities.

Local businessman Albert Okura, who created the Southern California rotisserie chicken franchise Juan Pollo in the 1980s, established the museum in 1998. Okura purchased the property from the city after he heard that it was slated for demolition. Okura's love of fast food and his admiration for the industry compelled him to convert the abandoned restaurant and adjoining property into a memorial to Maurice and Richard McDonald's legacy (and Juan Pollo's corporate headquarters). Lovers of kitsch, scholars of all things Americana, and hungry travelers misled by their GPS navigation apps gather on the very spot where the McDonald brothers perfected their million-dollar idea. They changed the American restaurant industry with a simple menu of hamburgers and French fries. The museum tries to narrate this with each photograph, paper cup, and tray liner. Outside of the museum entrance is a replica of an early McDonald's sign boasting the sale of over 1 million hamburgers; that number has since climbed to more than 1 billion.

Okura's ever-expanding collection records seventy years of evolving tastes in food, aesthetics, and children's popular culture in the United States and around the world, all emanating from one company and the assurance that everyday people can get a hot meal quickly for a low price. Okura and his team receive, catalog, and display hundreds of donated objects each year from site visitors worldwide. Former McDonald's crew members add to the Museum's extensive fashion exhibit of polyester-blend uniforms, standard-issue visors and paper hats, gifted manager's ties with embroidered Golden Arches wrapped in tissue, and commendation pins earned at their first jobs. International visitors offer cardboard pie sleeves for the dessert flavors only found in Asia: taro root, banana, and sweet corn. The museum's assortment of Happy Meal toys and McDonald's commissioned children's activity books range from an educational newsletter promising fun learning the metric system to plastic Chicken McNugget action figures dressed in Halloween costumes.

The museum is like the attic of a family elder with the presence of mind to label each piece of their personal collection of chaos. This corpus of McDonald's history is arranged chronologically in some places, thematically in others, and haphazardly throughout. To the left of a McDonald's Playland carousel that greets visitors when they enter are artifacts of early McDonald's history. There is a collection of steel utensils that were used to cut French fries and flattened shovels that placed the piping hot potato sticks into paper envelopes. The original mustard and "katsup" funnel used to dress hamburgers in rapid succession is identified as the work of the Toman Brothers, "Local Craftsmen." The walls display pictures of employees from the 1940s. Ruth Black, who worked at McDonald's in 1942, is captured in her uniform of a short skirt, starched white blouse, and black sweater. Her coworker, Helen Anderson, is pictured with a "frycook" only identified as Frenchy. The museum's 4,000 square feet can barely contain the collection, so objects from different times and places share whatever space is available. The very first "Orange Juice Machine" used at the location occupies a spot in a corner with a Captain Crook statue. Captain Crook bears an uncanny resemblance to the Captain Cook character that appeared in Disney's 1953 version of *Peter Pan*. Before the Hamburglar became the most wanted criminal in

McDonaldland, Officer Big Mac pursued Crook for stealing Filet-O-Fish sandwiches.

The tour also highlights McDonald's many partnerships, past and present. A commemorative plate from the 1984 Olympic Games featuring three American gold medalists and the silhouette of the Los Angeles Memorial Coliseum reminds visitors of the company's sponsorship of the global competition. A shelf of Happy Meal Beanie Babies and Muppet figurines highlights the fact that McDonald's is the largest distributor of toys in the entire world. The museum's sizable international section, which features cardboard poutine containers, vegetable deluxe sandwich boxes and menus in various languages, showcases the unifying power of a set of Golden Arches.

As versed as Okura and his curatorial team is in the story of the McDonald brothers, the Kroc family, the manufacturers of McDonald's ephemera, and the evolution of McDonaldland characters, there is a gaping hole in the museum's historiographical view of the Golden Arches. There is no recognition of the calamitous meeting between McDonald's and black America and the way this encounter shaped civil rights, transformed the health and wealth of entire communities, and directed sectors from advertising to education to labor policy. This untold history is not articulated in the glass shelves of the McDonald's Museum or told in most of the case studies on McDonald's rise, dominance, and recent missteps.

This is the missing piece of the story of how race, civil rights, and hamburgers converged and changed everything. This is the story of how McDonald's became black.

* * *

Maurice McDonald was born in Manchester, New Hampshire, in the fall of 1902; his brother Richard arrived seven years later in February of 1909. In 1902, eighty-five African Americans were reportedly lynched nationwide. Four days before Maurice's birth, the National Association for the Advancement of Colored People (NAACP) was founded by an interracial coalition seeking to eradicate the reign of Jim Crow terror over black America. These historical moments may appear disparate—the birth of two white entrepreneurs in what was then the rural Northeast and the racial violence meted upon blacks, largely in the Deep South, and the activist response to it. Yet everything that shaped their legacy in the fast food industry—their ability to move across the country without fear of racial violence, their access to second and third chances before they were able to strike gold in California with a hamburger stand, and the avenues available for their namesake restaurant to become a global leader—was dependent on systems that denied African Americans routes to social mobility and equal rights. In the early twentieth century, racism dictated that African Americans strategize how to provide for themselves, their families, and their communities without drawing the ire of white power structures that could deprive them of liberty, livelihood, or life. The McDonald's narrative that is captured in books like John F. Love's *McDonald's: Behind the Arches* and the 2016 film *The Founder* center on how innovative thinking, opportunities made possible by a booming wartime economy, and the American desire for expediency and novelty formed the company.[2] These stories are both accurate and deceptive. McDonald's—and its fast food brethren—illuminates the ways that many Americans live and what they enjoy and how they consume. For good or for ill, McDonald's can be a reliable mirror. But like many aspects of American mass culture, the centrality of race, its role in shaping what is possible for some and impossible for others, is obscured in the interests of forgetting what is painful, what is complicated, or what is merely hard to digest.

Maurice and Richard McDonald, having seen the ravages the Depression wreaked on their family, decided to head west in 1930 to seek their fortunes. The twenty-somethings were probably lured to California by Hollywood's images of cosmopolitan nightlife in a voraciously growing Los Angeles or San Francisco. Maybe they saw themselves in Gary Cooper's cowboy roles, conquering the West with a trusty horse and a gun at his hip. The men undoubtedly had an affinity for film, and after working as stagehands they opened a movie theater in Glendale, a few miles northeast of Hollywood. In addition to Westerns and over-the-top musicals, Hollywood churned out features that delivered the most insidious and harmful images of African Americans, Native Americans, Asians, and Mexican Americans. In 1915, the Los Angeles NAACP joined forces with other local civil rights groups to request the city council ban the screening of Thomas Dixon's film adaptation of his book *The Clansman: A Historical Romance of the Ku Klux Klan.* The film version, *The Birth of a Nation,* was heralded for the cinematic techniques infused into a disturbing, historically inaccurate telling of Reconstruction and the rise of the Ku Klux Klan. Fearful that the film would incite violence against blacks in Los Angeles, NAACP chapter leaders joined their colleagues across the country in pleading for a ban.[3] The city council's prohibition against screening the film was later overturned by the state supreme court, and *Birth of a Nation*—a film that depicted an attempted rape by an African American man on a white teenage girl, a group of bare-footed black congressmen eating fried chicken on the floor of the U.S. House of Representatives, and an image of Jesus superimposed on a scene of a cavalcade of righteous KKK members—was screened for an entire year at L.A.'s Clune Theater.[4] Between 1930 and 1937, before the brothers pivoted from the movie business to a drive-in venture, films such as Fred Astaire's "Swing Time" and Judy Garland's "Everybody Sing" presented the stars in blackface as they danced and sang in the style of African-American folk and jazz culture.[5] Despite the best efforts of the national and local NAACP, Hollywood rarely censored racist content or took seriously the claims that what was seen by white viewers on the screen had real implications for black people on the streets. To be sure, the McDonald brothers were not settling in a region as devoted to Jim Crow as the Deep South or a city as overwhelmed by the rural emigrants of the Great Negro Migration as Chicago or New York, but the West was not a land of racial harmony.[6] The McDonald brothers established themselves in a state built upon a history of Native American conquest and extermination, border wars with Mexico, a dependence upon and vilification of Asian and Middle

Eastern immigrant labor, and a hostility toward blacks likely only tempered by their relatively small population.

In 1937, the brothers and their father, Patrick, opened the Airdrome hot dog stand in Monrovia. Convinced that they needed to move to a place with more car traffic, the trio found a spot in downtown San Bernardino. The McDonald men struck out a few times before they found a bank willing to lend them $5,000 to move to the more populous and diverse town forty-four miles east of Monrovia.[7] In 1940, San Bernardino was well on its way to becoming a utopia for the fast food industry.[8] Its location near a military base, on Route 66, and in the center of growing lower-middle-class suburbs made it the ideal location for a restaurant that you could drive, walk, or ride a bike to, and with only a few coins in your pocket enjoy a full meal. Initially, the brothers departed from the austere menu they offered at the Airdrome and indulged their interest in barbecuing for the new location. Within a few years, patrons could choose from an array of dishes that included hamburgers, peanut-butter-and-jelly sandwiches, tamales, chili, and barbecued beef, ham, and pork sandwiches. The brothers assured diners that their meats were not simply "cooked in a stove" and passed off as barbecue, a sham they accused other restaurants of pulling, and they even welcomed guests to see the barbecue pit for themselves.[9]

The early menu was a hit with locals, and the offerings were versions of European (hamburger), Mexican (tamale), and Caribbean (barbecue) cuisine. Foods from around the world were adjusted and Americanized for mid-century taste buds. The origins and the popularization of the most iconic fast food staple in the United States, the hamburger, are often traced to German immigrants, who developed the idea of sandwiching the thinly pressed Hamburg steak served between slices of bread. Hamburger historian Andrew Smith argues "there are several contenders for the title of 'inventor of the hamburger' . . . [but] no primary evidence has surfaced to support any of their claims."[10] No one has definitively settled the debate about who first made and marketed the hamburger, but it is clear that the advent of the meat grinder and the ability to form, grill, dress, and serve hamburgers rapidly transformed the

American diet. The demonstration of the meat grinder to visitors at the 1876 Philadelphia Centennial Exposition introduced a far more economical way of feeding people than the tradition of butchering cattle into steaks and chops. "The meat grinder was a great asset to butchers, who could now use unsaleable or undesirable scraps and organ meats that might otherwise have been tossed out."[11] Cheaper meat meant that working-class people could incorporate beef—often enriched with additives and pieces of fat and gristle that were previously discarded or fed to animals—into their everyday meals. Soon, the hamburger sandwich was being sold throughout major cities, from carts, roadside stands, and automats.[12]

From the existing historical records of McDonald's businesses in Monrovia and San Bernardino, it is unclear whether the men served up their barbecue and burgers exclusively to white patrons. Both locations were home to African Americans and Mexican Americans. Monrovia's African-American community was founded in the 1880s. These freedmen and descendants of enslaved peoples believed their destinies would be met out West after the end of Reconstruction. Black Monrovians established churches, mutual aid societies, and their own NAACP chapter. Monrovia's shared name with the capital city of Liberia—the African nation colonized by emancipated black Americans—may have made it doubly attractive to blacks who looked west for greater freedoms. Despite Monrovia's vibrant black community and the fact that the city may have been the site of the first all-black jury to hear a case anywhere in the United States, blacks were still subject to the color line.[13] The archives of those that settled in Monrovia, and nearby Pasadena, chronicle separate schools, colored days at the local pool, a segregated cemetery, and battles over access to library cards and representation on the police force.[14] San Bernardino's Mexican-American community members were descendants of ancestors from the days when California was still part of Mexico. Mexican Americans in the twentieth century worked in the Inland Empire's agricultural fields and railroad yards, and they shared similar limitations as blacks in the region. Mexican Americans in San Bernardino also share a similar history with blacks of exclusion in the town. The extant oral histories and biographies of Mexican-American people and communities in pre-1960s San Bernardino attest to being barred from using public pools and being limited in their housing options. Mexican-American parents also organized antisegregation actions against public schools on behalf of their children.[15] In Okura's collection of photographs from the late 1940s, there are a few images of customers who may have been of Mexican descent visiting the drive-in. If blacks and Mexicans were served, they may have had to patronize the outlet on specific days, during certain hours, or wait for whites to order first before requesting their meals. Although there is no evidence to suggest that McDonald's was segregated in its service delivery or in its customer base, the dynamics that surrounded the building and expansion of McDonald's depended on racial inequality.

Within the confines of the McDonalds' drive-in, there were no reasons to be concerned about color lines, movements organizing against it, or the world outside of San Bernardino. For the first eight years of the brothers' success in their octagonal building, which had been split in two and physically moved from Monrovia to San Bernardino, they only had to focus on the immediate future and maintain their success. McDonald's was averaging $200,000 in sales each year, with the men splitting $50,000 in profits. The cold winters of their New Hampshire youth and the lean years in Glendale were long gone.[16] In 1948, the men began to take stock of the drive-in. They accounted for their unreliable workforce and the revolving door of carhops and cooks they supervised, the demand of replacing pilfered and broken dishware, and the money and time wasted stocking so many different foods and allowing individualized customer orders. The brothers rethought their approach. They wanted to serve families, not rowdy teenagers. The menu was too complicated. Competitors and copycats were beginning to sprout up along Route 66. The founders decided to close their business and spent three months gestating the modern fast-food restaurant that would mature into the McDonald's we know today. Maurice and Richard determined which foods turned the highest profits and were easiest to prepare, and designed or commissioned kitchen supplies to maximize efficiency. They dispensed with the carhop concept, believing young women were too distracting to customers and distracted as employees. Then, in a move that surprised their competition, they lowered the prices on their scaled-back menu. At the new McDonald's, you could purchase a 15-cent standardized hamburger, a 19-cent cheeseburger, a 19-cent milkshake, and a dime could get you a side of French fries (which ended a short-lived foray into potato chips), a paper cup of milk, root beer from a barrel, a fresh glass of orange juice (or an orange soda, called orangeade), a Coca-Cola, or a slice of pie. The new McDonald's, outfitted with a fishbowl kitchen staffed exclusively by men, introduced their signature Speedee Service System—an approach to making and delivering food quickly. Speedee came to life with a hamburger bun–faced cartoon chef in motion on neon signs, menus, and stationery.[17] The revamped McDonald's hamburger assembly line resembled the factory floors of the nation's post–World War II manufacturing centers, at a time when U.S.-made products dominated the global marketplace. The "new" McDonald's was so successful that within seven years the brothers had doubled their profits.

McDonald's success wasn't just a response to the menu and staff changes; the lightning-speed dominance over the local restaurant market was delivered by the rise in household incomes. McDonald's catered to the newcomers in town, who were drawn to the Inland Empire by the drivers of mid-century, middle-class prosperity: the military and the manufacturing industries. Each of these institutions were conduits for white families to surpass the class positions of their old-world immigrant, or native-born, working-class parents and become a part of the middle-class consumer republic. Although San Bernardino was not among the most affluent of the Southern California communities born from the suburbanization movements of the late 1940s and 1950s, the town and its beloved hamburger spot was one way an upwardly mobile person could exercise his newly obtained consumer power and spend a little of the discretionary income that came his way.

When military and manufacturing opportunities were opened up to blacks, they were segregated, racially discriminatory, or abusive.

African Americans, despite their long service in the military, trained and served on a segregated basis until President Harry S. Truman signed Executive Order 9981 in 1948, nearly a decade after the U.S. Army acquired the San Bernardino airport for its Air Materiel Command Center, which drew scores of military trainees and employees to the area.[18] San Bernardino's railroads, and its steel, metalwork, and machinery plants, created well-paying, union jobs for white workers.[19] But black workers, excluded from labor unions, found themselves routinely among the first fired and last hired. There is no indication that the Speedee system in San Bernardino refused to deliver to the city's residents of color, but there was no question that equal opportunity was not in full supply during the boom years. Even if black working-class families were allowed to also enjoy trips to McDonald's on weekend evenings, their experiences of job instability and earning lower wages may have prevented them from exercising this option very often.[20]

The McDonalds were prescient in their projection that highway travel would increase and that their restaurant was the perfect stop for a hurried and hungry traveler. Cars, car travel, and car ownership were key ingredients in the formula for growing a fast food empire. Outside, in the drive-in's congested lot, Henry Ford's dream of a car priced so that his workers could afford it could be found in real life. From the comfort of their cars, families waited for food that the motor company's workers could also afford. Inside the kitchen, Fordist work principles kept the cooking staff attuned to the rhythms of the flat-top grill, the Multimixer machine whisking milk and ice cream, and the deep fat fryers calibrated to render each French fry perfectly cooked and crisped. The revamped McDonald's was a suitable place for a family, children could run in and collect the evening meal—each component wrapped in disposable paper—and return to the car, which could double as a dining room. The prices and the burgers drew in customers, but the car also made it possible for the roadside eatery to thrive. In 1950, an estimated 8 million new cars were joining the already 25 million cars traversing the expanding highway system. By 1960, the number of cars in the United States doubled, and car culture from hot rod racing to drive-in movies characterized the sense of freedom and independence cars provided anyone seeking a quick escape from everyday life.

Car ownership, however, was not as simple as saving up money and visiting a local dealership to make a purchase. The color line and its extensions—lack of access to capital, racial discrimination in selling, and unsafe driving conditions for black motorists traveling far from home—made driving a fraught, and sometimes terrifying experience.[21] Black car ownership rates lagged behind that of whites, but even if all things were equal, where African Americans could travel to was determined by the "local customs" and their approach to still-legal racial segregation. The uncertainty of safety allowed black-owned restaurants, gas stations, and motels to distinguish themselves in the growing hospitality industry emerging from the creation of the highway and road improvements. Black drivers could rely on Victor H. Green's essential travel guide, *The Negro Motorist Green Book,* which was published between 1936 and 1967 and listed the addresses of hotels, restaurants, resorts, and entertainment venues that did not discriminate.[22] In a 1958 report titled "The Negro Market Potential: The U.S. Negro Market Today, $17.5 Billion in Purchasing Power," researchers described the "basic areas of human activities" for blacks.

> For the Negro of sophistication and poise, as well as for the Negro who is ill-at-ease and insecure, there is always uncertainty as to whether an otherwise pleasant evening will be marred by discourteous employee treatment in public places or whether he will be the victim of insults from the non-Negro patrons.

When McDonald's patrons returned to their cars with a full stomach, some drove to the newly built suburban housing developments that sprouted across the city and country in the late 1940s and 1950s. The opening of an air command center in San Bernardino in 1941 brought 4,000 members of the military and an additional 11,000 family members into a town of 43,000 people.[23] After the end of World War II, military personnel continued to move to the area, leading to a housing shortage on the base. In 1948, 4,000 more Air Force employees arrived for new roles in the one-year-old branch of the military. As the military scrambled to accommodate newcomers in hotels, campsites, and private homes, returning veterans of color struggled to find a place of their own. The *Los Angeles Sentinel*, an African-American newspaper, reported on the plight of Marvin Spears, a returning veteran who tried for two years to secure the home loan he was entitled to under the Servicemen's Readjustment Act of 1944, known as the GI Bill. The newspaper described his battle with the Veterans Administration as "typical of what Negro and Mexican veterans in Southern California face in trying to substitute homes for the shacks, trailers, and emergency housing in which they still live with their families." The *Sentinel* hoped that in publishing Spears's account of being denied an adequate appraisal for the home he wanted built and being forced to navigate several bureaucracies, "the loan guarantee division of the veterans' administration will get off its dime."[24]

San Bernardino epitomized mid-century America's many contradictions. A world war had been fought overseas to destroy fascism and totalitarianism. While one segment of the population was enjoying the fruits of a postconflict economy, others could only imagine what such prosperity felt like. White San Bernardino families were able to buy homes, purchase cars, and enjoy nights out for the family at McDonald's without fear or intimidation. Blacks and Mexican Americans would have to wait for a plethora of events to unfold before they could do the same.

* * *

As word of the McDonald's magic spread across the region, and national trade publications like *American Restaurant Magazine* featured McDonald's in its pages, businessmen with aspirations of their own began to visit San Bernardino and seek advice. Older franchises like White Castle and Howard Johnson's were doing well, but McDonald's volume and consistency in a relatively small location was a model of distinction. The McDonalds saw no harm in disclosing how they sourced their ingredients, commissioned specially designed equipment, or managed their crew members. It was a wide-open world, and they were not interested in growing McDonald's beyond a few additional restaurants in California and one franchise deal they inked in Arizona. Some visitors returned to their hometowns and tried to replicate the McDonald's System but realized that it took more than mimicry to make a successful business. The McDonalds possessed the hindsight of past failures, and then they could later afford to shut down and reopen their restaurant in order to make improvements. They forged trusting relationships with suppliers. They went to great lengths to institute and preserve the efficiency of their kitchen by demarcating preparation zones and timing production. But even those who couldn't replicate the McDonald's formula used McDonald's methodology to sell hot dogs, fried chicken, and roast beef sandwiches. Glen Bell, a San Bernardino local, was so inspired by the men he opened a fast food restaurant of his own but added a twist: tacos. Bell regularly patronized the Mitla Café, a Mexican restaurant across the street from his business, and he even visited their kitchen. Later he abandoned burgers altogether and created Taco Bell, the first national chain of Anglicized Mexican food in the United States.[25] By today's standards, it may seem bizarre, if not foolish, that the men with the winning ideas would be so willing to allow others to use and adapt them. But the growth of America's roadsides, especially after the passage of the Federal Aid Highway Act of 1956, convinced fast food pioneers that there was enough market share for everyone.

Highway developments were not only welcomed by the fast food industry. Housing interests that wanted to maintain segregation also used highways to protect the racial boundaries of the nation. Advocates for a national highway system saw it as essential to boosting the attractiveness of racially exclusive suburbs. Highway proposals often claimed that a network of roads could address the problems of overcrowded and dilapidated inner cities, which grew in black population from World War I until the early 1970s. From Harlem to Chicago to Oakland, Negro slums made city leaders anxious, but never so concerned that they took steps to fight the housing discrimination that limited where blacks could live. The building of highways provided the impetus for slum clearance, the demolition of unsightly, low-quality and dangerous housing, which also served to disrupt black communities, some that had formed before the Great Migration.[26] Seven years before the Federal Highway Act was passed, lobbying organizations like the American Road Builders Association offered that highways could accelerate the process of eliminating "slum and deteriorated areas." The primary target of this dual approach to transportation and urban renewal caused planners to "drive the Interstates through black and poor neighborhoods."[27] Racially segregated public housing replaced some slums; other "cleared out" residents moved into older housing that whites left behind. The targets of slum clearance became the food deserts of the twenty-first century.[28]

Ray Kroc was not troubled about the impact of highways on the nation's racial disharmony when he traveled to San Bernardino in 1954. Highways would help him make a fortune, but as he made the pilgrimage from his office in Illinois to McDonald's for the first time, all he could think about was milkshakes. The Multi-Mixer milkshake machine salesman had seen the piece in *American Restaurant Magazine* praising McDonald's. He knew firsthand that there was something special about this drive-in. McDonald's was among his best customers, having purchased up to ten of the five-spindle milkshake machines from him in a few years. Kroc was accustomed to supplying soda fountains and diners with one or two, and he heard from his West Coast colleague that McDonald's had to be seen to be believed; the customer lines snaked around the front lot, and they could serve thousands of people out of a 600-square-foot restaurant.[29] Soon Kroc was in business with the McDonald brothers. He replaced the McDonald's franchising agent, a position they needed to guarantee some level of uniformity among their handful of franchise owners in California and their one outlet in Arizona.

Kroc's original intention was to help McDonald's expand in order to boost sales of the milkshake mixers, in which he had a financial stake. Yet Kroc realized something bigger was afoot. In the spring of 1955, Kroc established McDonald's System, Inc., and set about recruiting new franchisees among his peer groups: fellow salesmen, first-generation suburbanites, and members of his country club that catered to the newly upper-middle-class. Kroc's strategy to entice new franchise owners was to keep the initial investment as low as possible, provide exhaustive detail on how to improve on the already breakneck speed of food preparation, and keep franchise fees at a level that ensured that franchisees could turn profits quickly and sustain their restaurants for the long run.[30] Kroc signed up new franchisees throughout the 1950s, but he did not take full control of McDonald's until 1961, after years of a deteriorating relationship with and tense exchanges between Kroc and the brothers. At the end of a flurry of correspondence between San Bernardino and Des Plaines, a wild goose chase for funding, and hours of meetings among attorneys, company executives, and accountants, Ray Kroc at last became the head of a newly independent McDonald's. Richard and Maurice each received a check for $1 million and dispensation from dealing with the sometimes harsh and impossible Kroc. Kroc lost access to the San Bernardino store in the sale. He exacted his vengeance by opening his own McDonald's one block away from the birthplace of the chain. Confused customers patronized what they believed was a relocated McDonald's. The "old McDonald's" was no longer the brothers' namesake; Kroc prevented the men from using their own surname on their store. Although longtime employees christened it the Big M, they could not compete against the brand name they created. In 1970, the property at 1398 North E Street in San Bernardino closed. Nearly three decades passed until Albert Okura resuscitated the lot where the first McDonald's stood and resurrected it into a fast food memorial.[31]

*　*　*

Three days after Christmas in 1961, Ray Kroc assumed the leadership of 323 McDonald's restaurants across 44 states.[32] Even before the McDonalds relinquished the business to Kroc, he was developing an aggressive expansion plan. Kroc boarded a single-engine Cessna plane with his trusted advisors and scouted locations for potential new franchises from the air. He took note of the neatly drawn grids of suburban towns, the highway exits and the vacant lots near schools and churches. As the men searched for places to build McDonald's, and for the franchisees that would implement the Speedee system, they took note of the land below them. McDonald's executive Harry Sonneborn presented the idea of circumventing the negotiation process for land leases and franchise subleases altogether. Sonneborn proposed that McDonald's purchase the real estate on which future restaurants would be built. Kroc liked the way that Sonneborn thought. With the establishment of the Franchise Realty Corporation in 1956, McDonald's acquired new assets and collateral as it fanned out into new territories. One biographer of the company credits the investment in real estate as "the most important reason why McDonald's . . . boasts a financial position" unmatched by other fast food companies.[33]

As Kroc flew over the country evaluating McDonald's next territory, his pilots probably didn't linger over the inner cities, which by 1961 were becoming less white and less affluent. Kroc called suburbia "where McDonald's grew up," and he expressed uncertainty about the urban landscape.[34] Despite his own reservations about the city, some of the early franchises were in fact in neighborhoods transitioning from all white to all black, and local franchisees in the new McDonald's hub of the Midwest advertised in African-American newspapers. In 1957, a location opened near Chicago's South Side Chatham community. Chatham had transitioned from a predominately white, middle-class enclave in 1950 to a mostly black, middle-class neighborhood by 1960. The franchise operator, Joseph Fine, appeared to have a cordial relationship with local black residents; his wife cohosted a community Chamber of Commerce event in 1959. In the pages of one of the most influential African-American dailies, the *Chicago Defender*, the McDonald's location used the image and recommendation of James North, an African American. "For a treat that can't be beat . . . I'll take McDonald's Hamburgers."[35] Another McDonald's franchise opened in the heart of black Chicago in 1961, in the Bronzeville neighborhood, and the outlet promised "plenty of parking, no car hops, no tipping," only the "tastiest food in town at prices that please!"[36] Throughout the 1960s, the Bronzeville location purchased *Defender* ads to entice locals to try French fries made from Idaho premium potatoes, sample the new Fish Filet sandwich, and tune in to local stations to see the McDonald's float in the 1965 Macy's Thanksgiving Day Parade. The next year, the newspaper published a story with a headline, "McDonald's Hamburgers Are Just Great," and a profile piece about Samuel Sheriff, a black McDonald's manager, at the helm of the company's fifth-highest-grossing store.[37]

Black Chicagoans with the means and desire to eat at McDonald's, or try to follow in Sheriff's footsteps as a manager, may have read the *Defender* items with interest. For *Defender* readers in the Deep South, the advertisements and stories may have been difficult to relate to. Wherever whites and "others" lived in proximity, a color line could be erected and legislated, but the most virulent application and defense of separation resided in the South. In the years that McDonald's was taking its model national, the struggle against Jim Crow was internationalized as television stations worldwide broadcast the violent responses to nonviolent sit-ins, boycotts, and marches. These protests, brought to homes across the world through television sets, radios, magazines, and newspapers, heightened awareness of the ways that blacks were relegated to second-class consumer citizenship. Black women had to use their imaginations if they spotted the perfect dress at a segregated department store, because they were not allowed to try it on. Black men had to defer to white children while waiting in line to order food to bring home to their families. Black children, including Martin Luther King Jr.'s daughter Yolanda, had to ask their parents why they were not allowed to go to amusement parks.[38] The national enthusiasm for the marketplace, and the local realities of segregation, separated black consumers from the nation's prosperity. Blacks and other people of color were in many ways social aliens in white America, observing a world they could never fully belong to or enjoy.

Public humiliation was commonplace in the Jim Crow era, and restaurants were the setting for a host of embarrassing experiences. Exclusionary and abusive behavior toward blacks in restaurants often began with a host or a manager ignoring an expectant black customer or simply stating that they do not serve black people at their establishments. Customers who challenged these policies and practices could be physically removed by restaurant staff or be arrested by police. African-American activists and writers have long reflected on the ways that segregation at fine restaurants, casual lunch counters, and even rundown barbecue shacks illustrated their exclusion from the small luxuries that consumer culture offered whites. In Melba Pattillo Beals's autobiography, *Warriors Don't Cry: A Searing Memoir of the Battle to Integrate Little Rock's Central High,* she recalled a family vacation to Cincinnati, where she ate at an integrated restaurant for the first time. She described it as dining in "the promised land." The following fall, as one of nine high-schoolers selected to integrate Little Rock Central High School, she again thought about restaurant segregation. Beals and her eight compatriots were targets of violence and harassment for their acts of bravery, and they were supported by the NAACP's legal defense arm. When NAACP lawyer Thurgood Marshall visited the Arkansas capital to meet with the students, Beals remembered feeling ashamed because the future Supreme Court justice could only "eat a greasy hamburger" for dinner. Little Rock's fine restaurants were closed to blacks, especially ones fighting for civil rights.[39]

Black people from San Bernardino to Selma were usually aware of the rules—spoken and unspoken—about where they could enter and be served. They protected visitors by preparing meals in their homes or listing the places to avoid or consulting a copy of their *Green Book.* Uninitiated travelers passing through racially segregated towns or visiting the United States for the first time were shocked and insulted by these experiences. This was the case when William Henry Fitzjohn, a Sierra Leonean diplomat, was refused service at a Howard Johnson's restaurant on Maryland's Route 40 while traveling between Washington, D.C., and Pittsburgh. This length of Route 40 was filled with segregated eating establishments and gas stations, and it was a Congress of Racial Equality (CORE) target of protests due to its policies against blacks. Fitzjohn and his cohort of African diplomats and exchange students who came to the nation's capital in the early 1960s had encountered difficulties renting apartments and being served at restaurants before. Sometimes a phone call from an influential white colleague or the simple clarification that they were African, not African-American, could remedy the situation. But Fitzjohn was far from Washington on Route 40, and he had no one to turn to in the moment. When he later reported on his journey, the State Department was compelled to respond. At the height of the Cold War, when U.S. interests wanted to promote democracy among recently independent African states, they knew that these racist incidents could contribute to the accurate and damning anti-American critiques made by Communist states. For President John F. Kennedy's White House and his brother Robert's Department of Justice, the inability for blacks to be served in restaurants was not only a national injustice, it exacerbated a global crisis.[40]

Many Route 40 businesses, like the Howard Johnson's that refused to seat and serve Fitzjohn, were based on the model of the sit-down dining experience, in which a customer interacted with a host, a waiter or waitress, and if problems arose or the service was particularly excellent, maybe a manager. Fast food in the early 1960s was still based on the drive-in model. With no seats, no wait staff, and a mostly outdoor or car-based dining experience, fast food did not feel as wedded to the machinations of separate and unequal. McDonald's did not begin to incorporate seating into new restaurants until 1963, and Kroc maintained many of the Speedee system elements that discouraged diners from lingering: no silverware, limited seating, and counter workers were told to be friendly, but to avoid small talk with customers. The building of McDonald's was still not race-neutral in its site selection or its reliance on a disparate set of racially informed federal policies and social practices. McDonald's restaurants developed a reputation as ahead of its time in its business processes and models, but when it came to race, especially in the South, franchisees did not rock the boat. While diplomats and foreign affairs officers could appeal to Kennedy's presidential power to mobilize advisors and cabinet members, everyday people relied on the strength of homegrown, unelected leaders to address the problem of restaurant segregation and other forms of consumer discrimination.

Activists used the sit-in strategy throughout the country to make a case for the end of segregation in libraries, churches, and, most famously, lunch counters. The sit-in, initially called a sit-down, has had a long history as a tool of nonviolence, with the strategy being used in anticolonial struggles and union work strikes. In the 1940s, CORE sat in at a segregated coffeeshop in Chicago.[41] Sit-ins were well-orchestrated, dramatic demonstrations of the injustice of segregation in their simple but precise choreography and staging. Civil rights organizers often instructed protesters to dress in their Sunday best. Women arranged their hair in neat styles, made up their faces modestly, and appeared as ladylike as possible. Men wore suits or their military uniforms to emphasize the reality that their patriotism meant nothing in the eyes of the Jim Crow state. Sitting took courage, patience, and determination. In the best-case scenario, a protester would be told to leave and quit causing trouble. If a mob was present, a favorite sweater could be ruined by a steady stream of mustard poured down a sitter's back. Carefully pinned hair could become coated in maple syrup. Every CORE and NAACP member knew that things could get worse. A member of the mob may strike a protesting student with a bat. A police officer may break a pastor's shoulder while trying to move him off a silver stool seat.[42] Some sit-ins concluded with no violence and quick resolution. Sit-ins in cities like Wichita, Miami, and Oklahoma City in the late 1950s opened up access to lunch counters and drugstores in cities with small black populations. These sit-ins gave advocates of nonviolent protest evidence that the act of remaining unmoved by jeers and threats could actually make a difference. But it would take the February 1, 1960, sit-in at a North Carolina Woolworth & Company lunch counter to inspire a critical mass of people to test its suitability and potency throughout the South.

Four students from the historically black North Carolina Agricultural and Technical College—Ezell Blair (now Jibreel Khazan),

Frank McCain, Joe McNeil, and David Richmond—grew close over the course of the 1959–60 school year by sharing their frustrations over segregation in Greensboro, North Carolina. After deliberating about the decision to challenge Woolworth's segregation and acknowledging that their actions could imperil their families and friends, the four well-dressed men set out for their local Woolworth's. After purchasing a few items from the five-and-dime section of the store, they headed to their target: the whites-only lunch counter.[43] The men remained unmoved after the restaurant staff, and then a hovering police officer, tried to instruct them to leave. The first day, the men stayed at the counters, as white customers began to leave and the lingering ones silently stared at them. The manager closed the store early for the evening, and the men promised to show up again the next day, and the next. The Woolworth sit-ins drew more A&T students, as well as women from the historically black Bennett College and white women from the Woman's College of the University of North Carolina. The sit-in benefited from the men's resolve and the emergence of more civil rights movement reporting in the South. Prior to the murder of fourteen-year-old Emmett Till in the summer of 1955, the black press was the only reliable source of consistent movement coverage. By 1960, civil rights news was more readily available, and organizations knew to alert the press about their planned marches and demonstrations.[44] The Greensboro sit-in was inspirational and generative, and in a day's time, it inspired southern college students to put their bodies on the line to push against segregation in their local communities. The sit-ins also helped define the purpose of the Student Nonviolent Coordinating Committee (SNCC), which was founded on the campus of Shaw University in Raleigh two months to the day that the men entered Woolworth's. The Greensboro Woolworth's—after closing their lunch counters on multiple occasions and becoming tethered to some of the most vitriolic scenes of white mob intimidation and violence—desegregated their store in the summer of 1960. Woolworth's waited for the students to go home for the season, and the first four black customers to be served there were black women who worked at the retailer but could not be served prior to the sit-ins.

Much of the public memory surrounding Greensboro and the invigoration of the southern sit-in movement is associated with national companies and local-level chains that have all but vanished from most American cities: Woolworth's, S. H. Kress & Company, and Rexall drugstores. There are fewer commemorations of the activists who devoted their energies to desegregating the fast food restaurants that are still with us today. After winning concessions with Main Street and central-city business, protesters began to turn an eye toward roadside businesses, which had largely avoided the attention and disruption of the sit-ins. Protesters had to improvise on the sit-in strategies because restaurants like McDonald's and its peers did not provide seating inside of their stores. Drive-ins either refused service to blacks or operated out of separate windows, which would only be tended to after whites had placed orders. Joe McNeil recounted that, at McDonald's in Greensboro, "you were required to go to the rear of a McDonald's and place your order."[45] The fight to end segregation required the same meticulous organizing and dedication as the first round of sit-ins.

Between 1960 and 1963, CORE, SNCC, and the NAACP branches organized protests against segregated McDonald's restaurants. In Memphis, movement leaders had already celebrated the removal of COLORED waiting signs at the Greyhound bus station and were engaged in a lawsuit to desegregate the public libraries when they began a campaign against McDonald's.[46] The group of protesters targeted the city's first McDonald's in March of 1960. The location had been open nearly two years, and as the twentieth franchise in his McDonald's System, Kroc must have been aware of the tensions between the franchisee, Saul Kaplan, and black customers.[47] There is no record of Kroc publicly acknowledging or addressing the sit-in movement. Each franchisee was responsible for QSCV, the shorthand for Kroc's top priorities: quality, service, cleanliness, and value. If protests disrupted the franchise's ability to make sales, keep the stores tidy, or make every hamburger according to the manual, then the franchisee would have to deal with it. Kroc stayed out of civil rights. But civil rights would not ease up on

Kroc's prized possession. Kaplan tried to stand his ground against the protests. But the NAACP won out after an eighteen-month, city-wide campaign against Kaplan and other discriminating restaurants. They not only opened the drive-in to black customers, but they also secured a guarantee to hire black employees.[48]

In the spring of 1963, CORE strengthened campaigns against McDonald's in North Carolina by assisting fed-up black customers in High Point and Asheville. In Greensboro, SNCC and community activists were not resting on their laurels from the 1960 wins. Asheville, North Carolina, native Lewis Brandon took the skills he acquired sitting in at Woolworth's and Kress's to the area McDonald's. Lewis was among a subset of Greensboro activists who set their sights on "attacking the problems with desegregation in the city" outside of the downtown core. In early May of 1963, Greensboro Movement activists gathered outside the McDonald's in a commercial strip at 1101 Summit Avenue, less than two miles from the Woolworth's counter. Armed with signs that said, "Mc—Don't Set America Back—Get on the Right Track," the group of mostly college students demanded that the drive-in that opened the previous year end its segregation practices.[49] On the first night of the protest, Lewis and other demonstrators had rocks thrown at them outside the McDonald's. When they returned to the A&T campus, they were harassed by people throwing glass bottles at their dorms. The protesters returned to McDonald's the next day, but this time Greensboro police were dispatched to deter their action. The arrests drew more supporters to the group, and they were joined on the third day by local high school students and community members. A minister involved in the McDonald's campaign told leaders: "Now, you've got something going here. Keep it going and I'll have a mass meeting at my church and we'll turn out the adult community."[50] Further mobilization would not be necessary. The McDonald's franchisee did not want any more negative publicity and relented within four days of the first protest. Blacks would no longer have to wait until whites had been served before they could order their meals.

While Greensboro was settling its dispute with McDonald's,

Chicago-based CORE members were meeting with the company's executives and explaining the urgent need to end segregation in southern drive-ins. CORE left the gathering with a commitment that McDonald's would order franchisees to "hire [blacks], upgrade, and desegregate all Southern units" by May 15, 1963. On May 25, McDonald's in Durham stopped segregating black customers.

Franchisees were often selected and retained based on their sense of duty to the restaurant's mandates. But some southern operators did not accept the new order, so blacks continued to apply pressure on their local McDonald's.[51] In the winter of 1963, SNCC took on a citywide desegregation effort in Arkansas targeting McDonald's #433. The McDonald's drive-in was in a residential area in Pine Bluff, a town forty miles south of Little Rock. The franchise opened the previous year on July 3, 1962, just in time for Independence Day celebrations.[52] Within six months of the grand opening, members of SNCC's Pine Bluff branch became aware that the McDonald's was barring black customers from service, and they folded the restaurant into its larger plan to transform the city.[53] The Pine Bluff contingent started developing a plan to demand that blacks be served at McDonald's. After exhausting their patience for polite requests and appeals to the city, SNCC mounted a four-day-long demonstration in early August of 1963. Vivian Carroll Jones and other Pine Bluff volunteers entered the restaurant one by one and formed a line in front of the order counter. They were ignored. Jones remembered, "the orders were served over our heads to white customers," while the demonstrators remained in line. As was common across the South, the protesters' passive resistance was met by a crowd's escalating emotions. The white patrons began pushing and cursing at the demonstrators. The protesters drew upon the training that SNCC provided on how to remain calm and unresponsive to the invectives, slurs, insults, threats, shoves, and slaps. The mob persisted. The SNCC team refused to respond. Eventually, their attention shifted to sounds coming from outside the restaurant, where a single-arch neon sign beckoned customers to McDonald's Hamburgers. Sensible drivers proceeding down Pine Bluff's Main Street toward the restaurant may have kept on driving when they saw a "mob of about two hundred white youth . . . carrying bats, bottles, and bricks." There were also plenty of people in Pine Bluff who wanted to teach SNCC a lesson. They were the same kind of people who had been harboring their outrage since Beals and her friends in Little Rock had the president of the United States protect their right to attend the crown jewel of southern high schools. Those folks headed to the parking lot or across the street and joined the mob.

Jones felt the temperature rise inside the restaurant; maybe it was stress that was making her sweat. She looked around and noticed that everyone looked flush and overheated as they breathed in the air thick with the smell of hamburgers left too long on grills and the perspiration of the workers, protesters, and customers. Someone had locked them inside of the McDonald's out of concern for their safety. But no one felt secure. A McDonald's employee had disabled the air-conditioning unit in the restaurant, and as the temperatures rose, Jones wondered if she would make it out alive. Anyone involved in SNCC knew that civil rights demonstrations, protests, and mass meetings, as well as car trips through unfamiliar territory, and even talking back to your boss or a storekeeper, could all have deadly consequences. Activism had taken the lives of people demanding the basic rights of American citizenship before—whether you were seeking a ballot or a burger, standing up for yourself could lead to your death. Then, the doors to the McDonald's were unlocked, allowing the group to inhale some desperately needed fresh air. But the respite turned into a brutal reckoning as local police charged for the SNCC members and arrested them for "failure to leave a place of business." The officers did little to protect the arrestees from the rabidity of their canines or the madness of the crowd of Pine Bluff's segregation advocates. Someone in the mob attacked three young women with a makeshift weapon of ammonia.[54] An injured Arkansas Agricultural and Mechanical student hoped that a handkerchief would soothe her burning face, but it would be of no help. Instead, the chemical devoured the cloth.[55]

The visit left protesters traumatized, injured, and with arrest records, but nothing had changed at the Pine Bluff McDonald's.

Nearly a year of strategizing and protesting yielded no changes, and the Pine Bluff freedom workers called for a "nationwide protest" against the hundreds of McDonald's locations coast to coast. Perhaps under advisement from McDonald's headquarters or local businesses, the Pine Bluff franchise operator used the courts in an attempt to dress down the activists and impede further demonstrations. The franchisee saw that SNCC would not back down from "mass arrests, beatings, and the throwing of acid," so he figured that an injunction banning further action at the restaurant may be the solution to his problem. Store owners, school boards, and cities filed injunctions against major civil rights organizations throughout the 1950s and 1960s to suppress boycotts, marches, and demands to enforce the laws equally. Even when judges ruled these injunctions unconstitutional, the process of responding to the orders in court could tie up precious movement time and slow momentum. If activists defied the injunctions, it put them at risk for arrests as they awaited the news if the order was indeed enforceable. In late November, two SNCC field secretaries accompanied Pine Bluff members to a hearing on whether a McDonald's franchise could permanently ban SNCC from protesting at the restaurant. The order was also filed to keep members of the Arkansas chapter of the "NAACP and Black Muslims" from mobilizing in front of the store. McDonald's inflexibility was particularly enervating considering that SNCC found "most lunch counters" in the area were racially integrated.[56] In February of 1964, after a full year of action, the Pine Bluff McDonald's moved to desegregate.[57] Food historian Angela Jill Cooley believes that fast food chains in the South were particularly loyal to the local customs of segregation even when maintaining it was against their own interests or was out of step with other businesses. Cooley discovered that "when McDonald's implemented indoor seating, in the midst of civil rights sit-in activism, many Southern franchisees practiced racial segregation even when other local eateries had abolished the practice."[58] Franchises with ties to profitable corporate brands may have felt less motivated to comply with federal antidiscrimination policies because their parent companies did not demand it, or because they did not feel as beholden to local community challenges. Regardless of how franchises approached the new law, the sit-ins and the signing of the Civil Rights Act of 1964 would not adjourn the conversation about restaurants and racism.

If Kroc and his associates knew about the Pine Bluff protests—which was highly likely as Kroc was known to be controlling to the point of obsession about his restaurants—then it was either too insignificant or too damning to be included in his biography and other official accounts of McDonald's history. If McDonald's executives remained silent about Pine Bluff because they believed that the racial violence and chaos in Arkansas was an outlier, an issue that had nothing to do with Speedee or his growing dominance in the burger market, then they would soon learn better. Kroc's McDonald's—only ten years old when President Lyndon Johnson signed the Civil Rights Act and made it a violation of federal law to keep people out of McDonald's, a Howard Johnson's, the local swimming pool, or a movie theatre—was maturing in a turbulent decade, and the company would have to grow up fast in unfamiliar territory: America's inner cities.

* * *

The July 2 signing ceremony for the Civil Rights Act was the sort of interracial gathering civil rights organizations hoped could then be replicated in restaurants and diners across the country. The Act made it plain that the federal government would have the authority to ensure that "all persons" would be "entitled to the full and equal enjoyment of the goods, services, facilities, and privileges, advantages, and accommodations . . . without discrimination or segregation on the ground of race, color, religion, or national origin."[59] After the president celebrated with the guests present at the signing—including an ebullient King, Urban League head Roy Wilkins, and the supporters of the bill who waited out a seventy-five-day filibuster against it—the hard work of implementation was still ahead.

The law was only as strong and meaningful as local compliance and enforcement, and a presidential pen could not compel obedience to the Act. Attorney General Robert Kennedy dispatched Department of Justice investigators to monitor adherence, and each month field reports from southern cities charted how much impact the Act was having on the local level. Uncooperative tavern owners and impertinent innkeepers got creative with their strategies of circumvention. Richmond's Emporia Diner offered two sets of menus to black and white customers with varying prices. Whites were offered an "order of southern fried chicken at $1.75 . . . and $5.25" was the price for "undesirable" customers.[60] While the Justice Department concentrated its attention on the South, blacks in northern cities were not sure what to make of it. Jim Crow–style segregation was not as much of a fixture in their lives, and they needed legislation to address their more urgent needs—fair or "open" housing, equal education, and redress for police brutality. Three months after he attended the White House ceremony celebrating the act becoming law, Urban League Executive Director Whitney Young summed up the limits of the public accommodations effort in his "What Negroes Want" column in the *Chicago Defender.* "Negroes are learning that even the passage of a historic Civil Rights Act is not sufficient to wipe out rats . . ." He accused whites of being delusional about the impact of the change in law, arguing that "frivolous inertia" and "conscienceless gentility" was a result of when "a human being tries desperately to believe that, by the removal of old signs and symbols—in this case 'white only'—that a new world has been created . . . the rats are still biting; the children are still in the worst schools; the prenatal care is absent; the landlord won't send up any heat, and the husband is doing the hardest, dirtiest work for the smallest pay and then labeled as 'lazy,' that is, if he's lucky enough to find work."[61] Young's editorial gave voice to the frustrating state of black America as the goodwill and hope engendered by the March on Washington for Jobs and Freedom and the passage of major civil and voting rights legislation between 1963 and 1965 yielded little in terms of employment, health, housing, and educational opportunity.

Young and other activists not only lamented the growing poverty among black communities devastated by bisecting highways; they were also connecting a growing disillusionment and hopelessness, especially among black youth, with increasing instances of urban uprisings and rebellions. Throughout the twentieth century, African-American communities resisting police violence or mobs of vengeful whites have borne the brunt of lost lives and property damage when their neighborhoods become the battlefields of racial unrest. By 1967, these confrontations were so prevalent and disturbing that the year's summer was christened "the long, hot summer." From June to August, uprisings broke out in Buffalo, Detroit, Atlanta, Cincinnati, and Birmingham. At the close of the season, at least 85 people were dead, more than 2,000 injured, and 11,000 had been arrested. The summer inspired the formation of the National Advisory Commission on Civil Disorders—known colloquially as the Kerner Commission after the committee chairman, Illinois Governor Otto Kerner. The commission was tasked with assessing the causes of the violence and suggesting ways to stave off future devastation.

The Kerner Commission determined that blacks living in the inner cities from Watts, California, to Newark, New Jersey, were partly prone to loot and riot out of retaliation for the abysmal condition of their neighborhood businesses. The commission's investigation asserted that blacks expressed "grievances concerning unfair commercial practices affecting Negro consumers," and they often encountered "inferior quality goods (particularly meats and produce) at higher prices and they were subjected to excessive interest rates and fraudulent commercial practices."[62] The commission advocated a plethora of federal, local, and private-sector funded programs to increase job training, educational opportunities, and better community-police relations. The two-paragraph "Conclusion" section of the report quoted Kenneth B. Clark, the noted black psychologist whose "doll study" poignantly linked the experience of segregation with the internalization of self-hatred among black children. Clark was among the first experts called before the august panel, and his words captured the skepticism of black Americans:

I read that report . . . of the 1919 riot in Chicago, and it is as if I were reading the report of the investigating committee on the Harlem riot of 1935, the report of the investigating committee on the Harlem riot of 1943, the report of the McCone Commission on the Watts Riot. I must again in candor say to you members of the Commission—it is a kind of Alice in Wonderland with the same moving pictures reshown over and over again, the same analysis, the same recommendation, and the same inaction.

Shaped by Clark's words, the Kerner Commission contended that it was "time now to end the destruction and the violence, not only in the streets of the ghetto but in the lives of people."[63] Five weeks after the first printing of the *Report of the National Advisory Commission on Civil Disorders* by the U.S. Government Printing Office, Clark's reflection about the cycle of racial uprisings and Kerner's declaration that now was the time, would be read with even more scrutiny and urgency. Martin Luther King Jr. had been assassinated in Memphis.

* * *

Martin Luther King's 1968 visit to Memphis was not about the business community's segregation practices—this time. King had visited the city throughout his tenure as head of the Southern Christian Leadership Conference, and he knew the contours of black struggle in Tennessee around equal access to the city's downtown shops, local colleges, and well-compensated jobs. Some observers considered Memphis a "racially moderate city" in light of the police brutality that met civil rights workers in Alabama and the proliferation of those deemed "missing," actually victims of racial violence, in Mississippi. In 1957, King joined Arkansas NAACP chairwoman and Little Rock Nine representative Daisy Bates to support a slate of black candidates for local office, the Volunteer Ticket, who were competitors for commissioner of public works, juvenile court judge, and two seats on the city's board of education. The pamphlet introducing the candidates displayed the group's slogan: "The Negro Has a Love Affair with Destiny."[64]

He returned again two years later, in 1959, to assist a Volunteer Ticket hopeful, civil rights attorney Benjamin Hooks (who would later play his own role in fast food franchising as the legal representative for Mahalia Jackson's Glori-Fried Chicken).[65] By 1968, locals had witnessed the end of segregation in restaurants, stores, public parks and libraries, and celebrated the first black graduate of Memphis State University. The black vote was also able to secure a victory for A. W. Willis, a member of the state's General Assembly in 1964, a first for a black Tennessean since the Reconstruction era.

Triumphs aside, King descended upon a depressed city, where sanitation workers were on strike. In the spring of 1968, Memphis was an apt illustration for the minister's concern about the next stage in the fight to realize racial progress. The COLORED ONLY signs had disappeared, but the signs of economic inequality were still clearly visible—and seemingly permanent—throughout the city. Black sanitation workers took to the streets to protest the unsafe conditions and poor pay they endured while keeping Memphis communities free from garbage and vermin. After the horrific deaths of Echol Cole and Robert Walker, two black workers who were crushed to death by a malfunctioning trash compactor, their compatriots and community were galvanized to strike. Thirteen hundred workers went on strike. Hundreds of the workers, costumed with sandwich boards covering their torsos that declared I AM A MAN, marched along the main thoroughfares of Memphis protesting the dehumanizing machinery of low-wage work and racism.

"The Negro Has a Love Affair with Destiny." Who still believed that in 1968?

Blacks in Memphis were not living out anything resembling a love affair with the city. The dilapidated housing. The schools that had yet to desegregate. The jobs, if you were lucky to have one, and their insulting wages. With no love lost between them, the city and the sanitation workers remained at an impasse as strikers continued to wear their signs and hold up their placards. As the work stoppage continued and the heightened tensions of the strike led to instances of violence during workers' marches, local organizers reached out to the SCLC and requested that King visit the workers and their supporters. King's presence could guarantee stirring and passionate words of encouragement, and the flash of news cameras at the very least.

On his first visit to address the sanitation workers and their supporters, King reminded them how essential the boycott was because black rights meant nothing without economic justice. He asked:

> What does it profit a man to be able to eat at an integrated lunch counter if he doesn't have enough money to buy a hamburger? What does it profit a man to be able to eat at the swankest integrated restaurant when he doesn't even earn enough money to take his wife out to dine? What does it profit one to have access to the hotels of our cities, and the hotels of our highways, when we don't earn enough money to take our family on a vacation?[66]

On his second visit to Memphis in April, King gathered the increasingly weary movement followers for a mass meeting at the Bishop Charles Mason Temple to expound on his meditation about black wealth and black economic power. The audience braved a tornado warning to hear King's electrifying message. The radical reverend spoke for more than forty minutes about the arc of history, from the chosen people's biblical march through the wilderness to the most recent turning points in the civil rights movement—from the sit-ins to the freedom rides to the securing of voting rights in Alabama. King reminded the crowd of their moral power when they practice nonviolence, as well as their economic import. This address—King's final public oration—is often noted for its prophetic declarations, including the haunting statement "I may not get there with you." Yet, the substance of the address also forecasts the ways that economic issues—from ending poverty to strategic boycotting of national companies to business ownership—would become central to civil rights visions in the 1970s.

King, in his fiery style, stood at the podium and said:

> Now the other thing we'll have to do is this: always anchor our external direct action with the power of economic withdrawal.

Now we are poor people, individually we are poor when you compare us with white society in America. We are poor. Never stop and forget that collectively, that means all of us together, collectively we are richer than all the nations in the world, with the exception of nine. Did you ever think about that? After you leave the United States, Soviet Russia, Great Britain, West Germany, France . . . the American Negro collectively is richer than most nations of the world. We have an annual income of more than thirty billion dollars a year, which is more than all of the exports of the United States and more than the national budget of Canada. Did you know that? That's power right there, if we know how to pool it.[67]

King spoke about initiating a "bank-in" movement in Memphis by withdrawing monies from discriminatory banks and moving accounts to black-owned institutions. He suggested an "insurance-in" to promote the handful of black insurance companies still in operation in the late 1960s, and gestured toward a young Jesse Jackson's experience with consumer boycotts.[68] King advised the group to boycott Coca-Cola, Sealtest Dairy Milk, Wonder and Hart's Breads. He continued:

As Jesse Jackson has said, up to now only the garbage men have been feeling pain. Now we must kind of redistribute that pain. We are choosing these companies because they haven't been fair in their hiring policies, and we are choosing them because they can begin the process of saying they are going to support the needs and the rights of these men who are on strike.[69]

The tragic accident that claimed the lives of Cole and Walker—eight years to the day that the Greensboro sit-in ignited a movement—ended a period of King's leadership and guidance of the nonviolent movement toward integrating explicit calls for an economic response to racial inequality. The distance between the Woolworth's counter in Greensboro and the pulpit of Mason Temple was bridged by the March on Washington's call for *jobs* and freedom. The route between Greensboro and Memphis was connected by the SCLC's Northern Campaign to end housing discrimination in Chicago. This ideological road was traveled by the architects of the Poor People's Campaign, King's ambitious second March on Washington to create a tent city in the capital where the poor from every corner of the nation could rally for economic justice.[70] At the close of the Memphis event, King bid farewell to the crowd: "And so I'm happy tonight; I'm not worried about anything; I'm not fearing any man. Mine eyes have seen the glory of the coming of the Lord."[71]

The next evening, an assassin shot and killed Martin Luther King Jr.

That night, the Holy Week Uprising began.

* * *

McDonald's store manager Roland Jones heard the news out of Memphis as he prepared to leave a suburban Washington, D.C., franchise and head into the District. The West Tennessee native moved to Memphis when he was ten years old, and he considered the City of Blues his hometown. He sat behind the wheel of his car and wondered what direction he was going to take. He knew he had to check on his boss's other restaurants, including the New York Avenue location that had always been a little tough because of the neighborhood.[72] As one of the few black people with a supervisory role with McDonald's, Jones had never imagined a career at a fast food chain. He didn't grow up eating in restaurants, and he had never been to a McDonald's drive-in until he became an employee. In Memphis, he learned early to stay on his side of town. The few times he tested the city's color line, he was harassed by police. He was careful in Memphis, and on April 4, 1968, he knew he had to remain vigilant in Washington, D.C.[73] For the time being, he decided to stay put and ignore the part of him that told him to turn around and head back south. Jones called the area franchise owners to see what he could do to keep watch over the McDonald's restaurants in the eye of the storm, as local and federal forces tried to compel order on streets across the country. Chicago's local authorities were not as successful as their municipal peers elsewhere in restoring order, and McDonald's executives housed in a downtown office building nervously fielded reports on how their city locations were faring during the unrest. Jones's success in keeping restaurants closed immediately after King's death, and later securing and cleaning up vandalized locations, brought him to the attention of McDonald's senior corporate leaders. After a series of phone calls back and forth between Jones and McDonald's executives in downtown Chicago, Jones was offered a promotion into an entirely new role with the company. Jones would travel around the country and search for someone to become the very first black franchise owner in McDonald's history. Jones had a feeling that what he was about to do was going to be important for McDonald's and for the black community that would get their "own" franchise.

Three years earlier, on April 21, 1965, McDonald's became a publicly traded company and the first fast food IPO. While investors on New York's Wall Street watched the offering climb from $22.50 to more than $30.00 a share, Martin Luther King Jr. was delivering a talk to the Bar of the City of New York. He spoke of an economic boycott in Alabama and offered that, in response to Klan violence, "the economic power structure of our nation can do a great deal to stop that kind of terror."[74] These two events—both reported in national newspapers—may have appeared in different sections of the papers and seemed worlds apart to the readers. But within a few years, McDonald's ambitions for its company and King's unrealized dreams for the nation would converge.

But first, Roland Jones had to get to Chicago.

CHAPTER TWO

Burgers in the Age of Black Capitalism

After Martin Luther King Jr.'s assassination in Memphis on April 4, 1968, cities across the country exploded in violence. Some black business owners tried to reduce property damage to their stores by indicating that they were "soul brother" outfits. Photo by Paul Sequeira / Getty Images.

The storefronts that lined the commercial boulevards of Chicago's black neighborhoods after the Holy Week uprising reflected the mood of a city distraught by a leader's death and disheartened by its familiarity with the destruction that followed. Along Madison Street and Roosevelt Road, the damage was incongruous, but the entire neighborhood remained bleak. KING IS DEAD and LONG LIVE THE KING painted on a partially boarded-up store window stood as an unrefined but heartfelt memorial. A burnt-out brick building was marked BLACKSTONE KILLERS, a reference to the Blackstone Rangers street gang that controlled pockets of Chicago's South Side. The gang had actually assisted police in cooling youth anger in their territories during the chaos. Both levels of the Madison-Albany Department store were gutted; the merchandise was likely looted and the windows were blown out in a fire. Eerily, the store's brightly printed sign advertising "Men's and Boy's Ready to Wear Shoes" was still intact. An undisturbed tailor shop or dry cleaner provided a glimmer of hope among the blocks and blocks of devastation. More than two hundred buildings had been destroyed; many of them would never be rebuilt.[1] Roland Jones surveyed all the broken windows, vacant lots, and debris, as he headed to the Woodlawn neighborhood, where a battered but still functional McDonald's waited for a new owner.

The Woodlawn restaurant was the eighth McDonald's location opened after Kroc began his leadership of the chain, and the store initially served mostly white diners. Rapid changes in the surrounding community's racial demographics transformed Woodlawn. In the spring of 1968, it was among the roster of white-owned businesses that attracted the irritation of its black neighbors and clientele during the uprisings. Jones and another Washington, D.C.–based manager, Carl Osborne, drew the notice of McDonald's executives when the men adeptly took control of the area's restaurants after white franchisees and employees fled their stores and were too afraid to return to their positions. Even after calm was restored in cities that were inflamed by King's death and stores could resume normal operating order, some white franchisees wanted out. McDonald's became the fast food market leader by being relentless, and this national crisis would not stop it. The sit-ins across the South were a minor disruption in years in which they continued to outperform their competitors. Why would this moment be any different? The white franchisees would be allowed to walk away. In lieu of retreating from the inner city, McDonald's would simply find translators. These new McDonald's employees would explain why they could be trusted and why they were different than the merchants that regularly ripped off and disrespected black customers. Although McDonald's corporate offices had previously discussed the possibility of recruiting black franchisees to open new, urban stores, the 1968 unrest hastened the process. King's assassination rendered some of their restaurants targets and they couldn't allow the company to be vulnerable if another event—another assassination, another tragedy, another explosion—like this were to happen.

McDonald's decision to seek black franchisees to replace white ones in predominantly black communities was affirmed by influential voices which suggested that national trends indicated that if the nation did not act, U.S. cities would experience more disturbances. Foundations, think tanks, and riot commissions published a spate of alarming studies on the pervasive economic and social problems that plagued black America. Meanwhile, Madison Avenue and Wall Street were evaluating advertising and marketing reports that advised that companies should capture a lucrative and growing market of upwardly mobile black consumers. The 1968 presidential election, slated for seven months and one day after King's assassination, opened up conversations about the federal government's role in protecting and financing equal opportunity. All of these forces informed McDonald's next steps in Chicago and across the country throughout the 1970s. The knowledge, rhetoric, and insight generated from these experts and industries pointed toward private business as the answer to a myriad of problems. Almost immediately after he was laid to rest in his hometown of Atlanta, King's death became inextricably tied to the advancement of capitalism, which he had believed "failed to meet the needs of the masses," and was on a par with the "evils of militarism and evils of racism."[2]

Jones had King on his mind when he met with Ed Schmitt, Chicago's regional manager of franchises, to accept a special consultant role on black franchising. Jones described Schmitt as "pretty liberal," and applauded his commitment to not only identifying black franchisees, "but also transforming the image of blacks in the system."[3] McDonald's had little information on its black consumer market, and with few black managerial or executive staff, Schmitt and his colleagues placed a lot of trust in Jones to understand how to best select someone who was willing, able, and determined enough to take on a restaurant that had been insulted, robbed, or even shot at in the past. The seasoned McDonald's manager believed that the right person would possess a mix of characteristics learned inside and outside of school. Jones recalled thinking that McDonald's needed to find someone "who could communicate with the corporate structure, and identify with blacks on the grassroots level." Familiarity with "grassroots" meant being attuned to what was happening on the streets and on the stock market. Grassroots businessmen were regular folk who managed to survive the ins and outs of Chicago's slums and who could command respect from gang members and corporate board members alike.[4] The search ended when he met Herman Petty, a recent visitor to a local franchising fair. Jones liked the way Petty carried himself; Petty could talk to the white managers and executives comfortably, which could be a challenge for men of his generation who grew up under some of the most rigid segregation. The Tennessean tasked with marching McDonald's into a multiracial future had never sat next to a white person or had a substantive conversation with one until he joined the military.[5]

Petty was a military man, too. He was even from Woodlawn and grew up at 65th and Evans, a little more than a mile from the McDonald's. Petty was a true son of the South Side, which was remade by the Great Migration, when nearly a million African Americans moved to Chicago between 1916 and 1970.[6] He was born at Provident Hospital, the historic black training facility founded in 1889 as a nursing school for black women.[7] He attended Roosevelt University, a consciously integrated school in Chicago's downtown. In 1968, he was among a generation of South Siders who tried to eke out opportunity in the Windy City any way he could. Petty made ends meet driving a city bus and running a barber shop. Neither job required a formal education, and both almost certainly underutilized his skills and training. But they were the types of positions that routed blacks into a solidly middle-class life in the 1960s. The high rates of unemployment on Chicago's South Side and waves of deindustrialization in the 1970s ravaged Woodlawn and surrounding communities. By 1975, Woodlawn's unemployment rate reached 30%, and the joblessness rate for youth was at 50%. Chicago's overall unemployment rate was only 8%. Nearly two-thirds of Woodlawn residents that year reported relying on some form of government assistance. Local activists believed that the numbers were actually higher.[8] Even before Petty attended a 1968 franchising fair, where representatives recruited curious attendees to invest in the next big idea in fried fish made fast or quickie oil changes, he was doing pretty well for himself given the city's economic picture painted by racial discrimination.[9] But solid jobs were just that, jobs, and for African Americans, how hard you worked was an independent variable in the calculus of how much wealth you were able to build.

Petty's work ethic and reputation would compensate for his lack of capital. In the excitement to place a black franchisee, McDonald's exhibited an uncharacteristic flexibility. Petty was already somewhat familiar with the restaurant business, having been previously approached by two white businessmen about opening a new venture. That eatery never materialized, but the men steered Petty toward learning about franchising. After a meeting with Jones and Schmitt, Petty agreed to take over the Woodlawn property and started his franchisee training program at Hamburger University, the intensive preparation program that was housed at McDonald's campus in Oak Brook, a Chicago suburb. Petty later recalled: "One minute I was in Oak Brook finding out more about McDonald's, and the next minute I was on the telephone telling my wife I'm not a barber anymore."[10] In McDonald's enthusiasm to install a black owner, they waived the requirement that a franchisee personally provide 100% of the contract fee. In the late 1960s, a McDonald's franchise license fee could cost up to $150,000 for a "turnkey" quality store.[11] The franchisee operated the restaurant for a fixed period of time, and then the corporate offices either renewed or denied the license. Black franchisees looked for help with the additional costs that came due each year after they first opened their restaurants. In the 1970s, franchisees paid a rental fee of no less than 8.5%, which was based on a store's annual revenues. McDonald's also collected an annual 3.5% service charge, and eventually franchisees had to contribute to advertising funds to support national and local campaigns.[12]

Petty was also given dispensation to partner with white investors to provide monies, as long as he was the majority owner and the public face of the store in the community. Franchisees were asked to be a presence in their stores, and they could not hold multiple jobs and responsibilities that kept them away from their patrons. Crudely called "zebra" or "salt and pepper" partnerships, these agreements designated white benefactors as silent investors and secondary partners. McDonald's did not stipulate the finance terms between white investors and black franchisees, and the parties with more financial leverage could charge whatever administrative fees, interest rates, and management dues they wanted. After a few years of bringing more blacks to the McDonald's System, Jones fielded complaints about reckless investors removing cash from registers at closing time.[13] Franchisees complained of neglectful silent partners who failed to make payments and settle debts. In the early 1970s, McDonald's eventually intervened and paid out half a million dollars to expel problematic investors.[14]

Petty's partnership with white investors was not the only delicate relationship he had to manage. The Blackstone Rangers, who had proved themselves helpful during the uprising, had claimed the Woodlawn McDonald's as part of their turf. They had intimidated the previous franchisee into hiring some of their members. The Rangers were not the best employees, and the presence of gang members in the restaurant deterred older people and families from dropping by for a milkshake. The Rangers also had a reputation for shaking down neighborhood businesses. White business owners often lamented that Chicago's gang members would threaten them with arson, violence, even death if they failed to pay them for diverting trouble from their stores or determining it untouchable in their robbery sprees. Rangers leader Jeff Fort, who famously applied for and secured a million dollars in federal and private funds for a combination of real and bogus South Side job training and business initiatives, used a variety of methods to extort businesses. In March of 1969 he formalized the Rangers business protection plan by forcing a Red Rooster grocery store to hire 22 of his members.[15] The Red Rooster was one of the South Side food stores that black residents and local civil rights groups accused of "selling poor quality meat, overcharging and short changing." Operation Breadbasket—the economic justice wing of the Southern Christian Leadership Conference—negotiated with the supermarket to improve the quality of its foods and hire neighborhood people, and the Rangers demanded a share of the jobs. After hiring the gang members, the store reported the Rangers to the police. The employment scandal propelled Red Rooster to write off doing business on the South Side, and in 1970 they closed seven of its stores, which led to the dismissal of 300 black workers.[16] Petty knew that he couldn't be equivocal in his stance with the Rangers. They had to be out. Petty leveraged some of his goodwill from his barber shop to level with the Rangers: The gang members had to leave, they couldn't negotiate any job guarantees, and no more loitering around the property.[17] The Rangers were not looking to fight Petty, and they may have been pleased to see the restaurant change hands from white to black.[18] They agreed to concede the sliver of gang territory to the McDonald's franchisee.

Once Petty resolved the Rangers situation, he had to find reliable employees. Like many African-American firsts, he had to depart from the McDonald's directives that were designed with someone white working in somewhere suburban in mind. Since the McDonalds revamped their San Bernardino restaurant by eliminating the carhop role, many McDonald's franchisees did not employ women. Even after the first woman franchised a Pontiac, Michigan, McDonald's in 1960, it was rare to see women at the grill or the Multi-Mixer station. Petty, having observed their abilities in the community, prioritized hiring black women to work at his restaurant, and he hosted restaurant operations trainings at local churches to prepare them before they applied their lessons in the store. Petty and other black operators are often credited with bringing women employees back into the restaurant and furrowing entry points into managerial positions and franchise ownership. Next on Petty's employment list were "guys who came out of the service," like he did. [19] Restaurant training often adapts elements of military procedure—formalities regarding neat uniforms, an emphasis on precision and efficiency, and a system of ascending ranks. As a black franchisee, Petty may have felt the pressure for his restaurant to outshine those of his white compatriots, and in selecting workers, he could not leave anything to chance.

Regardless of the strength or might of his crew, Petty confronted problems that were not solvable with street-level negotiations or discerning personnel choices. The physical state of his store, as was the case of all businesses caught in the crosshairs of the uprising, was poor. Jones found that black owners were usually assigned to facilities that were "run down and the equipment mostly broken." [20] This was a common problem for black franchisees; they inherited some of the system's most damaged city properties. As black franchisees' numbers grew, they watched enviously as white operators acquired well-maintained suburban stores with functioning exhaust fans, freezers that could preserve shipments of beef patties, and air-conditioning units that could match unseasonably hot summers. Blacks would wait longer to be paired with newly built restaurants, adapted for the newest trends in fast food: indoor dining, drive-thru windows, and PlayPlaces. For some black franchisees, acquiring a restaurant that a white person no longer wanted may have been reminiscent of how they had always lived their lives. On Chicago's South Side, even upper-middle-class blacks moved into homes that were abandoned by whites who were panicked about the possibility of having them as neighbors. In the South, black schoolchildren would learn from textbooks that had become too outdated or degraded for white children to use, so they were retired to "the colored school." In Great Migration cities, blacks worshiped at churches and synagogues that converted from Episcopalianism and Judaism to Baptist. Blacks were used to making the most out of what whites had cast off and what was left behind. The fast food industry was no different.

On December 21, 1968, Herman Petty opened the first black-franchised McDonald's in the country. As the tumultuous year drew to a close, Chicago was still troubled by the past spring's Holy Week. Compounding the city's springtime distress was the turbulent Democratic National Convention in August, where anti–Vietnam War protests overtook the downtown and convention gathering places. For the second time in one year, the National Guard was called in to assist local police in restoring order. The luxury hotels and restaurants that catered to the Democratic Party's nominees and delegates were a world away from Petty's McDonald's. But in a year in which many black Chicagoans felt ignored or disregarded, something (almost) brand-new, something in the possession of a black person, and something to celebrate may have been a welcomed change of pace. By the first anniversary of King's death, Petty had gained a hold of his business. He figured out how to upgrade the facilities. He was a regular fixture in the kitchen and front counter to oversee operations. At the end of his first year, his restaurant sales had increased by 75%.[21] McDonald's supported his bid for a second South Side property on nearby Vincennes Avenue, and they helped free him from his partnership with outside investors.[22]

Black franchisees' presence alone did not mean that they would automatically attract black customers, although it did make a difference. McDonald's was popular because it was cheap and it was among the few choices left in black neighborhoods eviscerated after civil insurrections. Mom-and-pop diners and catfish shacks, as well as larger outfits like grocery stores and furniture galleries, packed up and left for good in 1968. Even black franchisees were surprised by how well their restaurants performed. Wayne Embry, a professional basketball player–turned–McDonald's franchisee, gained his Milwaukee store in 1969. He was told that his restaurant would earn approximately $750,000 a year; he soon was earning $1.2 million.[23] His store's success reflected the research findings on black people and fast food. By 1972, one study found that "in the poor black neighborhoods, the cheap mass-produced food was more than a snack. It generally constituted an all-purpose meal. Not surprisingly, a disproportionate number of 'ghetto stands' belong to

Hamburger Central's 'million-dollar club,' the restaurants which do over a million dollars a year in business."[24] "Black stores," as they were called, on average grossed 25% more profits than "white stores."[25] Throughout the 1970s, market research reports found that black men displayed a "tendency" to eat at McDonald's more than any other demographic. Blacks were also more likely to be "heavy users," meaning they consumed McDonald's food at least once a week and tended to spend more money than whites on fast food. Although the data indicated that McDonald's was doing well with blacks, their studies cautioned that black customers generally "display more use vulnerability to competition," so they required concentrated efforts to maintain their loyalties.[26] Consultants recommended that McDonald's pursue several paths to expanding black market share through black franchisee induction. The suggestions included setting up "a high priority program to build more stores to serve black customers," increasing their use of "local store marketing programs" for their black-owned franchises, and establishing a Black Store Task Force to streamline the planning process and beat out Burger King, which was close on McDonald's heels in forging black franchising networks. McDonald's was even advised to find ways to make their reliable clown mascot Ronald McDonald more appealing to black children.[27]

Implementation of these ambitious ideas fell on the shoulders of black franchisees and the small number of black executives that joined McDonald's after 1968. Petty made the idea of a black franchisee viable, and McDonald's had a number of cities in mind where they wanted to recreate this model. McDonald's needed more people out in the field to identify black talent, and CEO Fred Turner invited Bob Beavers, a future board member, to talk about a new opportunity with the company. Beavers, a native of Washington, D.C., was initially taken aback by the office's demographics. "When I was being interviewed, I got the tour of our offices, which covered three floors of the building . . . there was not a single person of color in the entire building." The office did not give him a "comforting feeling."[28] Beavers had worked at franchises back home, and he may have heard from Jones and Osborne about McDonald's heightened seriousness about diversifying the operator corps.[29] Beavers was attuned to the changes in the U.S. business climate in the late 1960s, and he knew that franchise expansion would require McDonald's to capitalize on federal programs and acknowledge the distinct challenges of black franchises. Beavers proposed the 50-2 Program, which set a goal of opening 50 stores by operators of color in a 2-year span. To tackle this ambitious goal, Beavers worked with a black Small Business Administration bureaucrat to teach potential franchisees to tap into the federal agency's programs for minority businesses.[30] He also convinced McDonald's to establish a satellite campus for Hamburger University. With the expansion of black franchisees on Chicago's South Side, who in turn hired more black managers and crew shift leaders, traveling to suburban Chicago was not practical or comfortable. The demand for operator and employee training in Chicago's black centers was high, and improvisation like Petty's use of churches to meet staff was not sustainable. McDonald's opened a permanent classroom building on the South Side, where black operators took crash courses on the ins and outs of franchise management—registers, food handling safety, security measures, and scheduling. Black franchise owners in other cities traveled to the facility to catch up with their friends and learn from each other. Kroc, hardly a racial liberal, supported the idea and even offered the new corps access to a bus and the company's private airplane. Kroc did not quite understand the pressures that black professionals inside of his organization faced, and he may have not cared. But he understood the bottom line, and as long as black franchisees could deliver profits and deliver QSCV—quality, service, cleanliness, and value—he was willing to meet them where they were.[31]

In the three years after Petty assumed control over the Woodlawn location, the roster of stores operated by black McDonald's franchisees grew from four to almost fifty. Despite many successes, black franchisees had to manage a sometimes uncomfortable duality. They were enlisted to engender in the black community trust in a white corporation. Yet, they still struggled with their own feelings of being exploited and misunderstood within the McDonald's franchise system. The operators related to the reasons why throwing a rock at a grocer that never sold fresh meats or produce to your family could feel like a release, a triumph even. They also knew that few blacks had the opportunity they were given as franchisees—to actually own something (in part) and to be able to not just get by, but to really earn money. They were a minority within a minority. In 1968, *Time* magazine estimated that only 1% of the nation's 5 million private businesses were black-owned, and black business comprised mostly "mom-and-pop operations, catering to a ghetto clientele and providing a slim income for their owners and a few jobs for others," and that "a quarter of Negro firms [were] barbershops or beauty salons . . . mortuaries, restaurants, bars, small grocery stores and cleaning establishments," and "few manufacturing or distribution firms."[32] Many of those businesses would close, or they required their owners to have second jobs to stay open. Faced with those damning numbers, black franchisees sought every possible path to continue to succeed with McDonald's.

Black franchisees couldn't talk to very many members of the Oak Brook staff about how they felt, so every time another black operator was handed keys to a store, he joined a community that welcomed him with open arms. The first twelve black franchisees acquired restaurants in Chicago, Kansas City, St. Louis, and Milwaukee. They came from different backgrounds—some had business experience, others did not. Some had actually worked at McDonald's, others had rarely encountered it. But they all relied on each other to talk about the things that would be unfamiliar or unappreciated at Oak Brook. After meeting with each other at the "other" Hamburger University over the years, they decided to formalize their community. In 1972, they formed the National Black McDonald's Operators Association (NBMOA). The operators were well aware of the discomfort that black organizations elicited, regardless of the substance of their work. An early supporter of the group reasoned that McDonald's allowed the black organization to exist "as long as the BMOA was localized to the Midwest, confined to one field consultant, and focused on training and self-improvement, it had been accepted as a positive by the executives."[33] In the age of the Black Power movement's calls for separatism and a white resistance to efforts to integrate schools and neighborhoods, an all-black anything could raise eyebrows. In his description of the NBMOA, Petty emphasized that "they were not a militant group," which may have been his way of saying that the NBMOA would not challenge McDonald's too much or too quickly about the conditions of their stores or the lack of racial diversity within their headquarters. Gradually, as the organization expanded, they would take on McDonald's on issues of equity and parity among franchisees. By the time Hank Thomas entered franchising in 1982, the former civil rights movement activist described the NBMOA as "both the NAACP and SCLC for us."[34] For black organizations, whether it be a business group, an art league, or a concerned parents club, racism necessitates some engagement with the politics of access or the search to belong. Since its founding, the NBMOA has mitigated slights and oversight from McDonald's toward its members, and they have had to address demands from the communities that have enriched them. With time, they would increase in their capacity and sophistication in finding middle ground between the wishes that divided black politics and Golden Arches.

McDonald's risk of staying in, and expanding in, the inner city had paid off. Instead of closing their doors like their smaller business counterparts, they realized that they could maintain their investments—both in buildings and the real estate they sat upon. In 1967, McDonald's real estate holdings were valued at $100 million, which accounted for 35 to 40 percent of the company's business. Only a year after its debut on the New York Stock Exchange, and a year before it launched its first national advertising campaign, McDonald's was outpacing its competitors.[35] By installing black franchisees, McDonald's was able to tap into a consumer base that was watching the exodus of big and small business in their communities. They were also able to buy up land in the inner city at cheaper prices than in the suburbs. The uprisings had cleared commercial lots, and most business owners preferred to collect an insurance settlement rather than invest in a grand reopening. Between 1968 and 1973, predominately black neighborhoods declined in land values by 30% on average. It was cheaper to build in the inner cities, and the balance sheets from urban restaurants showed that their profits were increasing.[36]

Fast food franchising attracted the attention of both business and civic leaders in inner cities, because it was moving against the tide of business loss, and the profitability of well-run franchises could not be beat. In 1969, Chicago's Better Boys Foundation partnered with the community-based West Side Organization to franchise a McDonald's in the interest of both groups. Founded by business-man and Lawndale neighborhood native Joe Kellman in 1961 as a boxing gym for neighborhood boys, the Better Boys Foundation evolved throughout the 1960s as a community resource for one of Chicago's poorest areas. When Kellman grew up in the Chicago neighborhood, he was part of a predominately white ethnic enclave that by the early 1960s had become mostly black. Kellman remained a fixture in Lawndale, and he identified franchising as a vehicle for expanding the job-training and uplift functions of the founda-tion. The team used two franchises to employ teenage men from the West Side, where jobs were difficult to secure for youths, espe-cially those without high school diplomas.[37] The partnership took over an existing franchise, which was grossing about $200,000 a year in 1969; sales more than tripled when it was in the hands of the West Side Organization. By 1973, Westside Hamburger Inc. presided over one of the top ten franchises in the Midwest. Walter Pitchford, a NBMOA founding father, managed the outfit. Pitch-ford believed that the turnaround required them to change the "bad image that that store had under its previous owner."[38] Warner Saunders, the executive director of Better Boys, was happy to have the McDonald's as a training ground and funding source, but he acknowledged that the needs of West Side youth could not be solved solely with a boxing gym and a burger grill. "We have had a success rate among those with total involvement, but we don't have enough money to hire a large enough staff to reach everyone. We know how to solve social ills, but society has not made a total com-mitment."[39] The gaps between what was available to the West Side and what was needed grew as the nation's economy left poor, black

America behind, and social spending continued to shrink. McDonald's local-level gains were part of a larger political moment that would carry it into the next decades and affix it to black America.

* * *

Discounted burgers and swift service were integral to McDonald's popularity and brand recognition, but by themselves they were not enough to make an impact in black America. Fast food's entry into the inner city was also contingent on the alignment of federal policy and shifts in the ideological perspective on what black America needed at the precipice of the 1970s. The probusiness tune of Richard Nixon's administration coupled with a chorus of economists, activists, and researchers singing the praises of black capitalism scored the franchise age. If the 1960s was about ensuring each person's political destiny at the voting booth or guaranteeing a seat at the lunch counter, then the 1970s was about making business plans the new freedom papers.

The idea of black capitalism was by no means invented in the 1970s, although black capitalism was heavily debated and discussed during the decade. The principles connecting self-determination, economic sustainability, and black pride have been mainstays in African-American history. Groups like the National Negro Business League, founded in 1900 by black capitalism's great patriarch Booker T. Washington, believed that in the absence of full citizenship, full economic power would more than suffice; it was the quintessential way to escape Jim Crow's indignities.[40] Black capitalism's broad definitions and methods—government loans, coalition building with private industry, community-run business cooperatives—allowed programs under the label to receive support across a wide ideological expanse. In the late 1960s, the nation was still transitioning from the use of the word "Negro" to "black" in everyday parlance and in print media, so the declaration that blacks would be linked to and benefit from capitalism should have aroused anxiety or suspicion among white powerbrokers. "Black," when put next to the word "power," sent ripples of unease through white America. Capitalism, a system predicated on harsh inequalities, paradoxically softened the word "black," because capitalism's rough edges were smoothed by its association with Americanism and patriotism. Cold War anti-Communism made capitalism as comforting as an icebox filled with food and as gentle as a baby blanket purchased from Sears. If black capitalism meant that blacks would live well and earn honestly, apart from whites, then who could object? Perhaps the nation could awake from its racial nightmares without soul-searching, without being distracted by the moral challenges to segregation and exclusion that caused such uproar, especially after 1954. And if black capitalism meant that marginalized people would get a chance to earn more and spend more, what could be the harm in that? Black capitalism inspired black communities, while it united white ideologues. Historian Devin Fergus characterizes the 1970s as encouraging "liberals from Nelson Rockefeller to the editorial board of the *New York Times* [to] put aside initial concerns that black capitalism promoted black segregation and endorsed . . . that federal aid be given to minority enterprises as a means of growing the black middle class."[41]

If realizing separate-but-equal class mobility was more important than King's beloved community, then black capitalism could be directed by anyone, even Richard Nixon. Nixon was not a friend of civil rights, but on the 1968 campaign trail he presented himself as an admirer of black capitalism. A week before King's death, he told a crowd in Milwaukee: "What most of the militants are asking is not for separation, but to be included in—not as supplicants, but as owners, as entrepreneurs—to have a share of the wealth and piece of the action." Black capitalism's appeal to small-state conservatives was that it could ostensibly trickle down to the lower classes of black America as long as it remained segregated. The federal government had to play a part in clearing a way for "more black ownership," and deliver on the remaining demands of the times: "black pride, black jobs, black opportunity, and yes, black power, in the best, the constructive sense of that often misapplied term."[42] The more race-conscious campaigns of Robert Kennedy and Hubert Humphrey offered a black capitalism program that required white business interests to lend a hand. Howard J. Samuels of the Small Business Administration crafted Project OWN, which encouraged the kinds of transfers that McDonald's engaged in, where white business owners who wanted to leave cities would get special funding to sell their enterprises to blacks. The project failed because, as historian Robert Weems discovered, the program attracted "many existing businesses . . . [that couldn't be] operated profitably regardless of the owners' races."[43] The SBA did not want to appear to be using federal funds to simply give white businesses an easy exit out of black America. Under the cover of programs designed to promote black businesses, federal and local programs protected white business interests by incentivizing business transfers like the ones proposed by Samuels while ignoring racial discrimination in bank lending and the extension of credit. Additionally, federal and state funding subsidized costly public works that helped create suburban shopping malls and office parks.

Black capitalism was not a panacea. But in the aftermath of King's death, while progressive Americans cried for their lost leader and mourned those killed in the uprising violence and saw their neighborhoods in pieces, business renewal felt like self-renewal. Three weeks after King's assassination, Nixon delivered his "Bridges to Human Dignity" radio address to allay concerns that if he were to become the commander-in-chief, he would not leave the inner city behind.

It's no longer enough that white-owned enterprises employ greater numbers of Negroes, whether as laborers or as middle-management personnel. This is needed, yes—but it has to be accompanied by an expansion of black ownership, of black capitalism. We need more black employers, more black businesses . . . We have to get private enterprise into the ghetto. But at the same time, we have to get the people of the ghetto into private enterprise—as workers, as managers, as owners. At a time when so many things seem to be going against us in the relations between the races, let us remember the greatest thing going for us: the emerging pride of the black American. That pride, that demand for dignity, is the driving force that we all can build upon.

The black man's pride is the white man's hope—and we must all, black and white, respond to that pride and that hope. These past few years have been a long night of the American spirit. It's time we let in the sun.[44]

Nixon closed his invitation for black America to step into the sunshine by asking his supporters to let that same sun set on the past goals of the freedom struggle. He signed off by saying: "It's time to move past the old civil rights, and to bridge the gap between freedom and dignity, between promise and fulfillment."[45] Nixon was never a civil rights man, and the urgency of the unfinished business of King's legacy was not going to make him one. Nixon believed that "old civil rights" needed to be dispensed with in order to create that link between "freedom" and "dignity." The option of bartering civil rights for economic opportunity has been presented to African Americans for centuries. In exchange for silence, black communities could acquire a plethora of resources. The colored part of town could get a new high school if the residents didn't fight segregation. Funds for a county hospital was the reward for not registering to vote. A new law school at a historically black college could be offered to suspend a lawsuit against a public university that closed its doors to qualified black applicants. Nixon hinted that a new business may be the reward for abandoning the fight for school busing.[46] Once Nixon was in the White House, he directed federal assistance to black communities for business, and he signed an executive order in the spring of 1969 to open the Office of Minority Business Enterprise. The scale and size of these federal commitments were modest at best, and offices like OMBE were most concerned with hosting black entrepreneurs at White House ceremonies and dispatching positive press releases. Minority set-aside programs could passively enrich white-owned businesses. Minority bank deposit programs fell short. The OMBE's role was that of consultant to federal agencies and private business, rather than co-creator of black business.[47]

The Republican president's actions were weak, but the rhetoric remained powerful. With each photo opportunity or empty declaration about the importance of enterprise, black capitalism was able to gather more allies. Nixon's vision for black business was also energized by support from celebrities like R&B sensation James Brown and Cleveland Browns star Jim Brown. But, Nixon's gospel of black capitalism was most effectively reinforced by civil rights advocates who in one breath criticized his regressive racial politics and in another repeated his ideas about black capitalism chapter and verse. Jesse Jackson began calling for blacks to pursue their "silver rights." Jackson had seen the effectiveness of boycotting in the South to unlock the doors to public accommodations. Sit-ins also allowed for black customers to open up their wallets to spend at movie theaters and motels. Meanwhile in Chicago, Jackson and his associates at Operation Breadbasket, and later Operation PUSH (People United to Save Humanity), facilitated demonstrations, boycotts, and selective buying campaigns that unlocked jobs and put money in black wallets. If Nixon and Jackson disagreed on a million things, they could find common ground on the notion that economic development should be a key component in black visions of freedom.

While black capitalism was forging tenuous alliances with Washington, a circle of critics was gathering to unmask Nixon's cynicism and question how in the world would bank deposits and business loans feed the hungry or shelter the homeless. Scholars and anti–silver rights activists attacked black capitalism from a range of perspectives. Believers in capitalism found the business development dollars and the new businesses established under these plans far too low, and they also knew that a racialized marketplace would not be so easily defeated. Civil rights activists saw the embrace of capitalism among their peers as morally bankrupt, and they reminded organizations about the very inequalities that nurtured capitalism.

The Kerner Commission famously warned that the nation was "moving toward two societies—one black, one white." The consumer market was already there. The 1969 collection of essays *The Ghetto Marketplace* tackled this issue. The book's editor, Frederick Sturdivant, wrote that in suburbia, there was a "bountiful cornucopia that delivers to the nation the necessities, gadgetry, and playthings associated with its high standard of living" and this disparity reflected "the incongruity in the American economic system." This is where McDonald's imagined it would mature, a world with "huge department stores, ubiquitous supermarkets and gasoline stations, and modern suburban shopping centers." Meanwhile, poor blacks and communities of color were relegated to low-quality retailers with exorbitant layaway fees, vulnerable to predatory contract-leasing programs, and "often the victims of unethical or illegal merchandising practices."[48] Soon, McDonald's discovered that it could actually thrive in that America also.

Sturdivant and his colleagues did not have to wait and see what would happen when the federal government pledged allegiance to black capitalism: nothing large-scale, sustainable, or sufficiently funded emerged to make a difference. Post-riot cities were magnets for acronym-laden policy programs that claimed to be in the interest of rebuilding businesses, seeding manufacturing outfits, and bringing jobs to the jobless. Even Lyndon Johnson's alphabet soup of ambitious programs against poverty adopted probusiness development provisions amid its crusade. The SCLC worried that these black capitalism efforts were made at the expense of youth job and Head Start early education programs.[49] Black economists, scholars, activists, and business owners learned this lesson after the Watts uprising in August of 1965. Sparked by confrontations between residents of the South Los Angeles neighborhood and police officers conducting an arrest, the six-day rebellion claimed 34 victims and $40 million in property damage. Black business owners like Larry Brown painted the words SOUL BROTHER on their storefronts in hopes looters would bypass their location in the spirit of racial solidarity.[50] Sometimes this kind of tactic worked; sometimes it did not. What would stop this the next time people were upset at the police? Former-police-officer-turned-councilman Tom Bradley, who was on a journey to becoming Los Angeles's first black mayor, believed that developing more soul brother businesses would help. "The proper way to stop racism and return Watts to normalcy includes jobs and job training, inducement to business and industry to return to the stricken communities, federal tax inducements for relocation of firms to Negro areas, and reduction of insurance rates."[51] Federal and state governments could craft and implement enticements like tax relief for new businesses and rebates in exchange for hiring local people. But weary and traumatized business owners found the financial and emotional costs of rebuilding far too taxing, regardless of state support. After a community experienced a riot, the spike in insurance and security costs was often passed on to shoppers in the area, the majority of whom had nothing to do with the disorder. Watts was "caught in a cost-price whirl," reflected one economist.[52] Paying more for lower-quality goods and services was a common experience for blacks across class lines. Additionally, blacks were underwriting their own oppression when they paid taxes for the improvement and maintenance of schools that barred them or funded the salaries of police officers that terrorized them. Bradley's recommendations were contingent on local business owners' willingness to stay and expand in Watts.

The "white flight" of homeowners from central cities to suburbs is a historical phenomenon that has long been recognized and documented, but fewer Americans are aware of how the collapse of business districts created a parallel, racially based process.[53] When white business owners fled black neighborhoods or refused to reopen stores after unrest, the flight of jobs, tax revenue, and services constricted an already limited marketplace. While some whites held on to residential properties in black communities and profited handily from a discriminatory housing market, this form of absentee landlord arrangement was not as lucrative for commercial properties.[54] After collecting an insurance disbursement for a torched store, business owners simply relocated or moved on to a new line of work. Vacant lots remained as a sign of what once was. "Why should I reopen? So, it can happen again?" a white appliance store owner in Watts asked. He decided that he wasn't "going to give 'em another chance," and he started over in a whiter part of Los Angeles. He committed himself to trying "to forget Watts." His conclusion: "To hell with civil rights and all their causes."[55]

Civil rights and civil disorder became one and the same in the shop owner's mind, and reactionary policymakers and voters agreed. In forgetting Watts, Chicago, and Newark, the nation was also forgetting King's message and rewriting his legacy to fit with the desires of corporations, racist politicians, and wealthy people.

Some civil rights activists who had worked with Jackson, and others who pivoted toward black capitalism, refused to bend to the idea that it was the next step in the struggle. Former Student Nonviolent Coordinating Committee member James Forman took a critical stance on black capitalism and was wary of anyone swayed by it. If there was to be talk of money, Forman supported reparations for slavery, real recompense for centuries of subjugation. Grocery stores and drive-ins could never do that. Forman wrote in the spring of 1969:

> We must separate ourselves from those Negroes who go around the country promoting all types of schemes for Black Capitalism. Ironically . . . the most militant Black Nationalists, as they call themselves, have been the first to jump on the bandwagon of black capitalism. They are pimps; Black Power Pimps and fraudulent leaders and the people must be educated to understand that any black man or Negro who is advocating a perpetuation of capitalism inside the United States is in fact seeking not only his ultimate destruction and death, but is contributing to the continuous exploitation of black people around the world.[56]

Three years into Nixon's presidency, critics had more evidence that the movement to put businesses on every inner-city block was a failed one. Economist Frederick Case charted attempts to "attack the root causes of the disturbances and revitalize the economic lives of South Central and East Los Angeles" by "providing more and better jobs and increased opportunities for minority businessmen to enter managerial and entrepreneurial ranks."[57] The strategy yielded little more than an "abundance of publicity . . . of business and government rolling up their sleeves and combining to slay the dragons of discrimination, inadequate education, poverty, and privation."[58] Like the Nixon White House, local-level governments projected a semblance of economic progress at groundbreaking celebrations and ribbon cuttings. For the constituents, business-inclined and otherwise, new stores offered another choice or opportunity in a place constrained by race and economics. A minority of Angelenos of color drafted business plans and tried to open their own business. The majority exercised the few options they had and figured out how to make the most with less, or they packed up their lives and set out for other cities. Case pointed out that poverty in Los Angeles was not ameliorated by post-Watts investments; it merely migrated to other parts of Los Angeles County and the surrounding area. South Los Angeles's unemployment rate continued to rise after the uprising and didn't abate when business funding came to Watts; between 1965 and 1969, the unemployment rate in the area was nearly triple the national and regional average.[59] Black business owners' attitudes toward black capitalism were also varied. Their position on the local and federal programs was sometimes as much about the size and type of business they owned as about their opinions on Nixon or their ideas about how to fix black America.

Small business owners complained of complicated application forms, lending limits, and bureaucratic mismanagement when they sought help from or enrolled in local business development programs. One black bookstore owner became deeply skeptical of black capitalism fanfare after multiple attempts to navigate a small loans program. The Small Business Administration rejected four separate business proposals from him, and after consulting a "major investment company" about the matter, they were surprised that his plan was not funded.[60] Black capitalism initiatives usually assigned seasoned businesspeople to mentor or advise program participants, and these coaches rarely hailed from the communities they were tasked with guiding. The bookstore owner found his advisor unskilled in interpersonal communication and his unwillingness to "get down in his community and start setting an example for the young" bothered him. The man abandoned all hope that the business program would help him, and he deemed "minority capitalism . . . one of the biggest frauds ever perpetrated on the aspirations of the black people." The programs didn't serve the people, they catered to political cronies. "They're pork barrels for politicians to use for putting their people in jobs."[61]

Even influential black thinkers, who took no issue with capitalism itself, hesitated to support black capitalism. Save black insurance agencies and banks, black small business concentrated in urban cores had not proven to be an economic boon, and more of them would put more people at risk. Andrew Brimmer, the first African-American Federal Reserve Board governor, cited the high failure rates of small businesses and their inability to employ significant numbers of people as the key reasons why encouraging new business development was a fool's errand. The Harvard-educated economist had broken many racial barriers over the course of his education and career, and he didn't see black capitalism as solely failing the nation financially. Having grown up in a segregated, small town in northeastern Louisiana, Brimmer feared that black capitalism encouraged the separatism that dictated his youth and young adulthood. "In the long run, the pursuit of black capitalism may retard the Negro's economic advancement by discouraging many from the full participation in the national economy with its much broader range of challenges and opportunities."[62] Brimmer advocated for blacks to seek careers in corporate America if they wanted to make a difference in the lives of black people, because affirmative action, minority training programs, and diversity recruitment efforts promised far more stability than small business.[63] Brimmer's concerns about black capitalism increased after the arrival of recession in 1970. The nearly year-long downturn, and subsequent recessions, reduced allocations for OMBE-adjacent projects and initiated social welfare spending freezes, which caused black communities to fall further into the economic depths.

Black capitalism was down, but it wasn't out. Federal black capitalism programs failed to invigorate the barbershops, beauty parlors, barbecue takeouts, and Black Power bookstores that tried to anchor post-uprising business districts. But they boosted a powerful newcomer into the inner city: fast food. With the benefit of corporate offices staffed with attorneys, lobbyists, and business strategists, and good relationships with the White House, fast food companies encouraged their potential black franchisees to pursue OMBE programs to access loans and business advantages. Professional athlete and Nixon ally Brady Keys's business success exemplified the ways that black capitalism undergirded the expansion of fast food in black communities. His challenges also exposed how little capitalism could actually alleviate the problems of black communities.

Brady Keys was the unofficial spokesperson for Nixon's black capitalism efforts. The former Colorado State University cornerback played football with the Pittsburgh Steelers, garnering All-Pro status during his eight-year stint between 1961 and 1969. After leaving the National Football League, Keys wanted to follow in the footsteps of his teammates and devote himself fully to business. During his football career, Keys tried to franchise a car dealership and had difficulties securing financing. Banks refused him ten times, and he needed to leverage a Steelers connection in order to receive his first business loan. The post-King climate alleviated his credit crunch. Keys intimated that the post-unrest desire to quell tensions through business creation worked in his favor. "At the time, I was a professional athlete, and I had a lot of credibility as a businessman already . . . [but] I had real big problems getting financing—until right after the riots . . ." After Keys retired his Steelers uniform, he devoted himself full-time to his self-referential All-Pro Chicken, a takeout he opened in 1967 with the hopes of turning it into a competitive franchise. Keys was able to take advantage of the lack of fried chicken competitors on his block of Harlem. The low-overhead business was a smash hit, and Keys expanded All-Pro to thirty-five franchises across the country. [64]

National chains took notice of Keys's All-Pro, as they were probably keeping tabs on McDonald's inner-city campaign, and drafted Keys for their team of black franchisees. In 1969 he met with executives from Miami-based Burger King and took possession of his first burger restaurant, an unprofitable and failing location in inner-city Detroit. Like Petty, Keys was tasked with turning around the store, and after a strong opening year, Keys acquired his second Burger King. Keys, like other black franchisees, used his instincts and revised the company's directives in order to turn the tide for his restaurants. He revived waning Whopper sales in 1969 by selling the iconic burgers in his store on a made-to-order basis, which inspired Burger King's "Have It Your Way" tagline of the 1970s. *Black Enterprise* magazine praised him for developing "the innovations [that] turned his Burger King store into the top selling store in the nation. In just three months, the outlet's sales rocketed to $65,000 a month, up from a meager $25,000." Keys also lowered the average employee turnover rate from the fast food standard of 300% to 100% in a year.[65]

Keys's good ideas were supplemented with cash courtesy of the federal government's black capitalism platform. Between 1969 and 1973, the former NFL defensive back drew upon an estimated $9 million in federal funds for his various businesses.[66] He told *Black Enterprise* in 1974: "All the franchise companies want to go into the inner city now. And since my company has been successful . . . it's fashionable to give franchises to blacks."[67] The appeal of the inner-city market and the reality of it were vastly different, and Keys believed that due to franchise saturation in the suburbs, the industry had to find ways around the fact "that doing business in my area is hell." Keys contended with "cutting, shooting, killing" inside and outside the restaurants, and he believed black franchisees were used as conduits into and buffers from the inner city. The retired athlete realized that black franchised restaurants were extensions of a larger system that would always outprofit and overpower "little guys" like him, no matter how many profitable franchises he operated. Keys figured that franchiser logic reasoned: "Why don't we get this black cat over here and franchise him? It may cost us $100,000 [in aid] to get him in business, but it would put a whole bunch of stores up and we'll make that much in a year from royalties, advertising, and supplies we sell him."[68] The All-Pro founder hoped to earn enough money in the management of other franchises to finance his own businesses, but he knew that it would be a long time coming, as the 1970s economic downturns were exacerbated by oil shortages, rising food costs, inflation, and growing unemployment. Every dollar Keys earned was hard-earned, and with his stores in poor areas, he had to remain vigilant about price and operations. "We've come off a real bad year," he said. "About 35 percent of the people in the inner city are on some type of welfare. Their income doesn't go up. So where in hell do they find the money to spend on a luxury such as fast food?" Gradually, fast food was transforming from a luxury to a staple of the diets of Keys's target markets, but relying on this market meant responding to their resistance to changes to the menu and the prices of food. He told the magazine:

> And how much can you charge for a hamburger? Eighteen months ago, the meat was 55 cents a pound. Now it's $1.02 a pound, but it's the same hamburger. And you can only charge so much. As the price of all this food increases, you try to raise your price, so that you can keep your level of profit. But this year it seriously reached the point of no return, where you could no longer raise your prices. Because the people rebel. As the costs keep going up, you've got to keep raising your prices accordingly, but then your sales just drop, drop, drop—the people can't afford your food.[69]

The nation's economic crises provided one competitive advantage for Keys, Petty, and the first generation of franchisees of color; their customers were less likely to actually drive to a drive-in. Carless and public-transportation-dependent consumers usually could walk to their favorite fast food spots, unlike suburban diners whose lifestyles were shaped by car travel. Without cars, inner-city customers were also unable to stray too far from home in search of a hot breakfast or a quick snack; therefore, fast food companies did not have to worry too much about oversaturating population-dense cities. This difference between urban and suburban stores was magnified in the fall of 1973, when the United States entered an oil crisis that lasted until the spring.[70] The McDonald's footprint in cities was growing throughout the 1970s, but the company had spent the prior two decades investing in mostly suburban towns and locations proximate to highways. American car owners waited in long lines that snaked out of gas station parking lots onto the street in hopes they wouldn't be turned away. If drivers were lucky enough to get gas, they could plan on paying nearly double what they were used to and weren't guaranteed they could leave with a full tank. No matter how strong a driver's hankering for a Filet-O-Fish sandwich, they had to think twice about expending precious fuel to get one. Although some of its suburban franchises were hit by the embargo, McDonald's official word was that the Big Mac was stronger than global export conflicts and their spokespeople were coy about acknowledging the crisis. At the close of 1973, McDonald's CEO Fred Turner told the *New York Times* that they were in the process of expanding their "efforts to keep stores near population centers so that people can walk in, rather than drive," and he conceded that "the energy shortage" heightened interest in the new focus. But he remained steadfast in the assertion that oil prices were irrelevant to the bigger picture. "We never have been a roadside chain." Turner claimed that in a year in which McDonald's stock prices dipped, the company actually experienced gains in business during the nationwide Sunday gas holidays, the weekly moratorium on fuel sales. The rise in oil costs also elevated building and construction budgets, and McDonald's had to rethink new store locations in case the nation's oil and economic problems lasted into the following fiscal years. According to Turner, the shift in focus to "moving more into the cities" led the company to discover "black neighborhoods and poorer communities."[71]

Because of the lessons learned from black franchisee success and the memories of the previous decade's uprisings, these new stores would rely heavily on black labor, management, and franchisees to maximize their popularity in black communities and insulate themselves from criticism and harm. Black capitalism did not work for many black businesses, but it was a godsend for players in the fast food race to the top. Massive entities like McDonald's and Burger King could sustain the ups and downs of market changes. New restaurants could be built on cheap land, and old ones could be resuscitated at relatively low cost. Black franchises, even when given internal funding to enter the business, were eligible for federal support, and ultimately, they contended with the high costs of security and insurance as part of their leasing agreements. More important, by expanding into neighborhoods with few drivers and even fewer choices, McDonald's and Burger King were able to overcome some of the economic challenges of the 1970s by exploiting the financial perils of poor communities.

Since the first McDonald's opened in 1940, the company was able to shapeshift for the times. The McDonald brothers understood the importance of efficiency in the 1940s. In the 1950s, Kroc tapped into the desires of the suburban nuclear family and their fascination with cars and consumption. By the late 1960s, McDonald's was forced to take its cues from a culture in constant conflict with its stated principles and its inability to fulfill them. A burger company does not set policies or elect candidates. But under capitalism, a company's influence is broad and deep, and the most powerful companies synchronize their movements to the beat of social change, without ever acknowledging that it can hear its sounds.

In order to survive and flourish after 1968, McDonald's not only had to learn how to listen to black America; the company would also have to learn how to talk to black America. Black franchises were their interpreters. In April of 1969, Ralph Abernathy, King's successor at the Southern Christian Leadership Conference, visited Chicago as part of a nationwide pilgrimage to honor his friend. Months earlier, Abernathy had announced that a reinvigorated Poor People's Campaign would commence that year. The campaign was part of King's vision to gather a multiracial caravan to travel to Washington, D.C., to amplify the struggles of poor whites, Native Americans, blacks, and veterans. Emboldened by King's final year of life dedicated to critiquing economic inequality, Abernathy declared, "We don't want rich individuals; we want rich communities." Abernathy made it plain: "I don't believe in black capitalism. I believe in black socialism."[72] Despite these declarations, while visiting Chicago, Abernathy accepted a donation of $1,300—the equivalent of one-day profit from Petty's restaurant—to the SCLC. The donation was the first of many that flowed between McDonald's and civil rights organizations, and it further tied King's dream to Kroc's dream, despite the two men's hopes for the world being miles apart.[73]

CHAPTER THREE

The Burger Boycott and the Ballot Box

In 1967, Cleveland's Carl Stokes became the first black mayor of a major city. A conflict over McDonald's profitability in black neighborhoods led to a series of boycotts of the restaurant, and Stokes was called in to mediate the battle. Bettman Archive / Getty Images, 1967.

On the night Martin Luther King Jr. was killed, Cleveland's Mayor Carl Stokes would not let his hometown burn, not again. He was the first black mayor of a major U.S. city, and he knew that he was always under surveillance—by the black Clevelanders who organized to help him eke out a 50.5% victory in 1967, and by whites who were unsure if he would serve their needs at all. Stokes was also a subject of fascination and scrutiny by news media and businessmen. They wondered if the charismatic attorney could prevent a repeat of what happened in the summer of 1966, when the predominately black and overwhelmingly poor Hough neighborhood was nearly leveled in an uprising. That unrest started on the evening of July 18 after white bar owners allegedly posted a sign on their door's business warning NO WATER FOR NIGGERS. Some people said that the barkeep refused to give a black man a glass of water. Others reported that the business owners had thrown a grieving woman out of the establishment for collecting donations for her dead child. Or was it for her friend's child? Like most uprisings, the details of what started the commotion felt less important than the horrors of what unfolded. Fires devoured wood frame houses and the heat's impact exploded windows, hurling glass onto sidewalks and into the streets. The main strip of Hough Avenue drew the reckless, the curious, and the desperate. Hough was home to many hungry families, and when the windows and doors to the Gale's Super Valu market on Superior Avenue were destroyed, they may have seen the event as a mixed blessing. The fires at All-Brite pharmacy and Sav-Mor market may have consumed all the wares in the stores before it was cleared out, so no one would ever benefit from the bottles of medicine, packs of diapers, and assortment of shampoos that were difficult to afford. Hough was ablaze, but for a moment, in a warped twist of fate, Hough was able to provide for the community. Young men who had been hassled by police for years fought back and tussled with the Cleveland Police Department. The mostly white police force was not able to maintain order, and later 1,700 members of the Ohio National Guard were put on alert to contain the chaos within a fifteen-block perimeter inside Hough.[1]

As was the case in many city neighborhoods that became the final destinations for blacks seeking refuge from Jim Crow's chokehold on personal and political freedom during the Great Migration, Hough's racial composition had transformed from upwardly mobile whites to plucky blacks who learned that they had to be careful with each step they made. Carl Stokes must have remembered the scenes from an intact Hough Avenue, one of the neighborhood's main arteries, as he strolled down the numbered side streets with the volunteer cleanup crews that gathered to collect rubble and mourn what had just been there a few days earlier. Swift Dry Cleaners' brick frame sides remained strong, but without a roof. The wire grate that was supposed to shield Al's Cut

Rate Store off of Lexington was no match for the mobs, and the store that offered BEER TO GO was left dry. All that remained of the University Party Roller Rink Hall was the sign that helped mark it, like a headstone. In 1966, Stokes represented Cleveland as the first black Democrat to sit in the Ohio statehouse, and although the rebellion in Hough was devastating, it may have been no surprise that tensions would boil over there. At mid-decade, Hough was nearly 90% black and one of the poorest parts of the city, with residents earning nearly 40% less than the citywide average. The economic disparity in Hough was fueled by double-digit unemployment rates, and families tried to make ends meet with welfare benefits and charitable donations.[2]

On the first day of the Hough uprising, the future mayor asked his brother Louis to travel to Hough with him. The men were greeted by the sight of "flames leaping out of storefronts and billowing up into the darkening sky." They heard gun shots, police sirens, and screams. In his memoir, Congressman Louis Stokes recalled the mood in Hough in the years before the unrest. "The lack of jobs and health care, the absence of essential social services, the ongoing victimization by police, the general perception of black disenfranchisement and white entitlement fed a growing undercurrent of anger."[3]

Hough was not going to happen again. The mayor headed first to a news channel to plead with Clevelanders to "do honor to the memory of MLK by reacting to the tragic loss in the peaceful manner in which he lived." Then he traveled to Cleveland's East Side, walking the streets with other persuasive, civic-minded black leaders to reason with the angry and the frustrated. He asked that the police department deploy black officers onto the streets that night, knowing that the memories of 1966 and the realities of the present would make the appearance of white police officers a barrier to peace. Stokes and his associates spent four long days in Hough pleading for people to "Keep it cool." There were no reports of violence, property damage, or arson in Hough. Clevelanders were saddened by King's death, but Stokes's position as mayor may have kept them from turning their grief into full-on retaliation in the streets.[4] Stokes won over the city, and the nation, in the spring by keeping Cleveland calm and safe. But the favor curried during Holy Week would dissolve into bitterness over the summer, when a shootout in Glenville, a neighborhood northeast of Hough, claimed seven lives—four African-American civilians and three white police officers—during a two-day uprising.[5] After Glenville, Stokes knew that his reelection bid the following year would be tough, so he strategized how to convince voters that he could ably maintain relationships with a police force that had long antagonized black Clevelanders and appease a powerful white business community that saw uprisings cut into their bottom line. Stokes knew that his position as mayor required more than approving budgets and appearing at ribbon cuttings; as a black mayor, his job required him to juggle black expectations, reduce white apprehension, and tend to his personal ambitions for city politics. What he never could have anticipated as he prepared for his reelection bid in the summer of 1969 was that he would also have to cautiously maneuver a community conflict with McDonald's if he was going to realize a second term in office.

As McDonald's franchising opened up to African-American businessmen in the inner cities, these same cities were undergoing radical shifts in political power. Few blacks were moving into city hall like Stokes or Gary, Indiana's Richard Hatcher in the late 1960s, but African Americans were running for and winning seats on city councils, joining school boards, and securing statehouse seats by mobilizing black coalitions.[6] After President Lyndon Johnson inked the Voting Rights Act of 1965, southern blacks were able to exercise the power of their vote more freely in local and national elections, while experienced black voters in the North were finding avenues to translate voting power into community control of the institutions that were failing them. Blacks organized for more black police officers in hopes of reducing the problem of police brutality. Exasperated parents established alternative schools or petitioned school boards to ensure their children received equal access to public school programs, and to expel the vestiges of segregation-era textbooks and teachers. Blacks in Great Migration cities were for the first time voting for black candidates from their own communities, who were alternative choices to the same white Democratic machine politicians who had held their votes hostage by making sure that district and ward lines preserved the color line.[7] Black voters electing black politicians did more than externalize their desires to see themselves reflected in positions of power and authority. In electing black candidates, a number of black voters were also explicitly or implicitly supporting black capitalism. Capitalism relies on a political system that supports its interests and protects its excesses. For black political candidates like Stokes, who spoke to black voters about the importance of social revolution through black representation and opportunity expansion, they had to also craft a message to assuage white anxieties. One of the most effective ways to make white voters comfortable, if you were a first black mayor, was to assume a pro-business stance. By talking about black capitalism and economic development in the inner city, black elective leaders were able to secure their position of power without attracting too much opposition. But in the late 1960s and beyond, when there was a conflict between white-owned businesses and the black communities they profited from, black political leaders had to somehow mediate tensions without alienating either group. Stokes was no different in his embrace of private business development as a means of realizing racial justice. Historian Keeanga-Yamahtta Taylor notes in her assessment of black political ascendancy after the passage of the Civil Rights Act that the Stokes campaign became the "focal point of the civil rights establishment, whose leaders worried about the political drift of their organizations after the end of legal discrimination in the South and the urban uprisings in the North."[8] Nothing could be left to chance.

Although Hough residents were only spectators of the drama acted out in other U.S. cities after King's death, they were still in dire straits the year after King. Buildings that had been lost in 1966 had not been rebuilt, and the community understood well its neighbors in Glenville, who took to the streets after suspicions that police were in the area to harass members of the community. The exchange of gunfire between a supposed group of nationalists and police officers set Stokes into action again, and he tried to remove white officers from the area. The withdrawal did little, and white officers were soon back on Glenville blocks to maintain law and order. Community members were still unable to achieve financial stability and were regularly exploited by business. As one study poignantly described it: "One of the bitterest complaints among Hough residents is that white businessmen raise their prices on 'Mother's Day'—the tenth of each month, when mothers receive aid-to-dependent-children welfare checks."[9]

In the aftermath of the Hough and Glenville uprisings, neighborhood groups and local leadership began the process of rebuilding with even less than they had before. The new business climate not only necessitated physical repairs and cleanups, but also led to a spike in the cost of doing business in areas already plagued with higher security, insurance, and carrying costs. One study found that a Hough pawn brokerage and jewelry store owner faced an increase in his fire insurance after the riots. Although he was able to defend his property with a "shotgun and revolver," his $144 a year fire insurance policy skyrocketed to $621 for the same coverage.[10] In response to these and other challenges, Operation Breadbasket had come to Cleveland to do the type of work it was known for in Chicago, which included pressuring businesses in black communities to commit to improving the quality of customer service, hiring local people, and addressing discriminatory practices. From its offices at 11006 St. Clair Avenue (blocks from the site of a future McDonald's), Breadbasket established itself on Cleveland's East Side. In the winter of 1967, Breadbasket announced that it had entered an agreement with Pick-N-Pay Supermarkets, leading to 300 "new and upgraded jobs" for the community. The positions varied from store managers, department heads, meat cutters and wrappers, and "salaried employees," yielding payroll expenses of more than $1.7 million. The agreement stipulated that the supermarket chain post jobs with black community agencies, advertise in black newspapers, deposit monies in black banks, stock the store with products made by black businesses, and donate to the United Negro College Fund as well as an internal employee scholarship. The statement announcing the negotiation reiterated the goal of Breadbasket:

Any company doing business in the ghetto must radically reconstruct its employment practices commensurate with the profits which it is taking out of the community. For any company to receive sizeable profits from the Negro community while employing only a small number of community residents, and thus reinvesting only a small percentage of its profits back into the community is one of the factors which creates a slum.[11]

Operation Breadbasket did not have an easy time coming into Cleveland. Some leaders found the organization's tactics too heavy-handed, like Clarence H. Holmes, director of Cleveland's public-private employment program named AIM-JOBS, who said that "Breadbasket activities have had no noticeable effect on . . . efforts to place hard-core unemployed Negroes." Johnson feared that Breadbasket inadvertently created negative attitudes toward those who needed jobs. "Nobody likes to be coerced into action."[12] Some Clevelanders—black and white—believed that the line between coercion and community action was a thin one. The question of how to compel businesses to listen to black consumers lingered as Hough managed its introduction to McDonald's and the goals of black franchising. While black Chicago welcomed the arrival of the Golden Arches with little consternation, McDonald's entry into the East Side of Cleveland was incredibly difficult. An inexplicable homicide, a possible con artist, a tense mayoral race, and uncomfortable alliances frame the story of how McDonald's met Hough, and how Hough exposed what McDonald's meant for black people, possibilities, and protest. Uncertainty and instability blanketed Hough, and that meant one thing: McDonald's was on its way.

* * *

Toledo was the first home for McDonald's in Ohio, and in 1961, Ray Kroc saw growth potential in moving to other cities across the state. By 1965, Cleveland was already home to two McDonald's restaurants, and due to their popularity, the company committed to a major expansion in Ohio, bringing the total to ten drive-ins, second in locations after Kroc's home state of Illinois.[13] In 1969,

Kroc exceeded his earlier goals for Ohio with twenty-four profitable locations in the state. It appears that the white franchisees of McDonald's locations in black neighborhoods benefited from the calm Holy Week in 1968 and survived Glenville that summer, because there were no complaints of unsafe stores or attempts to leave the neighborhoods. McDonald's in Cleveland was big business, with the restaurants predominately on the East Side, where Hough was located, regularly ranking among the highest-earning locations. Three white businessmen profited nearly $2.5 million a year from four East Side franchises: referred to as the 83rd Street, Euclid, St. Clair, and Kinsman locations. Edward Bood, vice president and director of franchising for McDonald's, estimated that two of the Cleveland restaurants serving the Hough community alone exceeded the national average of profits each year. The bustling locations employed many locals and collectively paid black employees "more than $600,000 a year."[14] With an estimated 38% of black men in Hough unemployed, McDonald's offered badly needed jobs. After the loss of so many restaurants in Hough, McDonald's provided a place to eat. But, as some community leaders—energized by a round of conversations about what came next for the East Side—watched as the franchise locations filled cash registers day after day with money from black customers, eyebrows began to raise. Who was getting rich off all these people? Where did the money go? It didn't go to the public parks, the schools, or the people, that was for certain.[15] Besides, now that Cleveland had a black mayor, wasn't it time for a black businessman to have a chance at some of the wealth that had come from the East Side?

In the winter of 1969, Ernest Hilliard of suburban Warrenville Heights decided he would try his hand at this new fast food venture. The native of Uniontown, Pennsylvania, was known by most in Cleveland, and across the country, as radio evangelist Prophet Frank Thomas of the First Spiritual Christian Church of America. Hilliard shepherded his flock by using the airwaves as his staff, and he was visible in Hough with a religious goods store. After Hilliard decided that he would try to apply for a McDonald's franchise on St. Clair and 105th Streets, he consulted his friend and fellow religious leader David Hill, who called himself Rabbi Hill of the House of Israel. Black franchisee may have been the role that Hilliard wanted most, but it was Hill who would emerge as the interlocutor in an absorbing exchange between black Cleveland and McDonald's. Hill was part of a long tradition of urban prophets who offered black people an alternative explanation of the world, in which their racial origins could be traced to African nobility and offered a radical vision of their purpose on earth, which challenged salvationist views of Christianity that rationalized suffering as the price one paid for a glorious afterlife.[16] If slavery and Jim Crow were the price of admission for paradise, some black believers questioned the cost and worth of this precious ticket. They flocked to figures like Hill, whose problack ideologies not only instilled pride but also rejected any demands to surrender to the inevitability of suffering at the hands of a white man's racism. Hill's path to establishing the House of Israel wended through correctional facilities in the South and Midwest. Between 1951 and 1966, the native of the western Arkansas town of Nashville, a place vastly different than the similarly named city in Tennessee, had been charged with a host of crimes. He was convicted of forgery, grand larceny, fraud, and writing bad checks, and he spent time in the Lima State Hospital for the Criminally Insane.[17]

Hill's past did not disqualify him from becoming a self-proclaimed leader of black Cleveland. This house that David built rested on an amalgamated foundation of ideologies. The organization was loyal to black nationalism in its dedication to black institution building. They preached a vision of black millennialism, a belief that blacks should invest in the future possibilities of an all-black society within a larger racist one. They expressed their commitments to black radicalism by using protest to disrupt the status quo and demand social change. And when it came to what Hough needed, they embraced black capitalism. Hill was adept at not only preaching all of these belief systems, but he was also skilled in adapting them into political theater. In the fall of 1969, Hill announced that he would execute Santa Claus as part of the local Black Christmas Committee's attempt to have blacks boycott Christmas. Hill explained that in "typical Western custom," Santa would be paraded to the city's Public Square and found guilty of "exploitation and fostering white racism"; then he would be hanged. In typical Hill custom, the dramatics were meant to address the quotidian abuses felt by blacks in Hough and other parts of Cleveland, particularly reports that police officers intimidated black voters when they turned out to support Stokes on the most recent Election Day.[18]

Ever attuned to new opportunities for himself, in the summer of 1969, Hill believed that he and his fellow prophet had discovered something positive and profitable for their section of black Cleveland. Hilliard began the process to become a franchisee that year, contacting Mayor Stokes's office for help and arranging meetings with McDonald's regional franchise managers. Like many interested candidates, McDonald's recommended that Hilliard gain in-store experience, so he reported for duty to the St. Clair location. Hilliard discovered that actual McDonald's training occurred at Hamburger University, to which he never received an acceptance letter. Hilliard then hired an attorney and again tried to learn what was required to open a franchise, but the regional manager told him that he could not give Hilliard a franchise on the East Side because of territorial rights held by the current franchisees. In its early franchise days, McDonald's allowed franchisees to lay claim to large geographic regions, but ceased the practice when it was revealed to undercut their earning potential. Believing that he was a victim of racial discrimination, Hilliard appealed to Hill and his associate, activist and House of Israel Director James Raplin, for assistance.[19] Except for each being led by charismatic black men, the House of Israel and the mayor's office appeared as if they existed on different planets. But Stokes won his election by finding common ground with the more radical elements of black Cleveland, and as fixtures on the East Side, Hilliard and Hill probably felt at home meeting with McDonald's executives in the Tapestry Room of Cleveland City Hall under a Stokes administration. What use is a black mayor if the people can't use one of his meeting rooms? As tensions heightened around the issue of black franchising in Cleveland, the Beaux-Arts style building would serve as a neutral territory between McDonald's and a demanding public.

McDonald's did not come to the meeting prepared to offer anything to the duo, except for a request for names. If Hill and Raplin could generate a list of potential black franchisees who could pay a $2,500 application fee and $2,500 upon acceptance of their bid, then—after some vetting—an African American could possibly join the Golden Arches family in Cleveland. Hill and Raplin claimed to have already compiled a roster of twenty black Clevelanders for this effort, including football star Jim Brown, who patrolled the streets of Cleveland with Stokes that fateful April night that King was assassinated. Other hopefuls included an entire black investment club and a local public school system leader. While Hill and Raplin reported that the meeting was just a discussion of names, one Stokes biographer characterized the event as far more combative. Hill demanded that McDonald's "hand over the keys to all white-owned franchises in Cleveland's inner city."[20] A practiced provocateur, Hill knew that the odds were not in his favor that McDonald's would surrender anything to the men that afternoon. Hill and Raplin still wanted to know why their preferred members of black Cleveland had been denied and explore how and when Hilliard would get an opportunity to command his own franchise.[21] The meeting ended with little but an agreement to reconvene for another confab on July 7. By the time the assigned date and hour arrived, one man would be dead.

Three days before the meeting, when a shot rang out on Hathaway Lane in Warrenville Heights, neighbors may have thought they heard a lone firecracker left over from the Independence Day celebrations that evening. Hilliard's wife, Georgia, thought so too. But when she stepped outside her home to double check, she found her husband in the driveway gasping for air. Ernest had been shot. Georgia was in shock as she scrambled to talk to her dying husband. She started connecting the dots. Georgia later told the press that her husband was a victim of a "professional murder," a targeted killing that could only be tied to one thing: "the McDonald's deal." After Ernest was pronounced dead, his friends started to tell Georgia things. He had received a phone call from an unknown person who threatened: "We will let you make niggerburgers in hell." His wife remembered him mentioning "receiving threatening telephone calls," but Ernest didn't say much more. Georgia did not know who was behind the threats or just how disturbing the anonymous calls were to her husband, but she knew that the franchise was consuming a lot of time. As Ernest lay dying, Georgia asked, "Who shot you?" His reply: "White folks." Did she hear that correctly? Police later speculated he was actually saying "white Ford," because neighbors told authorities that they saw a white car speed away from the crime scene. But Georgia and Ernest's friends knew better. They were certain that this all circled back to McDonald's.[22] Hill decided that yet another white business—like that bar that put out the sign or the ones that marked up their prices on stale bread and rotting meat or the ones that refused to hire black teenagers—had gone too far. Hilliard's murder was never officially deemed associated with McDonald's or his franchising bid, but grief can activate old wounds. King's death had made some cities burn. Ernest Hilliard's death, at the very least, would make Cleveland change.

In a matter of days, Hill garnered support from an array of Cleveland-based community groups and local chapters of civil rights organizations to sign on to a new group, Operation Black Unity, headquarted at his House of Israel building. Hill and the members of the loosely bound OBU may have thought they would disrupt the flow of McDonald's traffic for a few days, find an avenue to get some blacks into franchising, and take their rightful place in Cleveland history alongside Stokes. Hill's first boycott flyer laid bare the enemy combatants in the war he was waging on fast food: "McDonald's Hamburger Corp versus Black People." On July 10, OBU directed concerned citizens to four McDonald's restaurants on the East Side to participate in staged demonstrations or to stay home and boycott the stores.[23] At one location, a group of young men outfitted in "black jackets and berets" told passersby not to enter a McDonald's. The store's manager claimed that ten carloads of protesters approached the store, so he threw in the towel and locked the doors of his restaurant at 12:35 P.M., the height of lunch-time service. Another location closed by the late afternoon.[24] The chapeau-clad young men may have been members of Afro Set, a local black nationalist group founded in 1968 that partnered with Stokes's Cleveland: NOW! economic development program. Afro Set advocated for developing the black community through busi-ness and social programs, so it could exist apart from the larger white economic power structure. Afro Set and Stokes were often opposed about methods and goals, but they were joined in their desire to see the East Side recover from its injuries. Black politics could bring board coalitions together for a greater good, whether to mourn a death or to seek healing for an ailing city.

McDonald's believed that the worst of doing business in the inner city was behind them. Restaurants in Washington, D.C., Detroit, Chicago, and Los Angeles rebounded from the property damage of April 1968 and the hot summers that followed, and by 1969, McDonald's corporate offices had constructed a well-oiled mechanism for transferring franchises from white to black hands. They were even getting good press for their bold commitment to black wealth building. McDonald's had "sent a directive to all white owners of inner-city franchises asking them to sell to blacks," and reported that the transfers were rapid and efficient. The scheme to shift operators across racial lines led to changes in nineteen exist-ing stores, and two brand-new stores were designated for blacks.[25] The NBMOA expanded out of its midwestern center and included members in Los Angeles and Kansas City.[26] Things were look-ing good for McDonald's. Until the frantic calls from Cleveland reached their headquarters.

If the Cleveland boycotters wanted to show McDonald's the power of the black dollar, it was working. Five days into the boy-cott, three of the stores had ceased operations and only one of the restaurants kept its doors open.[27] Accustomed to earning $400 by noon, a manager at Kinsman Road reported $36 in sales.[28] The next day, the newspaper business pages outside of Cleveland were tak-ing notice. Afro Set was performing its signature, choreographed drills. Dressed in bold print dashikis and necklaces with dangling African-inspired medallions, Afro Set sometimes performed with machetes and nationalist flags, and the sight of the young men heightened the tensions of managers and franchisees who did not care for the news cameras that began to gather around the restaurant. Four stores were "all but closed" by the boycotts. The OBU action was working so well that it was shaping business outside of the East Side. A fifth McDonald's location—which was not originally a target of the protest—also reported a decline in patrons.[29]

McDonald's tried to defend themselves from the accusations and insults leveled by Hill, the OBU's conductor and loudest mouthpiece. Black Cleveland—they argued—simply misunderstood what had happened. Months before Hilliard's death, McDonald's regional representatives claimed, they were trying to find black franchisees as early as March but couldn't find qualified operators. Cleveland's McDonald's outlets were not harmed or abandoned, like Petty's Woodlawn outfit. In fact, they netted more than their average stores, and those high profits contributed to the franchise's value. Cleveland's black business community could not clear the financial hurdle to qualify for a restaurant. Hill countered McDonald's claim by citing his list of twenty potential franchisees, as well as Hilliard's efforts to return the conversation to OBU's central argument: McDonald's wanted to dictate a process that belonged in the community's hands. McDonald's may have laid down the most valuable card in its deck when they strayed from the boycott and focused on its leader. McDonald's spokespeople shared with the *New York Times* and other news sources that Hill had used aliases for decades and had been arrested dozens of times between 1943 and 1960.[30] Hill may have been used to his criminal record becoming an inconvenient truth for him, and he simply reminded the public that McDonald's was no better than a white overseer of a plantation or any other predatory authority that did not respect black self-determination. Hill rested his case in the way he rested all his debates; there was no room for negotiation. "McDonald's people say they want to deal with some responsible and sophisticated colored people. They're looking for some good niggers," he retorted. Hill grandstanded: "If you don't meet with

Rabbi David Hill, then you won't meet with anyone. The black community will tell McDonald's who's qualified to run these things and who's not." [31]

The boycott continued.

McDonald's may have finally found a race-based challenge that they couldn't ignore like the southern sit-ins or capitalize upon like the damages of post-King cities. McDonald's representatives not only had to respond to OBU as boycotts imperiled their businesses, but they also had to address a news media that found the story noteworthy because of what was happening and where it was unfolding. Cleveland was rife with the appearance of racial contradictions. A black mayor was elected in a city that was only 37% black. He was smart enough to prevent a major catastrophe after King, only to have to manage a firestorm a few months later. McDonald's had seamlessly entered other inner cities in places that were larger, more racially polarized, and far more influential, but Cleveland was showing the country something different. If blacks were supposed to select what their freedom would look like off a limited menu of capitulation to capitalism or resistance to capitalism, then OBU was suggesting that they should customize it to fit their tastes. Black Power capitalism, as it emerged in Cleveland, prioritized black ownership, wealth building, and community connectedness.

The OBU boycott quickly revealed that the actions that shut down or disturbed McDonald's business were emblematic of black politics in Cleveland. Complaints about the mayor's cautious ways of talking about the protests—validating the right to protest without interrogating McDonald's responsibility to local communities—highlighted the disappointment with the limits of being governed by a black mayor. Concerns about Hill's suitability to speak for all of black Cleveland emanated from both his criminal history as well as his adoption of black radical ideals. McDonald's assertion that the boycott actually hurt black workers who could not collect paychecks when stores were closed exposed the unequal consequences of black political action in a low-income community. With each day, a new insight became visible or kernel of information was revealed about the nature of the boycott and black capitalism. OBU members and leaders had to wonder if the boycott was the right thing to do, and if a franchise could actually do very much for the East Side. Although OBU was forged out of a sense that McDonald's owed black Cleveland something, identifying the boycott's goals was difficult by virtue of the groups that came together over the McDonald's issue. On the whole, black advocacy groups sought the eradication of racism and organized themselves around ideas of racial justice, but there was no uniformity in opinion on how these principles should be manifested in the world, especially in the marketplace. In the ways that the term "black capitalism" could mean so many things to so many people, OBU's boycott expressed their opposition to McDonald's, but depending on each organization's history and political position, what they believed to be the solution varied greatly. The diversity among this group of black freedom seekers served to raise awareness of the boycotts and indicated that McDonald's had a formidable community to deal with, but that same diversity made it difficult to define the parameters of success.

As the boycott passed the two-week mark, an article in the *Cleveland Plain Dealer* captured the divergent ideas of what a black McDonald's meant to black residents. The newspaper reported: "Some members of the unity group want black owners of McDonald's franchises. Some want a structure of such a nature that profits will benefit the total black community. Some want McDonald's out of black neighborhoods."[32] A public-private development group founded to revitalize blighted neighborhoods, wanted to see a reduction in franchise fees. Franchise prices were based on annual sales, and there were questions and concerns about how a boycott could artificially depress a store's value. They repeated the claim made by black franchise applicants, who accused white operators of inflating the price tag on the boycotted restaurants. McDonald's accused OBU of using boycotts to "lower sale prices of the franchises" and held that black activists misunderstood why each franchise was offered at a different price—new stores and existing stores varied in the cost of investment because of differential profit margins, set volumes, and prior sales.[33] Boycotting, in McDonald's estimation, was merely a market manipulation trick. McDonald's argued in the court of public opinion that OBU activists were using the pickets to sink the franchises and snap them up for cheap.

Franchise costs were less important to the local Urban League, an organization founded on the principle of fighting racial discrimination. Urban League leaders did not get mired in the details of sale prices. An enthusiastic partner on many economic and housing development programs, the Urban League understood the boycott as a matter of blacks and whites being able to access franchises on an equal basis. Their position gestured toward the accusations that perfectly qualified black applicants were rejected out of hand from franchising. Civil rights mainstay CORE, which had been so integral in the sit-ins that desegregated the southern fast food industry, had pivoted toward economic development and black capitalism in the late 1960s. The Cleveland chapter wanted blacks to "define [their] own turf and control it." CORE Cleveland's spin-off project, Target City, also weighed in on the debate. Target City, which scholar Nishani Frazier has described as espousing "communal capitalism," believed that it was possible for franchising to do more than enrich individuals.[34] Target City's director explained, "We're not talking about making a half-dozen black millionaires . . . CORE is interested in a structure in which profits from the restaurants will benefit the total black community." Meanwhile, the Southern Christian Leadership Conference, which was still vibrant despite losing King a year earlier, was among the first supporters of the demonstrations, and they hoped that more restaurants and ownership opportunities could lead to better jobs for black people.[35] Each organization believed that if the boycotts could compel McDonald's to put the restaurants under the auspices of a black owner, some (if not all) of their goals for the community could be met. The fact that a fast food restaurant bore the weight of all these wants elucidates both the desperate state of black Cleveland in finding vehicles to address economic disenfranchisement and the pragmatism of some black leaders in using fast food's expansion as a way to meet community demands for jobs, as well as avenues to business ownership.

In the hands of the most talented organizer, the competing desires of OBU, McDonald's reticence to negotiate, and the uncertainty of how long the boycott would last would be incredibly difficult to manage. For Hill, whose strength was mostly showmanship, maintaining control of OBU became increasingly difficult. When McDonald's reached out to OBU to schedule a meeting after the first week of boycotting, Hill said that OBU was only willing to negotiate if McDonald's president Fred Turner came to Cleveland. Turner had no intention of boarding a plane to visit Hill or any other member of OBU. But McDonald's finally conceded to OBU demands and sent top-level McDonald's leaders, including a newly hired Bob Beavers, to the offices of the *Call & Post*, black Cleveland's trusted newspaper, to meet. The intensity that enveloped the gathering was on a par with a hostage negotiation or a wartime surrender. Guards stood outside the doors of the meeting room. The McDonald's representatives later revealed that they were advised to arm themselves with a gun in case someone made good on the threats that franchisers and franchisees had received since the boycott opened. The current franchisees had waved the white flag, and they wanted out as soon as possible. The offer to sell the franchises to a black businessman was not going to be accepted so hastily. Hill had been the public face and voice of the boycott for weeks, but McDonald's did not want to acknowledge Hill's leadership in the opening stages of the negotiation. Further, McDonald's refused his request to apologize for the various accusations they made about his character and criminal history in the press. Hill had already warned McDonald's that they had to meet with him and no one else would accommodate a request to talk. The Black community, Hill reminded, was in charge, and there was no question that they would win. McDonald's claimed that throughout the early days of the boycott, the corporation and its franchisees were recipients of threats and harassment. McDonald's executive Edward Bood assured OBU that they were supportive of a potential sale from white operators to black ones but wanted to avoid appearing as if they were rewarding "threats and intimidation," and he admitted that he didn't want to "deal with Hill" as the lead negotiator of the issue. When given the opportunity to talk to Hill directly, McDonald's representatives declined.

The McDonald's reps headed for the door, and they probably reasoned that any movement organized by Hill would eventually burn out. But as they began to measure the boycott in weeks rather than days, McDonald's grew afraid that if black diners took too long a break from their swiftly prepared burgers and perfectly browned potatoes, they would not return. Internally, McDonald's worried that the boycott was shifting the "eating habits of customers in the area" and making room for competing fast food outlets to enter their territory. They were not far off in their assessment; Mahalia Jackson's Glori-Fried Chicken restaurant visited Cleveland in the summer of 1969 to see if they could benefit from blacks taking a break from burgers.[36] Externally, McDonald's implored OBU to consider the ways they were imperiling black jobs by keeping the restaurant closed. The optics of the boycott may have been amplified because the employees and the boycotters were all black, highlighting the fissures among black community relationships to the burgeoning franchise. OBU supporters who wanted to realize black control of McDonald's in Cleveland could not ignore the fact that boycotts sometimes led to intimidation and violence between picketers and potential customers, as well as picketers and black employees. The consequences of picketing were a contentious issue for a community that often used this form of protest to access a restaurant, not to own it. An Urban League representative remarked:

> The objective is different from that of former picketing . . . it's to make them hurt to the point that they stop playing games and consummate the negotiation that has been going on for some time. I think this form of picketing is just as ethical and just as moral.[37]

McDonald's, of course, did not appreciate the ethical and moral imperatives of protest.

Blacks were welcome to try their hands at franchising, but ultimately the corporation would decide where, when, and how. Bood reiterated that they would do everything to "encourage Negro ownership," but criticized OBU for lacking "a responsible and reasonable approach" to appealing for the franchise. While Petty and others were encouraged to tap into Small Business Administration lending programs and McDonald's was willing to be flexible with other black franchisees unable to gather the requisite funds for stores, McDonald's would not bend in Cleveland. This was not about discrimination, they argued; they were uncertain about the OBU's capacity to cover the franchise's price. In 1969, franchise fees were set at $12,500 for a company-developed property plus 2.2% of profits for a "continuing service fee." Franchisees had to present approximately $45,000 to secure the deal, including up to $15,000 for "security on the leased property and building," in addition to a down payment of $8,000 "for signs and equipment, [and] $7,000 for operational items."[38] The only area in which McDonald's was willing to bend was that it would allow "responsible black community organizations to operate franchises," due to having "difficulty in locating financially qualified individuals." The announcement of the policy change toward allowing organizations to apply for franchises instantly piqued the interest of House of Israel members. Bood said Hill's church did not meet criteria. "The House of Israel in our opinion represents its own interests and objectives and not those of the black community in Cleveland." In McDonald's estimation, anything associated with Hill failed to qualify as responsible. As the boycott story remained on the pages of local and national newspapers, McDonald's may have worried that protests like these would multiply across the very markets they wanted to enter. McDonald's could not afford to have several of these actions dictate the future of their urban expansion.[39]

For the white franchisees in the middle of this fight, they were done with all of it: OBU's obstinance and McDonald's stubbornness. Bood claimed he was actively encouraging "white owners of franchises in black communities to sell to qualified black individuals" and assured that "many such sales have transpired." But Cleveland was not going to be that easy.[40] One white franchisee of the boycott's first targeted store, Orvin Benson, said that he was "perfectly willing to entertain any legitimate offer." His experience called McDonald's narrative of the boycott into question. Benson claimed that he was terrified by "shots through [his store] window," and for all of McDonald's posturing about supporting franchise sales, he had yet to engage in any "talk about a deal." Prior to the picketing, Benson said he actually tried to sell his franchise to Hilliard, but Hilliard could not get financing. Benson conceded that OBU's suspicions were correct but misunderstood. He did raise the price of his franchise for resale. His accountant valued the restaurant at $250,000 when Hilliard applied to franchise it. His location at 10411 St. Clair Avenue grew by 86% in one year, and Benson presented a letter from McDonald's stating that the St. Clair store witnessed "the biggest increase ever" that year.[41]

While McDonald's negotiated with OBU, the stores remained mostly closed as boycott activity entered its second month in August. McDonald's and OBU agreed to return to the drawing board, on the condition that McDonald's respect the request of the local chapters of the NAACP and Urban League: keep stores closed until after the two parties had a chance to meet. After agreeing to "carefully consider" the request, McDonald's fears of losing another day of sales receipts led them to reopen the stores. To add insult to injury, McDonald's paid for a full-page ad in the *Cleveland Press* announcing that stores were open for business.[42] Two weeks later, the OBU reopened conversations with McDonald's with a revised proposal for how the stalemate could come to an end. OBU ignored McDonald's earlier assessment of Hill and the House of Israel's suitability for franchise leadership, and they strategized how they would raise the capital to make a bid for at least one of the East Side locations.

But if OBU was to do any deals with McDonald's, they were not going to simply acquire a franchise, they were going to change how businesses entered black Cleveland altogether. Hill demanded that in addition to the keys to the properties, McDonald's give $10,000 to the black community of Cleveland for local projects and neighborhood resources. In recognition of their work in arranging the transfers, OBU also asked for a fee equal to 2% of the franchise sale price. Hill also requested that in order to prevent another instance like the one that frustrated Hilliard's attempt at getting his restaurant, OBU hold the exclusive right to determine Cleveland's future black franchisees. Exhausted and beleaguered white franchisees were willing to accept the 2% provision and turn over their stores, but McDonald's could not stomach the proposal. McDonald's, which had shown itself to be flexible with other black operators, believed that by accepting the OBU terms they would inflict "substantial harm" on other franchise operators, other business interests, and the East Side. By harm, Bood probably meant evidence that boycott was an effective means of challenging businesses and that black consumer power was still real after the sit-in movement had passed. In Bood's estimation, McDonald's "best contribution to the black community is being a good citizen and providing jobs and taxes, and encouraging our operators to support all worthy community programs."[43] OBU was willing to offer a slight compromise. If McDonald's didn't want to make a direct gift to OBU, each franchisee—acting independently of McDonald's—should offer $2,500 and collectively donate $20,000, which amounted to approximately 20% of the sale price of each store.[44] The two sides were approaching a compromise on sales to black franchisees, but McDonald's vice president demanded that no one give in to OBU's request for donations. McDonald's was willing to fund a community swimming pool, playground, or recreation center for east Cleveland, but no direct cash payment would be on the table. Besides, McDonald's argued, their initiative was worth far more than the original donation requests.[45]

The OBU would not be treated this way. Black people could determine their own destiny, and the group probably balked when a McDonald's representative listed its donations to the NAACP, the United Negro College Fund, schools on Native American reservations, and "educational institutions and local civic causes to the tune of $5,000." They would be open to donating to the Cleveland Urban Coalition, but not to OBU or OBU-connected projects.[46] McDonald's unquestionably would need to prioritize philanthropy if they were to expand in black America, but benevolence didn't mean that the company would acquiesce to every request or protest. The Cleveland crisis was actively shaping how McDonald's was establishing its community relations protocols for the future, and it was enhancing the expectation that black franchisees would function as peacekeepers and bulwarks between the corporate office and the community. The dynamic between OBU and McDonald's also foreshadowed the future of franchises in black areas, as their involvement in subsidizing swimming pools and neighborhood resources blurred the boundaries between company and community trust.

McDonald's rejection of the OBU plan momentarily reignited the fight. The week after Bood elaborated McDonald's good citizenship, OBU drew 500 people to a mass meeting about McDonald's. National CORE leader Roy Innis came to Cleveland to encourage the boycott. Innis was the only national civil rights leader to visit Cleveland during the protest. National Urban League and NAACP heads opted to have locals determine the way forward for themselves. Among the many lines that drew applause from the crowd, Innis said he was glad that Clevelanders did not ask for jobs at their local McDonald's—they wanted power. "The demand is to take over the whole damned instruments," he lectured.[47] White franchise owners were willing to hand over the instruments, but McDonald's was unmoved. Ed Greenwald, an attorney for a white franchisee, recognized that McDonald's would not concede to anyone even as their franchisees searched for an exit. "Big Daddy has final control and Big Daddy said no." The patriarchal will of the franchise over the franchisee was absolute: "If we want to sell our franchises, we gotta look to Big Daddy for the blessing. We can't move without their consent." Whether they were moved by the spirit of social change or collapsed by the stress of the boycotts, white franchisees agreed more than they disagreed with the transfer program, even if they did not initially seek it out. "Our franchise holders, after a lot of thought, have agreed that it makes perfectly good sense that these businesses should be sold to blacks because these are very different times," Greenwald said. "I have no guide for what is right in these times. Nobody has."[48]

The McDonald's franchise manual covered a myriad of topics, but challenges by black nationalists were not one of them. With "no guide" available on engaging groups like OBU, but an awareness that what happened in Cleveland may set a precedent, McDonald's continued to discredit OBU and their requests. Bood asked, with "no trust fund set up, no funds to be administered through any trust fund, no foundation or anything," how could OBU be trusted with thousands of dollars for the community? "Who are to be the officers? Who'll get the benefits of any monies collected from royalties?"[49] OBU was also without much of a blueprint on how to negotiate with a corporate entity like McDonald's. Previous large-scale boycotts among black communities were guided by the leadership of an Operation Breadbasket or an NAACP in solidarity with other groups. OBU imagined the organization to be an equal member of the boycott campaign, but Hill's dominance and the uncertainty of how each entity would intersect with the desired outcomes undermined the movement's strength.

As the summer gave way to a fall election season, the boycott's foundations began to crack. The wide range of OBU member perspectives, growing discomfort with Hill's assertive style, and the enlarging specter of the boycott on Stokes's reelection efforts began to disassemble the group.

Cleveland NAACP members grew outraged by Hill's alleged behavior behind the scenes of the boycott. Initially, his OBU compatriots did not address his criminal record, and he could rely on black establishment types in Cleveland to stand up for him when his character was in question. As an unnamed member of Stokes's inner circle told the press in response to revelations about Hill's past: "The man's not important but the issue of black control is."[50] The *Plain Dealer* summed it up: "OBU members were familiar with Hill's background, but they agreed with his position on black capitalism."[51] The possibilities of black ownership in Hough were too lucrative to let Hill's rap sheet get in the way. But eventually rumors circulated that Hill was asking for money to go into his pockets, not OBU coffers, and he may have been directing rogue boycotters to threaten franchisees. The NAACP wondered how their beloved organization was entangled with an "extortionist attempt."[52]

Urban League members were also becoming targets of criticism for associating with Hill. Leaders issued a joint statement from NAACP and Urban League members disavowing "extortion or blackmail." A member of a local business league offered: "We are opposed to any group trying to force others to sell their businesses. Negro people must build something of their own instead of taking from others."[53] One by one, the "mainstream" or "old-school" groups began to withdraw from OBU. In September of 1969, the Urban League broke from OBU.[54] A week later, Hill was ousted as the chair of the OBU Negotiating Committee. The group that expended significant social capital by supporting him unanimously accepted his reluctant resignation. Hill warned, "I don't share those beliefs, but they will soon learn that I am not the problem, but the enemy is." The final straw for OBU: Hill allegedly held onto $50,000 in franchisee applicant fees, a charge he denied.[55] Black capitalism could bring people together, but it alone was not enough to keep them united. McDonald's resistance to negotiate with OBU became secondary to Hill's reputation or the fear that the coalition would seem undeserving or overly greedy. In the struggle for black organizations to petition for resources—whether from the state or the marketplace—blacks always remained vigilant that they not conform to stereotypes of being idle or insolent, even when they were victims of injustice. Although Hill was a flawed leader in a variety of ways, OBU's defectors shifted their ire from the hamburger stand in their neighborhood to their neighbors who requested that the hamburger stand contribute to community resources.

Soon after Hill's ouster, a grand jury was assembled to determine if OBU violated extortion laws. Any opponent of black nationalism or the House of Israel lined up to make an example of Hill and to tell a black community organizing around boycotts and economic development that they would be watched. While anti-integrationist whites found black capitalism's comfort with separatism appealing, white authorities would not allow black communities to operate unchecked. Whether OBU was the real target, or the mayor heading into an election, the fallout around Hill and the boycott muffled black voices who took economic exploitation to task. A crusading state representative from the suburbs assured that if no specific laws were violated in this case because the OBU manipulated legal loopholes, then he would propose new extortion laws during the upcoming legislative period. Black Cleveland could agitate all they wanted, but ultimately the state could and would have the last word. In response to the threat of drafting new extortion laws to punish OBU activism, OBU supporter Hilbert Perry retorted that he wanted to impanel a grand jury to investigate racism in the city. "McDonald's can take $2.5 million out of the black community and not have the responsibility to help rebuild the inner city," and in his estimation, "this act of theft warranted some type of inquiry." Why stop there, Perry wondered. He also wanted someone to look into "the lack of fair housing . . . high inner-city unemployment rate, and current welfare programs."[56]

Having managed his own ups and downs with his colleagues in state and city government, Carl Stokes knew that some of his white detractors would rather spend time litigating OBU controversies than funding the construction projects needed in Hough and Glenville. He also knew the boycott was going to remain strong into September, and his primary race was on October 1. And he was aware that he had to stave off Democratic challengers, assure black voters he was still with them, and remind white voters that 1966 was behind them. Mayor Stokes did not have time for the back-and-forth with McDonald's, but he didn't get where he was without understanding that all things were political. He was feeling the pressure from the local party, which met in late August to express concern that Stokes was mum on the McDonald's issue, and the party formed a committee with the explicit purpose of discussing his strategy on managing it.[57] Then there were the newspapers with the embarrassing headlines that seemed to be making fun of the mayor. "Hamburger Hassle Imperils Stokes," cried the *Washington Post*. "Friends and advisers are praying that Mayor Carl B. Stokes won't trip over a hamburger between now and Election Day."[58] His campaign manager tried to keep his official comments strictly on the act of protest, rather than on the target. "They are exercising a constitutional right to picket. And they are sitting down at the negotiation table trying to settle their grievances with a company regarding what they consider to be an injustice in the community." Stokes called "picketing at McDonald's as American as apple pie."[59] The Stokes campaign's sanitized statement was vaguely supportive without choosing a side.

McDonald's was exposing how black politics, economics, and even identity could converge into high-stakes decision-making. The McDonald's boycott was about more than a business; it was testing the volume of black voices in setting the standard and expectation of their consumer citizenship in Hough and surrounding areas, which set the tone of how they could maintain their electoral power. Stokes's Democratic primary opponent Robert J. Kelly used the issue to blow a dog whistle toward white voters uncertain about a black mayor's ability to effectively control black communities. Kelly seized on the apple pie analogy: "This shows how little he knows about America or apple pie when he tries to compare legitimate picketing with extortion." Kelly asked which of Cleveland's beloved businesses would next fall victim to black irascibility? Would A&P, Pick-N-Pay, Sears, or the Cleveland Trust find themselves targeted by black ire? "Or will it be the little businessman in the neighborhood trying to make a living?"[60] Those closest to Stokes knew that white Clevelanders, maybe even some that voted for the charismatic mayor, had doubts about his ability to improve the city. Meanwhile black voters were perpetually reminded of how little had changed. One observer took blacks to task for believing too deeply in Stokes. "People thought that once a black mayor was elected, money was going to start falling from the sky, and jobs were going to be lying around in the streets."[61] Black Clevelanders were not so naïve as to think everything would change overnight, but how would change come if they didn't fight? Recognizing that there were battles to join across the city, black Cleveland turned out for their mayor in the Democratic primary, helping Stokes collect 60% of the vote to shore up his candidacy for a second term.[62]

The day before Stokes's electoral victory, he celebrated a smaller

win—the end of the McDonald's boycott. With Hill under investigation and a dwindling base of supporters, the mayor may have
realized that this was his chance to step in and settle the boycott.
The remaining leadership of the OBU accepted Stokes's proposal
that in exchange for the end of the boycotts, McDonald's would
immediately identify and turn over the stores to black franchisees.
OBU was probably unaware that McDonald's already had their
future franchisee in mind. In October, DeForest Brown Jr., president of the Hough Area Development Corporation (HADC), contacted what was left of the OBU to submit a bid to franchise two
locations. Founded by Brown, a minister and social worker, after
the Hough uprising in 1967, the HADC drew upon federal, city,
and private dollars to finance community-based projects, including a shopping plaza, affordable housing, and a small factory. The
HADC replicated a popular model created in the late 1960s, which
brought social service organizations in conversation with private
foundations and corporations to underwrite a host of initiatives that
matched the enthusiasm for black capitalism with millions of dollars.[63] Brown came prepared to offer $400,000 for the franchises,
with assistance from a local bank, more than $50,000 of HADC
venture capital, and federal resources from the Office of Economic
Opportunity (OEO). Once they acquired the restaurant, the HADC
would transfer ownership to the newly formed Ghetto East Enterprises, Inc., a for-profit corporation. Then, after a year, they would
transfer ownership to the larger Hough community by offering
shares in the franchise.[64] Hill and his faction were angered that the
HADC was granted a franchise before them and the list of twenty,
some of whom believed they were close to entering franchise agreements. The HADC's liquidity and its experience with tapping into
federal resources aligned with how McDonald's inner-city expansion plan had worked. Although the HADC was not opposed to
using protest to apply pressure to draw investments into Hough,
they were able to allay fears that McDonald's would be asked to
underwrite pools or parks. From the perspective of the HADC, they
would do that themselves by running a profitable business and putting the means of ownership in the hands of the people.[65]

After the deal was finalized, McDonald's revealed in the spring of 1970 that they had reached out to the HADC at the height of the protest that past summer. HADC's interest in McDonald's remained quiet, perhaps causing OBU to feel more confident about its prospects for acquiring the restaurants. McDonald's did not remark on this until a *Plain Dealer* article exposed that the HADC partnership was "part of a move to take over control of two McDonald's outlets in black areas." Fearing the boycotts would become "damaging to race relations in Cleveland" and could impede "acceptance of the restaurants" as truly black franchises, a local attorney admitted that he helped McDonald's contact the HADC. The lawyer also emphasized that Hill actually tried to undermine the deal, and he was grateful to Stokes for discreetly helping broker the process.[66] McDonald's refusals of the OBU were not only about their insistence not to capitulate, but also their awareness that they could find a better partner if they held out. By allowing their franchisees to fret, the community to become more incensed, and the mayor to contemplate if he was going to win reelection, McDonald's sent a clear message about how much community agitation they would tolerate. At the offices of the community development groups that sprouted up in cities across the country after 1968, the HADC McDonald's projects were inspiring them to think about how fast food could fit in their lofty plans to resuscitate the inner city. McDonald's had appeared unkind and unresponsive during the OBU boycotts, but soon after, they partnered with HADC and other community development groups to franchise restaurants in Hough, and McDonald's was able to seal its image as a socially progressive supporter of black capitalism.

McDonald's may have resolved their boycott issues, but for Hill and other OBU members, the final act of the drama was set in the courtroom, not at the counter. There was no grand jury assembled to think about poverty in Hough, as Hilbert Perry sarcastically suggested. A Cuyahoga County grand jury was, however, impaneled, and they called potential franchisees, OBU members, and McDonald's executives to answer questions about whether Hill solicited money for his backing their McDonald's bids. They all denied giving any money to Hill. Potential franchisee applicants all testified that McDonald's referred them to Hill before the pickets started, suggesting that they saw him as a valuable asset in finding black franchisees or an object of diversion to avoid engaging with the men.[67] The testimonies of Bood and McDonald's spokesman John Devitt probably convinced the jury to move forward with an indictment of four counts of blackmailing. In what was described as an "unprecedented move" by the prosecutor, the charge claimed that by initiating the boycott, Hill threatened to end the profits of the restaurants, which "carried the implicit threat of violence to anyone crossing the picket line," thus supporting a blackmail charge. For black organizations across Cleveland, the indictment may have alerted them to the risks of executing boycotts. James Raplin, Hill's right-hand man, was also charged with blackmail. The prosecutorial strategy was believed by some to be an attack on Stokes, who had lent support to other black boycotts.[68] Despite another court declaring him mentally incompetent, Hill stood trial for blackmail. OBU's attorney emphasized that the label of incompetence would have "no effect whatsoever on David Hill's position in Operation Black Unity," hinting that the gutted and discredited organization would continue on after the trial. Hill's defense attorney called the assessment of his client's faculties a "typical racist reaction to a black radical's efforts to help his people."[69] Hill's mental state aside, the attorney was accurate in describing the justice system's pathologizing of black anger and discord. State prisons and mental institutions housed black men and women who were labeled criminally insane, when in fact they were simply indignant over racist treatment. Protest would not die in Cleveland after a verdict came in Hill's trial, but the sheer power and influence of McDonald's and their ability to control the Cleveland crisis dampened the belief that gaining economic power meant gaining freedom from the racism found in other power structures.

By the start of 1970, the issue of black ownership of Cleveland McDonald's had officially come to an end.[70] The Hough Area Development Corporation was now at the helm of the East 82nd and East 107th Street restaurants. Kinsman Road went to

Charles E. Johnson, the president of CAM, Inc. Johnson had tried for more than a year to acquire a franchise, but he couldn't secure a loan until the OBU boycotts brought the ownership issue to the fore. The community-owned McDonald's locations were unable to maintain their hold on the businesses, especially after cuts to federal economic development programs depleted their financial and political power. In 1982, the HADC struggled to "replace 84% of its operating costs" after the OEO's successor, the Community Services Administration, was obliterated by federal budget cuts. Those locations, as well as more fast-food restaurants in black areas, would be franchised by blacks throughout the following two decades.[71] The *Atlanta Daily World* applauded the protests for showing "the viability of black power and the stability of appetites."[72] Each of these locations also showed the viability of fast food in environments shaped by economic, racial, and social instability.

As for Hill and Raplin, they would not know their fates until the winter of 1972. By then, Stokes had won the 1969 mayoral election, served his second term as mayor, and moved on to a career in broadcasting in New York City. Everyone had seemed to move on, except the pair. The men were found guilty, and then their paths diverged. Hill—who was facing up to forty-five years in prison for nine counts of blackmail—was determined not to serve another day in an institution after spending years in and out of juvenile and adult facilities. The Rabbi fled to Guyana, the South American nation that had long been seen as a promised land for American blacks.[73] In Guyana he established the House of Israel again, and in leaving Cleveland he not only fled the consequences of his McDonald's case, but he also evaded an unrelated legal matter in which he faced four counts of "larceny by trickery."[74] After years in Guyana, Hill found himself in trouble again and in a Guyanese prison for manslaughter. Hill was charged with ordering the murder of a House of Israel member's husband, and he served six years of a twenty-six-year sentence. In 1992, after verifying that he could not be apprehended for the Cleveland charges, and in accordance with his release agreement with Guyanese officials,

Hill returned to the United States. Hill, now calling himself Rabbi Edward Washington, arrived in New York on August 8, nearly a quarter century after initiating the boycott.[75] Hill was happy to leave Guyana, but he was warned that he could not return to Cleveland. A county prosecutor promised, "If he comes back, he's going to jail." In the fall of 1992, Hill returned to Guyana to craft his memoir of leading a congregation of 10,000 devotees, financing his church with Rabbi Chips—a banana snack—and serving Guyana's president Forbes Burnham.[76]

While his friend fled Cleveland to bask in the sun, Raplin set out to do his time for extortion and blackmail. On his first night at the Marion Correctional Institute, a "little disturbance" in the prison caused the kitchen to shut down. The correctional officers ordered McDonald's cheeseburgers to feed Marion's residents. Raplin wondered to himself as he peeled the paper wrapper from his dinner, "How did I get into this?"[77] Raplin was released in August of 1974, and he returned to his activist life in Cleveland. He joined the staff of a new Afro-American Studies program at Case Western Reserve University and organized an affordable and fair housing campaign.[78] In the revised, reconsidered, and reframed story of black franchises in Cleveland, Raplin (and Hill to some degree) were cast in the roles of unsung heroes of a difficult moment. At the seventh annual meeting of the National Black McDonald's Operators Association in Cleveland in 1978, the former mayor acknowledged the two men as playing an integral role in clearing a path for the city's black franchisees and their colleagues that came after them nationwide. Raplin was happy to accept some praise, and in remembering the coalition that formed under OBU, he believed the real feat was getting everybody together. Raplin acknowledged that OBU organized "the militant blacks, the almost militant blacks, the moderate blacks, the almost moderate blacks and even some of the most perennial Uncle Toms."[79] Raplin was accurate that black capitalism could bring a cross-section of a population in community, but regardless of business success or failure, maintaining coalitions was difficult. And when groups formed to negotiate or leverage their power with major corporations, the terms of the negotiation were sometimes far apart from the values of the group.

After the dust had settled from the tense negotiations over franchises in Cleveland, future McDonald's CEO Ed Rensi took his experiences as a field consultant in Cleveland to Chicago, believing that the corporation needed to learn from the debacle with the black community. Franchise recruiter Roland Jones and a fellow black management team member offered a mostly white office a presentation on "what it was like to be black in America." According to McDonald's insiders, the lecture—which some were concerned would be too divisive—proved to be beneficial in not only creating deeper understanding but also forecasting the ways the company was willing to be flexible and open to feedback in growing the "ethnic market." A future McDonald's vice president for diversity believed that the lesson learned was that "a proactive approach to minority licensing was the only way to avoid similar situations in major cities across the country."[80] The corporation hired black consultants to assist in redefining McDonald's corporate culture, from former Freedom Rider, and Southern Christian Leadership Conference member, civil rights legend C. T. Vivian, to future Secretary of Commerce Ron Brown. Brown worked with McDonald's in 1979 to assess how blacks could be part of what was described as a sometimes renegade and "wild and crazy" company.[81]

The Cleveland McDonald's boycotts encapsulated the central questions of how to ensure black economic development post-1968. Was it a matter of not unfairly enriching the already rich individuals Ralph Abernathy and James Forman cautioned against, or could franchises work in the service of creating rich communities? The Cleveland boycotts did not revolve around gaining access to a public accommodation, as was the case in the great sit-ins in Greensboro and Nashville years earlier. Clevelanders were protesting to *own* the accommodation. The Cleveland boycott reflected the convergence of differing political ideologies in black cities, contentions over ownership, the terrains in which the future of black struggle would play out, and the limits of black politicians and black capitalism. By the late 1960s, McDonald's and its close peers were not formally discriminating against black customers. In fact, from all reports blacks were enjoying spending their time and dollars at the drive-ins, and later drive-thrus. Rather, this boycott was about what was owed to black Cleveland in the form of economic opportunity and whether black capitalism could cover the nation's promises made to blacks, which Martin Luther King Jr. likened to a bad check at the 1963 March on Washington.

For black communities in the 1960s and 1970s, it seemed as if chaos was the only way to coax concern and maybe see change. Slum housing, overcrowded schools, and hungry children were all visible signs of poverty throughout black communities. But these scourges were magnified when buildings were on fire or businesses were looted. Activists who wanted to see improvements in their community's quality of life needed to learn how to capitalize on federal and state urgency to create businesses as a response to inadequate housing or health care. Whether a black leader found black capitalism hopeful or shameful was unimportant. Her ability to tap into the resources that black capitalism endowed made the difference between living in a community with a free meals program for children and the elderly or on a block filled with hungry people. Increasingly, as fast food expanded, the choice between a McDonald's and no McDonald's was actually a choice between a McDonald's or no youth job program. If McDonald's could be convinced to provide, why not find ways for them to become a member of the community? For boosters of black capitalism, the answer was self-evident. But for those skeptical of business, or at the very least invested in making sure that black dollars stay close to black businesses, fast food franchises still had to plead their case.

CHAPTER FOUR

Bending the Golden Arches

A protester outside of a McDonald's in the Albina neighborhood of Portland, Oregon. Albina was the center of black organizing in Portland and home to the local Black Panther Party chapter. City of Portland (OR) Archives, A2004-005.1808.

"Franchises: Boom or Bust for Blacks?"

The question posed on the cover of the inaugural issue of *Black Enterprise* magazine, launched in August of 1970, has been asked in the pages of the monthly for decades in different places and different ways. The bible of black capitalism always declares franchising a boom, and in this opening issue Brady Keys's All-Pro Chicken and McDonald's were presented as shining examples of the business model that seemed to effortlessly capture black dollars. Between the covers of the new publication, article after article reinforced its message to black America: it's time to get down to business. In a statement that ignored the long history of black business creation and wealth accumulation, *Black Enterprise* suggested that black people were just getting started on a path to economic success. "As a nation, as a people, we have begun in recent years to make modest beginnings toward making black people meaningful participants in our economic system. We feel that our people and our times require that we do more—much more—than settle for these modest beginnings."[1] According to *Black Enterprise,* fast food franchises were on the lookout for talent of color to open stores in their communities and help them achieve the Department of Commerce's 25x2x25 program goals of having 25 franchise companies offer 25 new franchises to minority applicants over the following two years.[2] With the private sector working so closely with federal agencies, fast food companies would meet and exceed their targets handily. Franchising had created a boom for black entrepreneurs. But, fast food still had hurdles to clear in some areas as movements emerged to ask critical questions of the industry and its representatives. Could a burger stand be a good neighbor? What did it mean to patronize a black-owned outlet of a white-owned company? What does it mean to buy black after all?

While the expansion of black-owned McDonald's franchises was a victory for the community development model in Cleveland and a coveted opportunity in Chicago, the movement of fast food into black communities was not uniformly welcomed or its potential problems mediated by the possibility of black financial investment. The presence of fast food franchises in cities from Portland to Philadelphia gave some black leaders an illustrative example of the problems of capitalism relative to black self-determination, while others held fast to the fantasy that the right kind of capitalism could clear the way for true racial liberation. The varied responses to fast food's encroachment into the inner city throughout the 1970s revealed that organized efforts to influence or altogether stop fast food in black neighborhoods became a proxy for talking about racial and economic inequality. Critics and activists believed that a new fast food restaurant in a black neighborhood wasn't just an addition to the marketplace of goods and services. Fast food represented larger structural and social problems, and the actions that some took against franchises demonstrated how much ground the industry had covered in relatively unfamiliar territory. The 1970s would usher in a decade of continued struggle against economic racism in local contexts, while the popularity of fast food was transforming how people viewed eating, working, and living. Franchise chains depended on their growing cohort of franchisees of color to buffer them from controversy, influence black consumer behavior, and acclimate communities to their foods. In the process, fast food franchises learned that blacks valued the very things—neighborhood control, care for community, or cultural authenticity—that fast food companies could never provide. Every fight wasn't about owning a franchise, in fact, most fights were not. The central question in all these conflicts: could fast food be a good citizen to, neighbor in, or symbol of black America?

*　*　*

The streets of Portland, Oregon, also managed to stay quiet the night that King died, but not very many people outside of the city or state took notice. Places with such small black populations rarely got mentioned in the somber national news stories about what was happening in and to the country in 1968. While Mayor Stokes was gaining nationwide praise for keeping things calm in Hough, the residents of the predominately black Albina neighborhood of Portland were quietly mourning King, too. Many of the residents remembered his Urban League–sponsored tour in 1961, when he visited one of the few black churches in Portland, the Vancouver Avenue First Baptist Church, a stately Gothic Revival building with stained-glass windows from the Povey Brothers Studio, the Tiffany & Co. of the Pacific Northwest. On that fall day, King told an audience at Portland State University, "We have come a long way toward making integration a reality, but we still have a long way to go." Folks in Albina knew that all too well. In the late 1960s, the population of blacks in Portland comprised only 5% of the city, but nearly 90% of them lived in Albina. King's legacy, in addition to recent memories of a 1967 uprising may have given people pause about going out on the streets again.

Albina was a testament, in many ways, to black resilience in a place that didn't want them there. Between 1844 and 1922, Oregon Country and later the State of Oregon (established in 1859) maintained laws that banned blacks from permanent residency.[3] By banning and expelling blacks in its early years, black sojourners were deterred from settling in the state even after they could legally live there. Oregon's cities observed racial, residential segregation, and blacks were mostly relegated to areas west of the Willamette River, which allowed black workers access to the railroad, defense industry, and domestic service jobs available to them.[4] The flooding of the river in the late 1940s, in addition to municipal expansion, highway projects, and the building of industrial centers, pushed black Portlanders across the Willamette into Albina. As the black population grew, white neighborhoods used the trusty mechanism of racially restrictive covenants to ensure their neighbors stayed the right color. Its proximity to the waterfront and expanding downtown also made Albina ripe for slum clearance and urban redevelopment. Where rows of houses once stood, the city of Portland sliced through Albina in 1956 to extend Interstate 5 and build Veterans Memorial Coliseum in 1960.[5] With so much compression, Albina became the only place where blacks who had to follow the employing industries could live.

On the same night that Detroit's 1967 uprising commenced, the Albina neighborhood was also kindled by confrontations between black youth and area police. The evening of July 20 brought a crowd to Irving Park for "Sunday at the Park," an interactive series of musical performances, lectures, and visual art that focused on the themes of Black Power, social revolution, and civil rights. The anticipated featured speaker, the Black Panther Party for Self Defense's Eldridge Cleaver, never appeared, and rumors spread that the Panthers' minister of information had been arrested. Although Irving Park was often busy on weekends, a nervous city leadership deployed police to patrol the park that day and kept the National Guard on standby, which only aided in riling the crowd. By early evening, tensions between the event attendees and the police reached a point of no return. The inexperienced police department lacked access to sufficient riot gear, so officers brought rifles and shotguns from their homes to reinforce the 200 officers deployed on the streets. Young men—white and black—fought with officers, threw Molotov cocktails at store windows, and spilled onto the streets. Residents locked their doors and prayed that a fire at a tavern or supermarket wouldn't spread to their homes. The uprising lasted two tense nights and claimed no fatalities, but many were injured or arrested, and neighborhood businesses were destroyed. After the $50,000 in property damage was totaled and the nearly 100 people arrested were processed, some Albina leaders hoped the incident could open up conversations about the way forward, as was the case in so many other cities. White Portland leaders chose to speak only about a disproven theory that outside agitators had caused the unrest, and they clung to a myth that Portland was a city for everybody, regardless of race. The Irving Park conflict did not inspire the same kind of large-scale urban investment plans, interracial rap sessions, or black business initiatives that emerged in blacker and more populous cities. In many ways, Portland's small black community was on its own.

The unresolved issues that surfaced at the Irving Park struggle inspired another round of disturbances two years later, on June 13, 1969, when a local member of Albina's National Committee to Combat Fascism (NCCF) noticed a confrontation between police and a group of black youths at Lidio's Drive-In, a hamburger stand.[6] That night, Kent Ford opened the door to a police cruiser and told the detainee—who Ford believed was only ten years old—to run, while he fought with police officers. Ford was then arrested, and officers drove him from the burger joint to another one, a McDonald's on Union Avenue. By the end of the night, officers had beaten the handcuffed Ford and placed him in custody. The five nights of fire bombings that followed Ford's arrest stopped when the weather changed. A rise in the temperature often led to a cool down of anger during riots. The streets of Albina were still by the evening of June 18, while a small group of white demonstrators appeared in front of City Hall to protest the arrest of five members of the Black Panther Party. Local business owners decided to arm themselves to stave off any bombers or looters, and others told the press that they would "move their businesses out of the fire and assault plagued area as soon as possible."[7] After spending more than two weeks in jail, Ford was welcomed back by his fellow NCCF comrades and friends. On the steps of the police station he gave a speech about police brutality and talked about the platform of the Black Panther Party. The NCCF transitioned into the local Panther Party by 1970, and they brought the signature initiatives of the then-four-year-old group from Oakland to the Rose City with gusto.[8] Even before they were officially chartered by the headquarters in California, the Portland NCCF was leading free breakfast programs, political education classes, and support for black students at the racially hostile Roosevelt High School.

Black Panther organizing illuminated a common theme in black life in America: survival in the face of suppression. The Portland Panthers were not only spreading the movement's message about self-determination and nation building; they were also filling a crucial gap between what blacks contributed to the system and what they were able to receive from it. No matter how hard African Americans worked and how many of their dollars ended up in public treasuries, basic services of the state were distributed in limited quantities, if at all. The Panthers filled voids for the hungry, the unemployed, and in Portland they were especially important to the sick. The 1969 establishment of Albina's People's Free Medical Clinic, part of a network of health care facilities operated and partially staffed by Panther members and a cohort of social-justice-oriented practitioners, transformed the health of black Albina. The clinic was later renamed for magnetic Chicago Panther leader Fred Hampton, who was slain by police alongside Panther Mark Clark in the winter of 1969.[9] In addition to offering routine physicals, the clinic could refer its clients to specialists in everything from dermatology to oncology. The clinic coordinated health education and offered sickle cell anemia screenings, helping African-American Portlanders understand the genetic disease. The clinics accommodated clients by opening on late afternoons and evenings, and trained medical and pharmacy assistants who were supervised by local medical and dental students. The Portland clinic was the only Panther project to provide dental services, in partnership with the University of Oregon Dental School.[10] Eventually, the Portland Panthers operated three medical centers—the Hampton location, a dental center named for Malcolm X, and the People's Clinic.[11] The clinics relied on donated supplies and volunteer time to ensure that vaccinations were administered and cavities filled.

The Portland Panthers were also dependent on the willingness and generosity of a wide swath of Albina to keep their initiative afloat, especially their signature free breakfast program. The first time Black Panthers served up a hot breakfast for area children was in Oakland in 1969, and they immediately discovered how desperately this meal was needed. The national school breakfast program wouldn't become part of the school day until 1975, so the Black Panthers' morning meal service became the most expansive of their offerings.[12] Free breakfast was highly visible and highly successful in bringing members of the community in contact with the group, and sometimes helped alleviate concerns about the Panthers. Educators appreciated being able to teach children without contending with distracting hunger pangs. While under the NCCF banner, the breakfast program promoted free meals as a means of chiseling away at the edifice of racial inequality in local schools. They critiqued the treatment of black children and the language used to deem them uneducable or ill-suited for school. "The root cause of the problem is not mental incapabilites or 'cultural deprivation,' but HUNGER."[13]

In the fall of 1971, *The Oregonian* reported that the Panther breakfast and clinic countered "the militant Panther image," and characterized Albina as approving of the Panthers' desire to "serve the people, body and soul." Kent Ford was quoted in the article, and he determined that the children who enjoyed the Panthers' meal "wouldn't be getting breakfast at home . . . not all of them are poor, but most come from homes where the mother doesn't have time to get up and cook in the mornings." He countered criticisms by arguing that "when the government steps forward and gives our people a balanced diet, we'll be glad to stop." The seemingly innocuous act of serving a hot breakfast to a child was a magnet for criticism, as anti-Panther forces believed it was a vehicle for radicalizing youth. Ford addressed the suspicions that the group was "indoctrinating" children. *The Oregonian* wrote that in the previous year teachers at a local school "complained that the breakfast program was making the children more hostile in the classrooms," but the complaints soon subsided. Black children conversant in Black Power ideology may have frightened their white teachers, but they couldn't argue that the children didn't arrive more focused and energetic each morning since the program started. Ford clarified that the children were only learning "by example, that socialism can work," as well as the stories of Panther icons, like the slain prisoner George Jackson, "for whom the meal program [was] named."[14] Decades later, adults recalled the breakfast program's meals and volunteers with fondness, because the organization's daily gathering spared them from the bland corn mush or toast doused in syrup sold at their local public school. The quality of the food, as well as the connection with adults, reassured children in a hypersegregated, and often ignored, community that they were cared for and loved. "The Panthers fed us well . . . pancakes or waffles, juice, and milk. Eggs with sausage was a staple. The Panthers served potatoes. The Panthers had a saying: . . . if a kid is hungry, he isn't thinking about learning."[15] Another frequent guest at breakfast recalled: "I loved going to the breakfast program . . . I remember Mr. Ford used to talk to us about staying in school, doing the right thing, and getting our lives together. I looked forward to seeing the Panthers. They always had something positive to say."[16] Albina's hungry children, their cash-strapped parents, and eventually their schoolteachers all came to appreciate what the breakfast program was doing for the community.

For Ford and the Portland Panthers, the breakfast program was not only rooted in their concern for children's nutrition, but also in their belief in redistributive justice. From their estimations, area businesses owed something to the Albina community that kept their doors open. When local Party members received cash donations or were gifted supplies, they were overseeing a little justice in a place where justice was in short supply. Ford explained that donating jugs of orange juice, cartons of eggs, and slabs of bacon to the breakfast program was the least that could be done by "the businessmen who take from our community," and the donations were one way they could "leave a little something in return."[17] Albina's businesses, especially the ones owned by whites, may have not fully supported the Black Panthers, but they figured that fortifying breakfast supplies could cultivate some amity with the local radicals, who some found confusing and others inspiring. In order for the program to survive, Kent Ford, and his wife Sandra Ford, had to constantly solicit businesses for support. After the last child was served hot chocolate and griddles were washed and dried, the pair would visit businesses to ask for help to maintain the breakfast, which some mornings drew more than a hundred hungry children. For the Panthers, the impact that the health screenings and hotcakes were having on the neighborhood spoke volumes about the community's rudimentary requirements and their ability to realize them. When the Panthers approached businesses for donations to sustain their programs, they offered business owners tours of the clinics and tallies of the pounds and pounds of food they were serving children each week at the Highland United Church of Christ.[18]

The Albina neighborhood McDonald's, located at 3510 N.E. Union Avenue, was under the charge of Al Laviske, who managed six other drive-ins across the area. Of all his stores, the Albina one may have presented the greatest challenge. The tensions that rose between his McDonald's and the Black Panther Party in the summer of 1970 can be traced back to a meeting that summer between Laviske and the Fords about McDonald's and the breakfast program. From Ford's perspective, he and associate Linda Thornton simply asked Laviske if he would be interested in helping them continue to feed children before school. Laviske claimed that he was the target of extortion, that Ford demanded $300 a month in cash from the restaurant, and they threatened him and the drive-in if he failed to deliver. The divergent origin stories of why the Panthers and McDonald's were at odds were difficult to prove then and cannot be proven now. What is clear is that Laviske's refusal led the Panthers to stage a boycott of his store, and that in the activists' estimation, it would be unwise to allow another white-owned business to profiteer from Albina without a sense of responsibility to the community. Kent Ford decided it was time to picket McDonald's. A Panther flyer called black Portland to

> Boycott!! Boycott! McDonald's does not support the FREE BREAKFAST FOR SCHOOL CHILDREN PROGRAM or MALCOLM X DENTAL CLINIC or FRED HAMPTON PEOPLE'S CLINIC.

As the protest intensified, McDonald's became a totem of the challenges that black people faced in Albina. The Panthers' protest exposed how the brand was associated with unchecked white domination, police brutality, and exploitative labor practices. The flyer also accused the McDonald's parking lot of doubling as a "base area for PIG attacks."[19] McDonald's, in the Panthers' view, not only refused to be a good citizen, but they also exacerbated the hyper-policing of blacks in Albina by welcoming law enforcement into its parking lots to transfer subjects, as was done with Ford the night the 1969 uprising started. Protesters chanted "No more pigs in our community" outside the restaurant, a critique of police relations in the neighborhood, which was especially on the hearts and minds of concerned residents after the winter of 1970, when a Portland police officer shot nineteen-year-old Albert Wayne Williams at the Portland Panthers headquarters, located a few doors down from McDonald's. Officers claimed they were trying to serve Williams an arrest warrant when he fired at them. Community members organized a "speech in" at a meeting at city hall, demanding that the mayor and city council respond to their suspicions about and anger over the shooting. Williams's shooting and the conflicting reports about it were emblematic of the strained relationships in Albina, powered by the pervasive police and informant surveillance in the community and the decision to send "beefed up patrols" to the neighborhood after Ford was acquitted of a charge of inciting a riot.[20]

The Panther protesters also took issue with the employment practices of the Albina McDonald's, as well as the nature of fast food work broadly. The demonstrators jeered managers for not hiring blacks and demanded that dismissed employees be reinstated. They passed out flyers that accused McDonald's of perpetuating a system of "unfair labor."[21] McDonald's expansion in the 1970s made it a frequent target of activists who believed that the brand suppressed organizing activity and used their business influence to shape labor policy. By the late 1970s, McDonald's employed approximately 150,000 people who had no access to any union representation. An investigative journalism project reported that the company subjected their workers to "arbitrary shift assignments, boring work, pressure from managers and customers, no paid holidays, and no hospital insurance," and they alleged that McDonald's used "sophisticated secret internal anti-labor apparatus effectively [rooting] out pro-union sympathizers from within employee ranks." The article also included accusations that managers regularly bullied crew members by forcing them to take lie detector tests and relied on an "interrogation technique."[22] The Panthers' concentration on labor issues stemmed from the treatment of individual black workers, and it may have been part of larger concerns about unemployment. In 1970, black unemployment nationally was at nearly 9% and would rise throughout the decade. Meanwhile, Ray Kroc tried to manipulate labor laws in his favor, which stood to undermine the earning potential of working youth. Kroc famously donated a quarter of a million dollars to Richard Nixon's reelection campaign, some believe in order to get him to support a proposed "youth differential" clause that exempted minors from the minimum wage bill being debated in Congress. When the donation was discovered and the brand was scrutinized, Kroc realized that he had to tread more carefully in political matters.

The Black Panthers' succinct enumeration of their community-based institutions that McDonald's chose not to support was a testament to Panther-led infrastructure in Albina, as well as a reminder of the many needs not being met by the state in a poor community. The health clinics and the food program were a direct response to the difficulty in securing quality health care in poor black communities and the continued nutritional challenges and difficulties experienced by black families, especially single women with children. In cities like Las Vegas and Los Angeles, black women—many on welfare assistance—organized campaigns to not only secure basic needs, but also to challenge assumptions about the black family's care for its own children and the political power of the poor.[23] The National Welfare Rights Organization, like the Black Panther Party, organized poor and working-class blacks to strengthen their capacities to provide for each other. They also crafted plans to maximize support from state and federal programs and cultivated relationships with philanthropic sources.

The Panthers picketed the restaurant between eight and ten hours a day, beginning at the lunchtime rush and remaining as late as 10 P.M. The protesters tried to stop customers from entering the McDonald's or cars from pulling into the lot. The protest continued for about a month. The Panthers were exercising their right both to organize and to demand that McDonald's be a good citizen. McDonald's workers and customers disagreed. They accused the Panthers of threatening patrons and scaring employees. At one point an employee asked a protester, "May I help you, please?" and the alleged response was "Be nice to me, I'm going to burn your place down."[24] It is difficult to know now if that exchange was a taunt or an actual threat. The Panthers often displayed their special kind of performative militarism with their unofficial uniform of fitted black leather jackets and berets. The Black Power newspapers they sold were filled with pictures and illustrations of armed revolutionaries. Their chants of black power taking over may have also been more provocative than predictive. Regardless of the intent, in the eyes of racist, fearful, or uninformed whites, the Panthers were always up to trouble.

From the remaining records on the protest, it is clear that the boycott did not hamper the Albina restaurant to the extent the Cleveland boycotts did, but McDonald's executives may have learned not to allow issues like these to fester for too long. The Portland Panthers were in no position to lobby for a franchise, and although other Panthers were proponents of black capitalism for their own communities, this chapter did not seem interested in investing itself in business like Operation Black Unity. In the investigation documents about the protests and Laviske's extortion accusations, it is clear that McDonald's corporate executives were attentive and aware of a conflict in Portland.[25] At some point in 1970, Laviske claimed that "two black representatives" from McDonald's traveled from Chicago to Portland to look for Ford, perhaps to see if he would ease his protest, but the meeting never materialized. Laviske testified that "they spent the entire day in the Albina area trying to locate Ford without success."[26]

Laviske and Ford were left to their own devices to end the boycott. The McDonald's manager continued complaining that he was being threatened by Panthers and their supporters. Laviske may have been without McDonald's corporate on his side, but as a white Portlander doing business in Albina, he turned to the power of the police and the courts to protect him, in a similar tactic as the Pine Bluff franchisee who sought legal protection against SNCC protesters. Laviske sought a restraining order against Ford; he brought copies of protest leaflets as evidence of his being harassed.[27] Laviske was not granted a protection order, and an ongoing police investigation of Ford for extorting other Albina businesses yielded insufficient evidence. A district attorney suggested that Laviske seek an injunction against three Black Panthers for protesting in front of his store and disturbing his business. While filing the paperwork, his assistant manager called from the McDonald's. Nine picketers were handing out pamphlets again and trying to convince customers not to enter the restaurant. With no injunction in hand yet, and no case against the picketing, the manager decided to close the store nearly six hours early "due to the forcefulness" of the boycott. The next day, Laviske's injunction was delivered, and the protest moved across the street.[28] With the protests now away from the store's entrance and parking lot, Laviske may have believed that it was only a matter of time before the Black Panthers relented, or at the very least, his customers would be able to avoid them and resume enjoying burgers and fries as before.

Then, disaster struck.

Around 2 A.M. the morning of August 22, someone threw four sticks of dynamite through the Albina McDonald's front window. The blast was powerful enough to hurl a metal picnic table eight feet from its perch across the parking lot. Most of the windows on the restaurant's north side combusted and scattered shards and specks of glass across the property.[29] No one was hurt, but the bombing unnerved other local businesses, who had monitored the McDonald's boycott and nervously anticipated an upcoming peace rally outside an American Legion conference. The store managers reported to police that someone made good on threats to "blow the place up."[30] Immediately, the local police—who were collaborating with a covert FBI investigation of Ford and the Panthers—swarmed the McDonald's to collect evidence. After businesses were reopened the next day, detectives fanned across Union Avenue to ask local grocers, pharmacists, and store managers if they were threatened by Ford or any other Panther members. From the investigators notes, it's clear that Albina's business community regularly butted heads with their black neighbors. Black teens were not trusted inside stores. Black residents were overlooked for jobs. The police may have been shaken, but they were not surprised by the bombing, having been tipped off by an undercover report. An agent noted:

> He overheard . . . that they were going to get McDonalds on the 1st or 2nd day of the upcoming Legion conference. Informant believes this to mean that they will bomb or burn out the McDonalds establishment at location at NE Union and Fremont and that they also indicated they might possibly hit other McDonalds establishments.[31]

The police tip may have been about a number of radical groups that had settled in Portland to protest the Vietnam War, take down capitalism, and, most recently, disrupt the upcoming visit by the Legion. Portland was also home to a chapter of the White Panthers, a radical group of antiracist whites who were also subject to FBI watch and a raid in December 1970. The extant investigative notes about the McDonald's bombing and the Black Panthers are not necessarily conclusive, considering that throughout the period black activist organizations—moderate and radical—were subject to state-generated misinformation, interference, and even assassination campaigns. The files confirm that the Portland Panthers had an adversarial relationship with some business owners, and donations made to them may have been acts of insurance more than generosity. But there was no evidence that Ford and the Panthers bombed McDonald's. The group denied any connection to the bombing. After canvassing the neighborhood, police compiled a suspect list that included "white hippies" who used assumed names to purchase explosives days before the bombing. Similarly, FBI agents, under the auspices of J. Edgar Hoover's COINTELPRO program, were directed to use any means necessary—from drugs to violence—to disrupt Black radical groups, especially the Panthers. In light of this history, it is impossible to rule out agent provocateurs as staging the bombing to discredit Panthers.[32]

With little evidence on Ford or the Panthers, the group was able to proceed with their projects. Within a month of the bombing, the contentions between the Panthers and the McDonald's actually waned. The restaurant eventually began supporting their initiatives with "fifty pounds of meat and five hundred paper cups, weekly."[33] Accounts in the years following the bombing indicate that McDonald's franchises forged a workable peace with the local community. At a sickle cell anemia testing drive organized by the Black Panthers, people who visited the McDonald's parking lot received one of 1,500 donated coupons for a hamburger, fries, and soda courtesy of their local franchisee.[34] After the bombing, Nate Proby, a local civil rights activist and leader of the United Minority Workers organization, was welcome to use McDonald's reinstalled picnic table to register voters. The picket and the bombing were minor disruptions in the much larger context of Albina, where blacks were constantly negotiating with local business owners, police forces, and political figures to have their voice heard. By using the consumer boycott to assert their position about the way that life was managed in Albina, the black population discovered a means of communicating how racism shaped the conditions and possibilities of the community.

Portland's Black Panther Party and McDonald's represented the pragmatism that allowed black radicalism to survive day to day, especially where blacks were at a population and power disadvantage. Although African Americans were small in number across the entire city, segregation concentrated their influence in mostly one location in Portland, which required them to find ways to challenge and reconcile with existing power structures. Kent Ford denies bombing the McDonald's, which he said was close to fulfilling his request for assistance. His colleague Percy Hampton believed the FBI told businesses not to pitch in for the breakfast program. "They said we were strong-arming businesses for donations. None of that was true . . . [The FBI] stayed one step ahead of us and one step behind."[35] What is most helpful to understand, in hindsight, are the ways that, on the local level, activists knew that critique or conflict didn't foreclose future collaboration. The Portland Black Panther Party, like their friends in Cleveland, used protest to air grievances and injustices about McDonald's, and then found ways to capitalize on their power relative to McDonald's. In prioritizing the breakfast program over his battles against McDonald's, Ford showed that even blacks with the most radical of imaginations could recognize the realities of the few choices black people had under capitalism. Eventually the destabilization of the Black Panther Party's national leadership would undermine the work of local chapters. Between 1975 and 1980, the controversies and transgressions of national Black Panther leadership in Oakland led to rudderless and embroiled chapters. Former Panthers were also subject to continued surveillance, police brutality, and tightening financial resources for the clinic. All these factors contributed to the Party's dissolution by 1980.[36] The McDonald's on Union Avenue (which was renamed Martin Luther King Jr. Boulevard in 1989) didn't make it either. By the early 1990s, the restaurant closed. Depopulation of the commercial strip and a rampant infusion of drugs in the immediate neighborhood drove out people and businesses that were privileged to have the choice to begin again in another place.

* * *

While the Portland Black Panther Party was renegotiating the terms of its relationship to McDonald's, thousands of miles away, the much older city of Philadelphia was on the precipice of its own political action against the Golden Arches. The expansion of McDonald's and other fast food restaurants along highways and beside the shopping malls and plazas that bookended suburban developments was met in most places with excitement and curiosity. A place to eat along a network of interconnecting expressways and toll roads was convenient. An affordable destination for a family's dinner night out meant more special outings for budget-conscious families. A fast food place where teens could get a bite to eat before a school dance seemed like harmless fun to an ever-growing fast food republic. As consumers grew accustomed to picking up buckets of chicken for a picnic or devouring an entire meal kept warm by Styrofoam, the environment's great enemy, the experience of eating outside the home became an everyday activity that required no planning and little thinking about the hands that prepared foods or the planet that provided it. Yet a national wave of environmental activism, movements that questioned the very foundations of capitalism, and citizen efforts to reclaim local policy and decision-making galvanized to halt or at least slow the march toward a fast food future.

Organizations like Cleveland's Operation Black Unity and the Portland chapter of the Black Panther Party believed that there was room for negotiation and mutual agreement with fast food restaurants. Other black-led entities believed that fast food had no place in community life. Some arguments against fast food focused on combating juvenile delinquency and reducing gang activity. Similar to Herman Petty's concern about his restaurant remaining Blackstone Rangers territory, fast food restaurants could be easily claimed by street gangs, especially after the development of dine-in facilities. Truant and troublemaking teenagers could linger in parking lots in the summer, and when temperatures dropped, they could park themselves in a molded plastic booth for hours. Urban

McDonald's locations often kept late hours, and franchisees under pressure to make money may have felt as if they couldn't do anything to alienate problematic, but paying, customers. Some black franchisees were able to win over gangs, like Harlem franchisee Lee Dunham, a former police officer who met with members of the Savage Skulls, the Wild Bunch, and the Saigons to ensure that they didn't disrupt his store, the country's third-busiest outlet in 1972. The first four months after he took hold of the franchise, he developed a rapport with the gang members, who marked his restaurant near the famed Apollo Theater as theirs by wearing their designated gang jackets and even firing guns inside while guests tried to enjoy their Big Macs.[37] Other stores couldn't handle the chaos. In the fall of 1976, at another New York City McDonald's, a group of twenty white teenagers brandishing baseball bats and sticks gathered outside of a McDonald's at West Third Street and Avenue of the Americas before setting out on a series of racist attacks in Washington Square Park. What started as an attempt to avenge a marijuana sale gone wrong turned into the young men screaming, "Get the niggers out of the park," and didn't end until a black teenager suffered a fractured face and eye.[38] News items of this kind were all that concerned parents and critical activists needed to convince their neighbors to join their crusades against hoisting another pair of golden arches or a giant bucket to hover over their neighborhoods.

Anti–fast food campaigns—in both affluent white and poor black communities—converged in the assertion that their neighborhoods warranted protection from the nefarious presence of burger stands and chicken joints. In an era in which racial disparities in quality, and even duration, of life calcified, there were few issues that could unite such defuse populations. Both parties agreed that no matter how profitable, popular, or even publicly altruistic these businesses were or could be, they ultimately undermined the elements of community that residents valued. The Small Business Administration classified fast food franchises as small businesses eligible for minority funding grants, but neighborhoods did not experience them like a mom-and-pop bakery that whipped up a beloved pineapple upside-down cake or a family enterprise where everyone knew the shopkeeper's name and her children. Fast food restaurants exported dollars outside of their communities with franchise fees and high-volume purchase orders that rarely, if ever, landed on a local business's desk. Researchers at the Institute for Local Self-Reliance estimated that in 1979, for a typical McDonald's restaurant, "only 17 percent of the store's expenditures clearly remains in the community where it is based: 15 percent for local labor (always hired at minimum wage) and 2 percent for local taxes." The remaining 83% went to McDonald's special suppliers, land leases, the national advertising fund, the company's management fees, loan repayments, and taxes. The study suggested that if "buildings were owned locally, management hired from local residents, and supplies purchased locally, some of this leakage could be effectively plugged."[39] While fast food benefited from tax breaks and cheap land, in some cities the franchisee and company contributed to the community at their discretion, not by mandate. Restaurants were known to attract litter, worsen traffic, and perpetuate youth misbehavior. When the tony community of Martha's Vineyard organized locals and the vacation home set against a proposed McDonald's in 1978, they submitted evidence from a Canadian researcher who "determined that an average purchase at McDonald's entails a minimum of ten pieces of trash, much of it nonbiodegradable—plastic straws, plastic covers for the paper cups, Styrofoam burger containers and plastic condiment containers." Opening the restaurant, the anti-McDonald's group argued, would add more than 5 million items to the Martha's Vineyard waste management system.[40] Cohesive, strategic communities believed that they could take steps to hold off McDonald's, but when the communities were black and lacked wealth, the task was far more difficult.

In the summer of 1970, the Ogontz Neighbors Association (ONA) invited residents to "Save Your Community!" The plea was a bit more ambitious than the actual matter at hand, but residents were moved to attend a meeting to discuss an issue that had been lingering for a while: the city of Philadelphia had authorized a permit for McDonald's to open a location at 6100 North Broad Street.

Ogontz in the 1970s was a working-class neighborhood of North Philadelphia that had felt some of the sting of the dual forces of residential and economic white flight in the previous decades. What made Ogontz distinct from other sections of major cities was that the residents went to great lengths to preserve the multicultural nature of the community. Having been particularly vocal in school integration efforts and projects to reduce housing discrimination, the ONA's strong tradition of organizing since the late 1950s would come in handy as they waged a new war on the North Broad Street construction project. The ONA argued against the McDonald's on a number of grounds, and unlike the protests in Cleveland or Portland, the ONA was not concerned about their ability to own a franchise or reap the rewards from its profitability. Rather, the ONA believed that the increasing commercialization of their neighborhood amounted to the city and private sector allowing a business to strip citizens of their power to determine the community's priorities. In their campaign against a new McDonald's, they cited the saturation of existing fast food restaurants in Ogontz, the threats to the historical significance of the area slated for rezoning, the socioenvironmental safety of Ogontz, and the fact that they had no opportunity to weigh in on the proposed restaurant. In a sophisticated, multipronged assault, the ONA used various organizing tools from nonviolent direct action to media outreach to municipal appeals to halt the building of a McDonald's. Campaign leaders also studied the OBU's fight in Cleveland to plan their own fast food resistance movement.

After the McDonald's construction crew first broke ground in 1969, the ONA deployed weekly "picket lines" to attract neighborhood attention to the building and its shift from residential to commercial. HOMES NOT HAMBURGERS! MCDONALD'S MAKES CHOPPED MEAT OUT OF A CHOICE COMMUNITY. If passersby asked about the protest, the ONA demonstrators explained that the McDonald's would "be detrimental to the health, safety and welfare of the residents." The ONA also bristled at the chosen location. The McDonald's would be built near the De Benneville Family Burial Ground, a private cemetery established in the 1750s, and the final resting place of Christian Universalist Dr. George De Benneville. In a city that prided itself on being older than the actual nation and its founding documents, the ONA believe that it could make a claim about respect for the city's history, as well as its departed notables.

The ONA wasn't expressly anti–fast food, but they were concerned with the proliferation of fast food joints in the area. Ogontz was already home to a Gino's Cheesesteak outlet, the Marriott hotel company's two franchise concepts, the hamburger-and-ice-cream specialist Hot Shoppe, and a Roy Rogers. Adding a McDonald's drive-in to the mix meant "more air pollution, littering, noise, traffic hazards, congestion, crime" they did not "want or need."[41] Anxieties about public safety often followed the opening of new fast food restaurants in the 1970s. The umbrage the McDonald brothers took about flirting and defiant teenagers in post–World War II era San Bernardino seemed insignificant in cities grappling with increased drug sales and substance abuse. Street gangs relied on all-night establishments to serve as a base for their operations, convene their members, and sometimes shake down store owners. In a letter opposing McDonald's, an ONA representative emphasized that Ogontz needed real community resources, not convenient restaurants. "The 24th gang slaying occurred in our area," wrote Kelly Miller, a minister and ONA advocate. "We have sufficient problems with gangs now without adding another hangout for them such as McDonald's . . . our organization has been working on constructive problems for youth for many years. We are opposed to adding to the gang problems."[42] Chicagoans had waged a fight against McDonald's in 1963 based on the same argument that the fast food restaurant would promote gangs and interfere with education because it was a magnet for truants. In a flyer headlined "Hamburgers vs. Education," a group of concerned residents of the West Side made it clear that they had "nothing against McDonald's putting up a hamburger stand in our community," but they believed that the location across the street from Marshall High School would exacerbate "cutting classes . . . gang fights . . . and other serious problems."[43]

The Ogontz collective connected the upcoming McDonald's opening to another form of lawlessness—the Mafia. In a July 1970 letter to the Federal Trade Commission, the ONA requested that the agency investigate the "Mafia penetration into McDonald's." Having noticed that the Commission investigated McDonald's for fraud claims associated with a sweepstakes contest, ONA member Robert Smalls hoped that the chair's office would investigate the ownership of 6100 North Broad Street. The location had been partly owned by a realtor who was also the nephew of a man believed to be a Philadelphia organized crime head. He closed the letter by referring to a current issue of *Reader's Digest*, which published an article about A&P grocery stores and organized crime. Another crusader appealed to the Licenses and Inspections Review Board using the Mafia angle to ask how the site developer was able to get the permit to build; the man had been indicted for perjury and bribery in the act of purchasing the building. [44] The ONA's savvy in attacking McDonald's from multiple angles, from its placement to its financers—reflected the diverse swath of talents that the organization possessed. The ONA believed that local people should have a say, if not the final say, in what their community needed and should look like. In an era in which the destabilization of civil rights groups, slum clearance, and failures in postriot leadership left inner cities voiceless or at the mercy of unethical business development, the ONA offered an example of the strength of racially mixed coalition building.

The ONA's protest provided the greater public with information about the fight. Behind the photographers' flash and away from neighborhood watchers, the ONA drew upon their bureaucratic knowledge to delay the start of construction on the new McDonald's building. The ONA requested that the city's Department of Licenses and Inspections investigate the permit process for the project. Their search uncovered why the McDonald's seemed to materialize out of nowhere; it was initiated by a councilman who did not represent Ogontz. The reclassification of the site was done without consulting the actual councilman from Ogontz. "We have more than enough eating places in the area," the ONA wrote in their petition. "We desire to maintain high residential standards in our community and oppose increasing . . . commercialization . . ." The ONA did not comprise the wealthiest or most politically connected Philadelphians, but that did not mean that they saw themselves as unworthy to drive municipal matters. When the maneuver was discovered, the ONA was able to halt further development on the site. The city issued a stop-work order, and combined with their picketing, the ONA stalled the construction for so long that the original building permits expired.[45]

For African Americans shaped by the promotion of self-determination found among black nationalist groups, community control in the 1970s was a hot-button issue. In a newspaper feature about why the ONA opposed McDonald's, respondents shared their fears about the deterioration of public services available to residents, as well as a rich pride in their sense of place and collective power. Distance from fast food restaurants was not only a sign of affluence for the Philadelphians, but keeping them at bay was an indicator that communities had the power to determine their own destinies. To be forced to live within the sight lines of arches or under a pungent cloud created by deep-fat fryers was to be without influence. One member of the association offered: "I don't see why these business people who don't live here should keep coming into our neighborhood and destroying the residential nature of it. Something constructive should be done with this land—like building low-cost housing on it." The rector of a neighborhood Episcopal Church highlighted the racial elements of the struggle. "It must be recognized that because a community changes racially, it's still a community to be reckoned with. When a community becomes predominantly black, there seems to be no need to be concerned with the feelings of the people there, but America must realize this is a new day, and this is definitely no longer the case." In a survey of opinions about the McDonald's project, it is clear that the restaurant issue was a vehicle for communicating the ways that Ogontz felt it would be left behind by the forces of urban neglect and overpowered by fast food's dominance. One local woman added that in addition to having to contend with traffic and trash with so many drive-ins in Ogontz, she added, "I don't see why we can't have a mental health clinic on its land." "Many people moved here to get away from the ghettos," she added. "Now the commercial interests who don't care about the people are coming in here and trying to make this a ghetto too." One resident cited gang concerns and suggested another institution that could actually help the community. "They should build a recreation center here. We don't have one in the whole neighborhood—and we don't have a library either."[46] The ONA was not swayed by arguments that the McDonald's would provide jobs to youth or exist as a partner with the community. They believed that it was not only their right, but their duty, to fight for what Ogontz truly needed.

It was a tough fight, and the ONA ultimately lost the war. The city's zoning decision was upheld in July of 1970, after the Philadelphia planning commission determined that the proposed site was already being used for commercial purposes and would not interfere with the historic cemetery.[47] Eventually, the 6100 Broad Street McDonald's became a black-franchised location, part of a six-store portfolio belonging to businessman Ed Johnson. By the 1980s, there were several McDonald's restaurants dotting the communities around Ogontz, and local attitudes toward them had seemed to shift. In 1983, when McDonald's corporate officials relieved Latino operator Juan Miranda of his franchises citing financial mismanagement, the nearby North Philadelphia Neighborhood Association mounted a boycott to show their gratitude for Miranda's impact on the community.[48] In the intervening years from the start of the ONA boycott to the show of solidarity with a franchisee of color, Ogontz bore the brunt of the wave of issues that made black, low-income neighborhoods less suspicious of fast food as recessions made people poorer and opportunities more scarce.

* * *

The competition was keeping tabs on how McDonald's inner-city campaign was going. For every headache acquired in Cleveland, Portland, or Philadelphia, there were opening day parties, sometimes a few blocks away from a boycotted store in the same city.

Other fast food chains took modest steps to see if opening in predominately black neighborhoods could pay off in the same ways as it had for Ronald McDonald. Recruiting and retaining a trusted member of the community to be the face of the franchise was essential, and in cities with sizable black populations, finding the right person was never as challenging as ensuring potential customers could trust the brand.

In the case of a doomed Dairy Queen franchise effort in Atlanta in the 1970s, the fast food industry slowly learned that the recipe for creating a profitable outlet in the inner city required more than a prominent African-American folded into a black neighborhood with a splash of soul talk. Dairy Queen and McDonald's share a birth year. John Fremont McCullough offered the newly invented soft serve ice cream in Joliet, Illinois, in 1940. McCullough and his business associate, Sherb Noble, were early adopters of the franchise model, and Dairy Queen stands—sometimes operated seasonally and other times year-round—multiplied at an impressive speed more than a decade before Kroc established the McDonald's franchising arm. By its eleventh birthday, Dairy Queen had captured a third of the soft-ice-cream market and reported that you could order a cone at one of their 1,400 franchises in a mix of small towns, suburbs, and cities across the country.[49] In 1957, they introduced the brazier concept, which converted Dairy Queen from a place to get sweet treats to a place to enjoy a full meal of hot dogs and burgers.

Dairy Queen, unlike McDonald's and Burger King, did not appear to have attracted external pressure to open their franchise opportunities to African Americans. Dairy Queen had a history of maintaining white and colored takeout windows in the past, and some black people may have still been apprehensive about the brand after they shifted to equal dine-in restaurants. But if Dairy Queen officials had access to the consumer market data on their peers, they would likely embrace the interest, because black consumers were the heavy users the industry hoped to cultivate and retain. Black consumers—even in a city like Atlanta with some black leadership—still had fewer choices of where to shop and where to eat.

In 1968, Georgia state legislator Julian Bond decided that the time was right for him to do something about this. The son of a black college president and graduate of the esteemed Morehouse College, Bond was born in Tennessee, but he was treated like a native son of Georgia. As a member of the courageous group of activists who tested segregation in interstate travel during the Freedom Rides of 1961, Bond risked his life to challenge the fact that despite the illegality of segregation on buses and in transportation stations, southern facilities still hung signs pointing to colored- and whites-only restrooms, waiting rooms, and seats. Court rulings in *Morgan v. Virginia* (1946) and *Boynton v. Virginia* (1960) should have protected the Riders, but when they stopped in bus depots across the South, the activists were met with screaming mobs, barking dogs, and exploding bombs.[50] Having played a role in establishing the Student Nonviolent Coordinating Committee, Bond was a civil rights notable before his twenty-fifth birthday. In his transition from freedom struggle leader to franchise business operator, Bond was joined by fellow Freedom Rider Hank Thomas and white civil rights advocate and dentist Gerald Reed. While Bond was fighting his expulsion from the Georgia statehouse for opposing the Vietnam War, Thomas was overseas fighting in it.[51] Thomas earned a Purple Heart for his service. Reed continued his work in interracial organizing; while practicing dentistry, he helped establish a branch of Operation Breadbasket in Atlanta. The three men were committed to the principle of nonviolence, and although they each took divergent paths after the Freedom Rides era and their activism changed, their shared experiences within the movement inspired them to use business as a means of continuing their commitments to racial and economic justice.

Bond's state house seat was restored by the time his friend Hank returned to Atlanta after fulfilling his military obligation. The doggedly focused Thomas sought an opportunity to build something of his own, but with little money and rigid barriers for blacks who wanted to join the owner class, Thomas's ambitions were stalled. The Jacksonville, Florida, native settled into a series of jobs that taught him various aspects of business. After work-

ing for the Army, a part-time gig at Sears and tenure as a fire-
man, Thomas finally found an opening when he learned about an
opportunity to manage apartment laundromats. Drawing on his
experience as a protester and an activist, he appeared at banks and
began "threatening to go all the way to Washington and demonstrate, if necessary," in front of the Small Business Administration
office to show how serious he was about getting a business loan.
Reed, who may have known Thomas from movement work in the
past, saw a commercial for the army veteran's laundry service and
reached out to the budding entrepreneur. Reed believed that part-
nering with Thomas was a powerful symbol of interracialism, one
of the values he carried with him as a supporter of civil rights.
Schools, residential communities, and churches were slow to integrate. The men may have hoped that businesses could lead the
way. Reed also contacted Bond, who would hold a smaller stake in
their efforts. From there, the Reed-Thomas Enterprises was born,
and the men set out to find the next big thing to bring to inner-
city Atlanta. Reed offered Thomas access to a plot of land that he
owned on which the men could build a Dairy Queen franchise.
Thomas sold his interest in the laundromat and entered into business with Reed. For Georgians who wanted to separate the state
from its associations with their most racially regressive southern
neighbors—namely Alabama and Mississippi—Atlanta was a crucial exemplar of what was possible in the New South. In the 1970s,
Atlanta—King's birthplace and place of rest—was attracting educated blacks on a reverse migration course out of the North and
back to their Southern roots. The excitement about Atlanta's possibility in expanding its black middle class, fortifying its historically black colleges, and opening businesses that could revitalize
poor communities motivated civil rights movement alums to pursue fast food franchising.[52]

The trio's new Dairy Queen opened in 1970, and it offered the
features of the most modern of the chain's brazier concept with an
air-conditioned dining room and a parking lot that could accommodate more than thirty cars. The menu introduced one of the
newest fast food concepts, "a kind of a chicken—a chicken pat-

tie," that Thomas assured Georgians, many of whom believed that they perfected fried chicken, was actually "very delicious."[53] In a feature on the Dairy Queen's groundbreaking ceremony, an *Atlanta Journal-Constitution* real estate writer explained that the restaurant on Ashby Street, S.W., near the hub of the city's black colleges, was a mechanism for helping to "finance other Negroes who want to go into business for themselves." The initiative was framed as a matter of investment and business, not white benevolence, and the article captured a great hope in what the newspaper called "Hank Thomas' Black Capitalism." This version of black capitalism placed Reed as the "catalytic agent" in the Negro community, in a "marriage of white capital with black initiative." This was not necessarily a new or novel approach to projects believed to be a realization of black capitalism, but Reed's presence and their desire to broadcast to whites that they could and did have a role to play in building black community wealth would soon become its own liability. Purists were concerned about the way that Reed fit into a black endeavor, and whites unable to see the value in Reed's efforts with Thomas and Bond, saw his actions as an example of white liberalism run amok.[54]

The thrill of the new Dairy Queen—and the subsequent second Dairy Queen and two Wishbone Fried Chicken franchises the men established—was short-lived. The brazier became a magnet for crime and protest, and the partnership became untenable due to the financial inequality among venture investors. By the time temperatures started to rise in Atlanta, and more people were flocking to the cool relief of a Dairy Queen treat, the business was in jeopardy due to community resistance. A headline blared: "Bond's White Associate Forced Out of Business." After a series of terminations of black employees, a group had begun to form a picket line in front of the partnership's restaurant, where a year earlier the men smiled at news cameras as they broke ground. As was the case in other cities, the fast food franchise was the place where communities litigated their frustrations with Atlanta's racial politics. Protesters called Reed a "filthy rich white racist[s] [*sic*] . . . sucking blood out of the black community." Thomas and Bond's participation in the endeavor was irrelevant; the picketers believed that they were being sold a black business that was actually replicating the way that whites lorded over blacks in Atlanta. Thomas's authority over the store operations was not compelling to the protesters, and vandals constantly targeted the restaurant. The black partners believed that the community had painted them into a corner, and regardless of their feelings of camaraderie with Reed, the business would not be able to survive him. "We told him (Reed) it wouldn't be settled until he got out and he agreed," Bond told the press. "He said pickets raised the issue of whether whites could do business at all in the black community—not if they could help and then withdraw." The beleaguered dentist hoped that the city's four-year-old Community Relations Commission, a community action group, would get involved, but they declined to get in the middle of this skirmish. Reed also used the Dairy Queen to punctuate his laments about what he perceived as a "rising tide of 'anti-white hatred' in the black community." Reed was no longer welcomed at black neighborhood and organizational activities as he was in the 1960s, and as a result, he was no longer sure where he fit. SNCC lost white members in a massive realignment in 1967 in which the organization decided to pivot from integration as a goal and instead encouraged whites to organize among themselves. Black Power and other nationalist movements' calls for black self-governance alienated some white liberals, who felt excluded or betrayed. Although black capitalism was a largely interracial movement in its enmeshment with white bureaucrats and even a racist president, the optics of black ownership were sometimes more important than the realities. Black businesses in black communities created to serve the needs of black people did not support the presence of well-intentioned men like Reed, regardless of their personal commitments to black wealth building. Feelings of white ostracism tested the limits of interracial solidarity politics throughout the period, and it played right into the hands of conservatives who relished the perceived failures of whites who were foolish enough to engage in what they saw as futile attempts to ally with blacks. *New York Times* columnist Jon Nordheimer believed that the partnership's dissolution proved that there was "a growing concern about the anti-white feeling that has emerged among Southern blacks." Accusations that groups committed to black self-sufficiency were particularly antiwhite could be heard across the country as some observers "discovered" what they believed was a new black radicalism.[55] "The heart of the matter," in the columnist's assessment, was the fact that Reed had secured the $100,000 worth of financing for the businesses, and he was unjustly moved out of the effort. Reed and Bond were no more than "noble jerks," who were hung out to dry by the "moderate black leadership" who refused to defend them in the attacks on the Dairy Queen. As franchises sought minority partners, civil rights organizations and community foundations who had their eyes on establishing their own stores may have been cautious not to rankle the regional franchising managers. Black conservative George Schuyler also seemed to revel in the Dairy Queen misfortune. Schuyler represented a strain of anti–Black Power, anti–Black Is Beautiful thinking that questioned the premise of black nationalism. Once a socialist, Schuyler's opinions of the Atlanta incident were forged after decades of deliberation on what black America should and shouldn't do. He called the Dairy Queen a "pipedream . . . [of] setting up a chain of food stands primarily to give managerial employment to promising young Negroes. A laudable ambition, but scarcely a basis for economic enterprise." Schuyler charged that the men's arrogance, ignorance of business, and misinformation about how capitalism worked led to their undoing. Critical of the activists' second acts as businessmen, Schuyler charged that "Bond and Reed violated about all of the laws of free enterprise . . . they knew nothing about business, and were experts in disturbing the public peace . . . They thought all they had to do to succeed was to get a little capital, yell 'Race,' and hire some blacks."[56]

Reed did not fully disavow black self-help, but he suggested that "the black community destroys its own . . . because the robber feels he'll get better from a white judge if he steals from a black business." Reed may have been attempting to garner sympathy, but he also exposed the pervasive racism that blacks faced in the courts, as well as on Main Street. Bond maintained his focus on structural issues, but his resentment also came through in his comments:

> Any business needs capital and there's not much of it available in the black community . . . I'm against having white businesses in the black community, but this will mean a black can't get any white help . . . when Gerry and I started out in this I didn't think we had anything to risk . . . we had the mistaken idea that we were performing a service in providing 80 jobs.

Businesses in other cities empathized with the partners. When Washington, D.C.'s T. M. Alexander Jr. entered into a 50-50 arrangement with a white colleague, they were proud to offer "more than average salaries to [their] car wash, liquor store and restaurant employees." But the wrath of the neighborhood soon surfaced and his businesses were targets of "harassment and intimidation from a local black minister and so-called leader of the people." The businesses couldn't survive, and the partners decided that they had no choice but to close their many doors. Alexander predicted that "local financial institutions are going to become more and more dubious of making substantial loans to blacks."[57]

Reed's departure did not immediately solve any problems. Within three days after Reed's exit, Dairy Queen was still contending with pickets during the day and burglars at night. The Dairy Queen had been robbed fifteen times during the winter of 1970. By spring, Bond was breathing a sigh of relief that the "armed bandits" were no longer attacking his restaurants, but the protests were far from resolved.[58] The protesters were organized by the Enterprise's former bookkeeper and five fired employees. The men were fired for "spreading dissension among the other employees" and "mismanagement of funds." Thomas enlisted Atlanta police to supervise their dismissals to stop the employees from taking anything else from the store and hopefully keep cooler heads.[59] The men, perhaps having learned about the elements of demonstration in the civil rights center, mounted a "one hundred percent effective" picket line by targeting the Dairy Queen in two-to-three-hour blocks twice a day, during its busiest hours. The men then adopted the name Black Unity Association and began organizing other community groups against the Dairy Queen, including men from Bond's alma mater to recruit students to their cause. The pickets began to alarm the men more and more when they learned that the Association was armed, and Thomas believed that the group likely had stolen the gun he kept in his car's glove compartment. The weapons, coupled with the threatening calls he and his wife began receiving at home, heightened their nervousness about the business. The Black Unity Association said that Thomas's business "would not be just another front for white men . . . ," and in an effort to further discredit Bond and Thomas, the group stole "records in its possession to support its contention that Dr. Reed controlled and dominated the business."[60]

At Reed's final meeting as a part of the Enterprises, the three men assessed their debt, which extended across three franchises and was owed to a number of banks across the country. Their total payroll costs were estimated at $100,000. The Ashby Avenue Dairy Queen had $30,000 in debt alone. They were behind on payments for the Dairy Queen on Bankhead Highway. The Gordon Road Wishbone Fried Chicken had an $850 debt due in a few months, and $450 was owed by the Simpson Road chicken shack. A note worth $15,000 was owed to Citizens & Southern National Bank and the Northwest Bank of Minneapolis. They were also paying the Internal Revenue Service $1,000 a week to pay down an $18,000 tax bill. Soon the men would discover they didn't have a clear sense of what was really owed, but what was indisputable was that Reed had underwritten all of these loans.[61] Over the course of the following three years, the men's lawyers would try to settle the matter, with Reed taking the most substantial financial hit. Reed was pensive at the end of the transfers, having expended considerable financial resources with very little to show for it. In an October 1971 letter to Bond hoping to collect some assistance with the efforts' outstanding debts, which Reed figured cost him $160,000, Reed wrote "the nightmare actually happened and the community remains the real loser," and he expressed regret at the collapse of the enterprise. "Julian," he told his former comrade in struggle and friend in business, "neither of us asked for or deserved what happened . . . the failure of our plan was a keen disappointment to me, for we had such high hopes for helping the community."[62]

Despite the unpleasantness with the Dairy Queen deal, Thomas remained committed to the franchising model. In a segment on the Atlanta University Center's radio show entitled "Economic Literacy," Thomas was celebrating four years at the helm of what was now his own Dairy Queen, which was among those with the "highest volume of service" in the country.[63] Thomas was glad that he stayed the course. Fast food was a sound business, he argued, because "a higher percentage of blacks spend more of their income with fast food services than whites who can better afford the higher tablecloth restaurants." Thomas eventually transitioned to franchising a Burger King, then he took the reins of six McDonald's restaurants throughout the South, including a High Point, North Carolina, location that denied him service as a young man. In the 2000s, he sold his restaurants and became a hotel franchisee.[64]

Bond never returned to the franchise game, but he did lend his voice as the narrator of an official National Black McDonald's Operators Association video that celebrated the organization's history and linked the franchisees' fight to win franchises with Bond's earlier career for fighting for black political and social enfranchisement.

* * *

Franchising and the question of black ownership lingered as new restaurants tried to enter black neighborhoods. Shrewd researchers and marketing experts helped major franchises obscure their corporate ties or the very nature of the franchise arrangement to convince black customers that they were supporting black business in earnest. In the summer of 1981, a new Sisters Chicken and Biscuits restaurant exemplified this approach on Cleveland's East Side, the epicenter of the McDonald's boycotts more than a decade earlier. Residents were concerned that the franchise was pretending to be black-owned, and the allegations led co-owner Tom Henning to respond in the pages of the *Call & Post*.[65] The newspaper suggested that "with a name like Sisters, and the fact that the stores sells beans and rice as well as chicken, makes it obvious that the chain hopes to attract a large black clientele."[66] Sisters riled concerned community members because of a comment made by advertising account executive Tim Robson: "Church's Chicken is the most profitable fast food operation in black America, because they go into black neighborhoods where they can get cheaper real estate . . ." He continued: "Church's cannot compete in a marginally black or suburban area; they can't compete against a white-oriented fast food market." The executive may have been talking about a number of fast food restaurants, as the cheaper access to purchase or lease land allowed the building of more franchise sites, which could then become available to black operators, who would assume the decidedly high costs of insurance, security, and sometimes repairs if the store was older. The *Call and Post* also challenged why Henning would call the Sisters effort an investment in the black community when ultimately there were no black construction workers on the $300,000 building project. The newspaper concluded that "the only thing left for blacks will be part time, minimum wage jobs that only serve to maintain the status quo." Having been out of jail for nearly a decade, activist James Raplin reminded Clevelanders that they couldn't "retrogress to pre-1969 conditions in which blacks were denied ownership in fast food restaurants in our own neighborhoods."

Sisters was still in the experimentation stage of the restaurant concept in 1981, and they had not established any minority franchising initiative. They did clarify that they were interested in local people operating stores, did not want to franchise to cooperatives or development groups, and they wanted people with significant experience in fast food. Franchising aside, the word "sister" was an issue of contention, whether the name of the restaurant was to reflect black modes of addressing black women or, as a co-owner suggested, "the main concept of the name Sisters has to do with chicken you would eat on your sister's front porch." The editorial concluded:

Whether the name Sisters was chosen because blacks will relate to it is really unimportant. What is important, however, is the message black neighborhoods are trying desperately to communicate to white fast food entrepreneurs. That message simply states: "come on in but, we want a slice of the economic pie not just a piece of your pre-packaged micro-wave oven pie!"

Sisters, a subsidiary of Ohio-based Wendy's, did not expand much after the Cleveland experiment. Wendy's sold the concept in 1987, and by 1994 the company closed the restaurants with the distinctive wrap-around porches and slanted roof.[67]

The various resistance strategies to the growing reach of fast food in the early 1970s all point to the diversity of black communities and leadership models that emerged in the period. Some of the strategies are familiar to us—boycotts, protests, and pickets. But some anti–fast food movements emerged in unlikely places, created new coalitions, and were inspired by concerns over a wide array of agenda items—including fidelity to the letter of the laws of black capitalism and the future of the environment. From Portland to Philadelphia to Atlanta, the fast food resistance movement took many forms, and taken together, it is clear that fast food's attempt to colonize black America was not unchallenged. Opposition to fast food was not solely about the industry itself, but rather who was profiting from it.

In Albina and across the country, fast food, racial politics, and competing demands—separately and together—could ignite the powder keg enflamed by tensions over community control and business citizenship. Even though the bombing in Albina was a foretold event, the responses to it were still revelatory about the economic, social, and political dynamics of the period. The relationship between the fast food restaurant—still in its adolescence—and a small, black community grappling with being infantilized and silenced in an overwhelmingly white city, exposed the tensions that the "urban turn" in fast food franchising would engender in working-class and poor neighborhoods of color throughout the 1970s. As conflicts over race and policing, access to good jobs, and the rightful role of businesses in communities continued to grow among black America, fast food restaurants could symbolize economic possibility or structural perniciousness and bigotry. This was all a matter of perspective. While McDonald's was able to win over black Chicago with the installation of Herman Petty at the helm of the Woodlawn location and the Cleveland boycotts yielded black franchise ownership, in Portland and other cities, concerns and conflicts over McDonald's were not so easily mediated. Some community groups took their critiques to city councils and municipal planning boards instead of the streets.

The 1970s was every bit as bittersweet as the decade that preceded it. Each year, African Americans were running candidates for mayoral races and city councils in greater numbers, and winning. Yet, federal programs were not addressing black unemployment. Organized parents' groups were battling boards of education, and sometimes teachers' unions, for community leadership of their children's schools. Other parents divested entirely from public schools, and creative parents established alternative, Afrocentric schools to circumvent a system they believed was harming their children. Meanwhile, busing was under attack at the highest levels in Washington.[68] A new generation of black doctors and nurses found greater employment opportunities in newly built community hospitals and clinics, but African Americans were still dying younger than whites. The Black Arts Movement inspired innovative theater, visual arts, and television shows with black audiences in mind, but mainstream entertainment was still fixated on stereotype and caricature. While black America was continuing its fight against the old problems of racism in jobs, schools, housing, and health, its entanglement with the fast food industry was still brandnew. And no one could predict if the drive-thru was a window that looked out onto a new world of possibility, or just provided a view of the same old problem-plagued street.

The Portland drama highlighted the ways that local politics would start to shape how McDonald's corporate would nationally address and cultivate black communities in the face of their own internal research reports that black consumers were key to their success. As they gingerly navigated opposition, they were devising strategies that would allow them to continue to grow the critical black consumer market. Portland's struggle also helps us understand that black militancy does not mean a total rejection of business influence or largesse, rather a way of being radically pragmatic and manipulating the flow of limited resources.

The transition from civil to silver rights was not seamless. Objection to fast food's desire to dominate the "urban market" was articulated in a number of ways as blacks strengthened and exercised their consumer citizenship. Many communities and organizations decided to play the role of objector, as well as competitors in the market. Both approaches required black people to define themselves in relationship to big business, as equally entitled to a number of explicit, as well as more nebulous, rights—from safe neighborhoods to a clean planet to black economic investment and healthy foods. Black neighborhoods and organizations challenged the presence of fast food and tried to set the terms of engagement on how the fast food industry would treat black communities. What was at stake for black America in the 1970s was whether a generation of citizens testing the strength of civil rights legislation, economic opportunity, federal policy, and corporate responsibility would let fast food become part of their worlds.

CHAPTER FIVE

Black America, Brought to You by . . .

Contemporary artist Hank Willis Thomas uses images from advertising to capture the complex relationships between the marketplace and race. In *So Glad We Made It, 1979*, Thomas has removed the branding from a vintage McDonald's advertisement targeted toward black consumers. These ads were crucial for McDonald's success in capturing black diners. © Hank Willis Thomas. Courtesy of the artist and Jack Shainman Gallery, New York.

The Spirit of '76 needed some soul. So a group of black McDonald's franchisees offered "Soul of a Nation," a more inclusive history lesson to its customers on the occasion of the nation's 200th birthday. Black History Month received official White House recognition that year, after scholars at Kent State University made a case for Negro History Week's extension in 1970.[1] In the bicentennial year, red-white-and-blue jelly glasses were offered at gas stations. Uncle Sam top hats and Betsy Ross–style wigs adorned sports mascots and corporate logos.[2] Outside of the burgeoning Afro-American studies programs on campuses scattered across the country and the small black history collectors that turned community centers and trailers into museums, black history was not easy to learn about in the deep, rich ways that would emerge in the late 1980s. Black history had to be learned and enjoyed where it could be found, including McDonald's. A group of franchisees underwrote "Soul of a Nation," described as "an illustrated collection of historical narratives reproduced from McDonald's special Black Bicentennial Radio Series." The radio show, broadcast from stations in Atlanta and Los Angeles, provided an interruption to the dominant, Founding Fathers–heavy celebration of the nation. In an era when slavery was scarcely acknowledged at historical sites and textbooks described the peculiar institution as a benevolent one, a black Bicentennial program proved meaningful to black customers, and the initiative illustrated the relative independence of black franchisees to determine what would work in their markets, as well as the cultural work of the fast food industry in the 1970s.

"Soul of a Nation" brought together scholars from Cleveland State and Wayne State Universities, which established black studies programs in 1969 and 1970, with black artist Carl Owens to create twenty-four historical profiles for the booklet. Comedian Bill Cosby lent star power to the recorded component as the narrator, and music sensation Ray Charles scored the show. The series applauded exceptional individuals and institutions in the nation's history, including Mary McLeod Bethune, "a woman who kept the faith"; George Washington Carver, "a man for all men"; the "unsung hero of the American West," the black cowboy; and "The Black Church," which had been "leading the way for nearly two centuries." The list of notables is, on its surface, inoffensive and may seem mundane, but even suggesting that African Americans deserve a laudatory history was not commonplace thinking in the period. The printed accompaniment to the radio program may have been drafted to quell any concerns about a hidden agenda. White audiences could be particularly sensitive that the word "soul" was a weapon of exclusion. "Soul of a Nation" wanted everyone to know that this effort was just about including African Americans in the national narrative. Cosby's note in the recording's guidebook clarified that "the word 'soul' means different things to different people. But to Black men and women, 'soul' means something very special. McDonald's Restaurants recognize this, and more importantly they have done something about it."[3] If you missed the "Soul of a Nation" on the radio, you could stop by a participating McDonald's and receive a copy of the program's script. Each profile reminded readers that the nation would not be possible without the diligence, wisdom, and insight of African Americans. There would be no nation's capital if it wasn't for "the good memory of one Black man," Benjamin Banneker. There would be no Will Rogers without the black cowboy Bill Pickett, who taught him "his famous rope tricks." And there would be no bicentennial without the courage of Crispus Attucks. "Soul of a Nation" re-created his fight in the Revolutionary War by making it clear that his battle was not "just another street fight."[4]

"Soul of a Nation" was one of a myriad of locally sponsored forms of outreach financed by franchisees and used to supplement the national advertising campaigns dictated by McDonald's corporate headquarters. Funding national advertising was a contentious issue for black franchisees of McDonald's and Burger King, and it was likely a problem in other franchise systems. Every franchisee contributed a percentage of profits or a fee for ads, but national campaigns that only used white actors and models, or were only played on radio stations that did not explicitly cater to black musical preferences, amounted to black franchisees throwing good money after bad. Brady Keys protested paying his Burger King advertising fees, and he purchased air time in 1978 to broadcast his own commercials on local television.[5] Franchisees with the means to do so could follow suit, but most needed to either create small-scale promotions to reach their target audiences or advocate for the inclusion of special advertising to their markets. Franchisees undertook both approaches, and in doing so—leveraging what was called ethnic advertising and underwriting creative projects—they were making an impact on the cultivation and dissemination of black culture.

"Soul" was hard to define precisely, but fast food marketers were hopeful that black customers could recognize it when they saw it in their attempts to reach black diners. In the late 1960s, black celebrities lent their names and likenesses to a number of businesses. These franchises suggested that they were truly black-owned and, in their spokesperson's authentic soulfulness, better poised to make black consumers happy and even improve black communities. All of these short-lived efforts failed because the brands were built on unstable foundations. Sometimes insufficient capital and poor planning led to a business closure. A few years after Mahalia Jackson's Glori-Fried Chicken was introduced in 1968, the business folded. The company's masterminds—two white lawyers from Nashville—structured it like a Ponzi scheme. Muhammad Ali's Miami-based ChampBurger, also introduced in 1968, only lasted a couple years. Friend of black capitalism and singer James Brown launched the Gold Platter restaurant franchise in 1969, which later spun off into a convenience store concept. After he convinced his fans that franchising would be his brand-new bag, the restaurant closed its few locations. Each of these companies assured black customers that in choosing the Negro Songbird, the Greatest, or the Godfather of Soul over Ronald, the Colonel, or the Burger King, they were choosing to not only support a black business, but they were also celebrating their own blackness.[6]

The collapse of each of these ventures animated the issue taken up by the Dairy Queen protesters that surrounded Julian Bond's brazier: in America, there were few truly black businesses. Between the time the first business plan was drafted and the moment the first profit collected, one could encounter white financers, white franchising representatives, white federal agency heads, or white French fry distribution company owners. If one could not buy black authentically, then the very least a black customer could do was look for products tinged with soul. For fast food companies that counted few franchisees of color among their ranks but recognized the power of the black dollar, building the soul market was a top priority. As the "soul businesses" flopped one by one, white-owned national chains took note of the centrality of amplifying soul in communicating to blacks. The 1970s and 1980s created a vital demand for the work of firms that could provide advertisements, consumer research, and product development focusing on black sensibilities. The line between appealing and offensive was a fine one in the corporate effort to integrate soul style into the selling of fast food. Businesses entrusted this delicate translation to a burgeoning generation of black professionals, who were beneficiaries of the opening of more opportunities to attend college and earn business degrees, ascend career tracks commensurate with their talents, and establish businesses predicated on their desire to improve the representation of blacks in mass media. Fast food's explosion was advantageous for franchisees and in-house professionals, as well as for a rising creative class of blacks looking to share their art, scholars hoping to spread their passion for black history, and black cultural institutions seeking to extend their reach. If black people were indeed the soul of a nation, then the fast food industry was determined to feed it.

McDonald's believed that its marketing strength came from its franchisees. Ostensibly, as members of the community, franchisees could best assess which charities were most worthy of free apple pie coupons or what Kiwanis Club had the most clout in town. Franchisees were better positioned to know which Fourth of July parade float or Little League team to sponsor than any bean counter or consultant in Oak Brook. The autonomy afforded franchisees in developing their community outreach was unusual, considering that every part of the McDonald's operations and business process was scripted by the corporate office. From its very beginning, McDonald's set the bar high for community outreach. Franchisees hosting children's days at the zoo, visiting hospitals, and offering scholarships were ways, according to a biographer of Ray Kroc and his wife Joan, to "counter the negative association with fifteen-cent hamburger joints." Serving up a few trays of free cheeseburgers and presenting oversized novelty checks now and then was also "cheaper than advertising," especially in the years before national television commercials dominated fast food marketing plans.[7] McDonald's approach to philanthropy has been accurately described as "carefully constructed" and "a master stroke of public relations in an age long before the trendy catchphrase, 'corporate social responsibility.'"[8] These franchisee activities occurred in different contexts. For black operators, their community outreach delved into areas that exposed the power of charitable acts in places where people struggled with profound powerlessness.

From the very beginning of their entry into McDonald's franchising, black franchisees were visible in various social aspects of community life. Black franchisees could be counted on to support the schools near their stores, which were most likely to be majority or entirely black. In Cleveland, franchisees initiated a series of summer events in 1972 in which the operators paid for buses to take neighborhood children on tours of the city, supplementing the field trip experience for low-income students.[9] Wilson Rogers, another Cleveland operator, adopted Paul Revere School after parents asked that the businessman help with litter, vandalism, and behavior problems among their students. Rogers used "a sizeable personal contribution" to organize a coalition of business leaders, elected officials, and parent-teacher association members to intervene in the school's troubles. Students were enticed to participate in antilittering campaigns with gift certificates to McDonald's. The McDonald's partnership with local schools spread, and the "be my guest card" became a standard prize for students with perfect attendance and academic honors.[10] McDonald's encouraged these appeals to children because they knew that youngsters held sway over whether a family would stay in or grab up a few burgers for dinner. One study found that "in three-quarters of the cases where a family decides to eat out the children choose the restaurant," hence much of "McDonald's advertising [appealed] directly to young TV viewers."[11]

Outside of school, McDonald's franchisees were regular funders of extracurricular activities, especially sports. On the local level, franchisees created new sports leagues, subsidized expenses, and hosted victory parties at their restaurants. McDonald's established the McDonald's All-American Game in 1977, where the best American and Canadian high school basketball players showcased their talents in tournaments. Being a McDonald's All-American athlete was a valuable distinction on the dossiers of the nation's best African-American high school basketball stars, including Magic Johnson in 1977 and Patrick Ewing in 1981. In a pre-Internet era, the games allowed an array of young black athletes to travel and capture the attention of college recruiters. The majority of these national youth sports opportunities were closed to girls' athletics until the 2000s, but one female-dominated sport made a splash with McDonald's earlier. The American Double Dutch League (ADDL)—conceived by two New York police detectives searching for a youth activity that appealed to girls—highlighted the athleticism and performative strengths of black girls through jump rope. In 1980, a collaboration of franchisees from New York, New Jersey, and Connecticut promoted the McDonald's Dynamos, a quartet of Double Dutchers. The ADDL-McDonald's partnership helped local communities establish rope-jumping leagues at rec centers and parks across the country. Three years later, McDonald's announced their support of the ADDL as a part of their official youth sports program.[12] Between 1979 and 1985, Double Dutchers were featured in McDonald's commercials, singing songs about their favorite items on the McDonald's menu. In one of the first ads featuring girls Double Dutching in New York City, the accompanying music was as much of an affirmation of the targeted black audience as it was a sales pitch. "McDonald's knows your Double Dutch is really hard to beat, cause when you're jumping you do something magic with your feet," crooned the commercial's voiceover. The 1985 "Jump to It" commercial featured the team in a McDonald's parking lot wearing red, white, and yellow uniforms, singing the praises of the Chicken McNugget. "Down at McDonald's where the arches glow, they've got Chicken McNuggets and they're hot to go." The team added cartwheels and complicated hand games to their already intricate choreography as a rap-style vocal described the delicious attributes of the poultry dish. The commercial ends with the jingle, sung in the style of R&B, "It's a good time for the great taste of McDonald's." For audiences unfamiliar with Double Dutch, the ad was an entertaining introduction to the impressive tradition of black rope-jumping. For black audiences, the ads that portrayed scenes of the Double Dutchers turning rope in front of an elder's house during a family gathering or on a strip of city street suggested that McDonald's also appreciated the ways that rope-jumping was familiar and joyful in black communities. Even activities that didn't necessarily have an exclusive association with African Americans were avenues for McDonald's to connect with black audiences. The McDonald's All-American High School Band, formed in 1967, was part of a cultural diplomacy effort to advertise a then-relatively-new brand. In 1980, when legendary band director William Foster was named the head of the All-American Band, he integrated elements of black marching band style into the competitive corps of 104 high school musicians. Foster, who also led the Florida Agricultural & Mechanical University Rattlers marching band, directed the group at national events like the Macy's Thanksgiving Day Parade, and some of the performers were featured in national commercials. For viewers with little experience of the rich tradition of historically black colleges, the All-American band may have been their first experiences of the moves, motions, and music of this black performance tradition.[13]

School programs and sports tournaments were some of the easier issues for black franchisees to tackle. In addition to offering free Happy Meals to children with straight A's and new goal posts for the local high school football program, black franchisees also responded to the fact that a mass of their clientele were earning low incomes, and sometimes assisted in helping families meet basic needs. In 1972, Cleveland's black franchisees partnered with three neighborhood Opportunity Industrialization Centers— a public-private partnership concept pioneered by Philadelphia's Leon Sullivan—to distribute more than 4,000 pairs of shoes across the East Side.[14] Each year, the franchisees marveled at how quickly the shoes were claimed and how many people were turned away because the demand significantly exceeded the supply. Black franchisees often pointed to their value to communities in not only providing charity, but also creating jobs for youth. Youth unemployment was, and continues to be, a chronic challenge for black communities. In the 1970s, inner-city youth joblessness rarely migrated below 50%. The teenagers and young adults who couldn't find work were often more susceptible to dropping out of school and finding themselves locked into a cycle of poverty. Federal assistance for youth jobs distributed through state agencies could only provide so many entry-level positions, and corruption in the administration of these programs sometimes diverted opportunities from youth to experienced workers. McDonald's franchises partnered with some of these state programs to staff their stores, and the high employee turnover rate of the fast food industry ensured constant openings. Working at McDonald's could teach youth, especially those who had not completed high school, a variety of skills. Some franchisees, however, noticed that their workers struggled with basic math when a register failed or a customer complained about being shortchanged. In the fall of 1979, at Caesar Burkes's Carnegie Avenue location in Cleveland, the operator invested more than $12,000 to build a training center inside his restaurant. He purchased two computers programed to teach employees how to operate newer models of cash registers.[15] Burkes said that educational deficiencies led to a 300% turnover rate among his crew, and the computers would allow employees to complete modules at their own pace. That year, the U.S. Department of Education reported the black high school dropout rate was 21.1%, compared to 12% for whites.[16] Burkes hoped that the training would not only strengthen their skills, but it would also "have doors open to them that are normally closed."[17]

While black franchisees tried to remedy the problems in inner-city education, there were times they were called upon to respond to immediate crises exacerbated by the lack of attention poor black neighborhoods endured. In the spring of 1974, in Chicago, residents of the Altgeld Gardens Homes public housing development observed a strange cloud lingering over the complex, which housed 2,000 families. Bordered by factories and a landfill, the Altgeld Gardens community had long been exposed to chemical hazards from neighboring plants. This eerie, gray sight in the sky was the result of a silicon tetrachloride leak from a nearby chemical company. A breach in a 500,000-gallon storage tank caused hydrochloric acid to mix with moisture in the air and gather above the South Side neighborhood. The acid made the residents susceptible to respiratory and gastrointestinal problems, especially children, pregnant women, the elderly, and people with asthma and bronchitis.[18] Many of the Garden residents reported feeling a burning sensation in their throats and used towels, handkerchiefs, and whatever cloth they could find to cover their mouths and noses. Fifty people were taken to the hospital for the day. A University of Illinois toxicologist advised the state's branch of the Environmental Protection Agency to begin evacuating the housing site in the late afternoon, but officials delayed the process for hours. Concerned residents called the police, who had little to offer by way of advice. When one resident called for help, she realized her actions were in vain. "They didn't send anyone. . . . If I'd known what this was, I could have been ready to take my family out of here. They should have told us so we would have been ready."[19] Eventually, the city dispatched public transit buses and police vehicles to Altgeld Gardens to start the evacuation process.[20] Some residents were unsure if they should leave, fearing that their homes would be robbed if they were gone for the night. The mayor dispatched police patrols to watch over the Garden homes. The only thing that the residents could depend on was a meal from McDonald's. A local black franchisee brought more than a thousand hamburgers and drinks for the evacuated Chicagoans, who waited for further instructions at a local high school. At the end of a long day that included being ignored by authorities, evacuated, and then moved to three different shelter sites, black McDonald's franchisees emerged as heroes. In a statement to the press, the National Black McDonald's Operators Association remarked, "We at McDonald's are sincerely interested in community involvement and can always be counted upon in a crisis."[21] Memories of the 1974 leak, which led the city to file a $5.4 million lawsuit against the responsible company, helped Altgeld Gardens resident Hazel Johnson recruit people for her environmental justice group, People for Community Recovery. Johnson, who is credited as the mother of the urban environmental justice movement, devoted her life to holding the city's housing authority, as well as the chemical and industrial plants in the surrounding area, responsible for the high rates of environmental illnesses in her community. Having lost her husband to lung cancer, Johnson later worked with a young community organizer, Barack Obama, to seek justice for the community's long-term health and economic suffering from pollutants and deindustrialization. For blacks in underserved areas, crisis was a constant. When McDonald's managers could be relied on more than school administrators or police officers, then the lines between where leadership and power rested in a city could become so blurred that a fast food restaurant could begin to look like a solution instead of a symptom.

Community outreach was effective advertising, but McDonald's had realized in the late 1960s that in order to remain dominant in the fast food field, they needed to do more. The company could not maintain its prowess in the market without the help of broad-based national advertising efforts, and they debuted their first coast-to-coast commercial in 1967. The spot featured children singing the refrain "McDonald's is our kind of place." The commercial's narrator assured parents that their spillproof cups and full-size bibs prevented stained shirts or messy car interiors. With each year, McDonald's advertising would feature higher production values, sleeker camera shots, clearer narrative structure, and more celebrities. Until actor John Amos (of *Roots* and *Good Times* fame) appeared in a McDonald's commercial in 1971 as part of a singing McDonald's crew, the television and print ads featured white people living in nearly all-white worlds. This did not sit well with the growing number of franchisees of color who were dutifully paying into the advertising fund but seeing few advertisements in the pages of the magazines they read or the radio stations they listened to. As was the case with most issues involving McDonald's, a small group of black operators had to advocate for themselves. This required them to return to where it all started: Chicago.

In addition to being the birthplace of some of the most celebrated black periodicals, like the *Chicago Defender*, *Ebony*, and *Jet*, Chicago was also the home of the very best in black advertising and market research.[22] Founded in 1971, black advertising pioneer Tom Burrell's agency, Burrell Communications, transformed the way the nation's largest retailers talked to black America. After a brief and mixed experience with a Philip Morris campaign to make the Marlboro Man more "soulful," Burrell received its most lucrative and impactful client—McDonald's. Burrell's first independent foray, a partnership named Burrell-McBain, focused on helping companies understand that "black people were culturally distinct enough and profitable enough as a consumer group to be worthy of a separate advertising initiative."[23] Burrell had to overcome the racial biases of the advertising industry that often treated black advertising talent as tokens or failed to take their advice into account. Historian of black advertising Jason Chambers described Burrell's success as a result of his refusal to accept "corporate handouts then used by some companies as a kind of community-relations effort . . . in which they gave money to black-owned companies but required little in the way of professional execution or actual deliverables."[24]

Under the leadership of an NBMOA founder, Columbus, Ohio's Carl Osborne, the black franchisees gathered with Roland Jones to discuss their being shut out of the McDonald's advertising strategy. McDonald's conceded that they should provide some avenue for black-oriented commercials to reach their customers, especially considering the importance of the urban stores to the chain's expansion. As black franchisees were making a case for more advertising, McDonald's was learning a lesson about simply recycling campaigns and pitching them to blacks, when they tried to circulate their popular "You deserve a break today" campaign to black outlets. Tom Burrell personally studied consumer reaction to the slogan, and he believed that black customers were not getting it. Black customers were confused. There were no breaks in their America. Unlike white suburban families that traveled to McDonald's to indulge their children's fancy, black families went to McDonald's to satisfy hunger momentarily before heading back into the challenges of their work and home lives. A history of Burrell Communications found that "the idea that the restaurants were only useful when one needed or wanted a break was meaningless to blacks."[25] Burrell Communications steered the advertising strategy in a wholly different direction. Burrell crafted the "So get up and get away to McDonald's" tagline, which anchored the first promotional material to feature blacks exclusively. The print advertisement featured an intimate moment between a stylish black couple, both sporting perfectly coiffed Afros. The woman looks directly at the viewer, while her companion is caught in the middle of saying something to her. The advertisement did not merely replace white faces with black ones. The woman's Afrocentric jewelry and the man's patterned shirt reflected popular black clothing styles of the time. Burrell was not holding back, and he struck gold. The ad worked, and from that moment onward, Burrell would set the standard on how to market to black America. Even with a team of black copywriters, photographers, and creative directors, this was no easy task.

Burrell's appeals to McDonald's to learn the language necessary to talk to blacks was supplemented by research from Chicago-based ViewPoint, Inc., which was founded in 1976 by Felix A. Burrows Jr., a Florida native who earned a master's degree in food chemistry in 1967. Burrows took his expertise to the food industry, working on quality control for dairies, and later attempted a Ph.D. in food chemistry, but the racial climate of the academic program led him to leave without a doctorate. His entry into market research came after being hired as a senior chemist by Kraft Foods in suburban Chicago. After executing a survey of housewives' perspectives on Kraft foods in development, he left the company for one of the area's leading consumer analysis firms. A few years later, Burrows decided to hang his own shingle and established ViewPoint, Inc., which grew to employ more than fifty researchers and staff, consulting on "food product acceptance and marketing dynamics" among blacks. ViewPoint broadened its scope to conduct market research for companies as diverse as Amoco, Coors Brewing Company, and Sears.

Agencies like Burrell and ViewPoint were essential in helping companies construct the dream worlds their advertising presented to consumers, who were frustrated with limited representation in commercials and campaigns. This lack of representation was cause for concern for civil rights groups, who recognized mass media as integral to buttressing their vision for a peaceful, integrated society. In 1967, the NAACP Legal Defense and Education Fund reported that "of 351 commercials monitored, 17 included Negroes," and among that group, "only three involved a principal role for a Negro." The New York City Commission on Human Rights conducted a similar watch and discovered that only 4% of commercials created between the fall seasons of 1966 and 1967 included blacks or Puerto Ricans. The study reported "minorities in TV advertising . . . instead of progressively increasing each year [in] integrated advertising, had actually fallen behind."[26] Occasionally, advertisements featured scenes of racially mixed community life, which viewers of all colors found forced and unrealistic. In a focus group about the "Coke Adds Life" campaign for Coca-Cola, one respondent said that interracial commercials were sometimes nonsensical. In reaction to a 1979 ad featuring a doo-wop group on a stoop of a Harlem brownstone, a viewer asked, "When have you ever seen a white dude harmonizing like that?" The resulting report on the study of the advertisement recommended that companies not resort to the "overuse of slang" and recognize that there was "no inherent magic in using black personalities in advertising" when crafting appeals to black consumers. The analysis concluded that "blacks are very skeptical as to whether the business establishment is sincerely interested in black customers."[27] Increasingly, as the experts weighed in about what blacks wanted to see, the few scenes of racial harmony were being replaced with black-only scenarios, perhaps mirroring a move away from interracialism as an aspiration. Although public alarm about separatism or black militancy, as it was called, was exaggerated, the advertising from the period reflected a more accepted idea that black life could evolve and reflect progress independent of the white gaze or approval. By the mid-1970s, African Americans were becoming more visible on network television and in commercials, but the desire for more black representation did not mean that black consumers were confident that their marketplace experiences would be free from the discrimination that was supposed to be socially and legally unacceptable. A president of a marketing consulting firm described the change in attitudes of black consumers as a matter of moving away from white ideals. "A decade ago, the typical successful black adopted the white man's middle-class style. The black from Tuskegee was more Ivy League than the Brahmin from Yale. Blacks are no longer emulating whites. They are expressing their black consciousness."[28]

Black consciousness and what the Burrell firm termed "positive realism" were the dual muses that inspired their oeuvre of ads. Burrell's team believed that they could subtly counter more than a century of racist depictions of black people and racist modes of addressing black consumers by highlighting the aspects of black cultural and social life that made people proud.[29] Burrell followed that first successful ad with the slogan "Get Down with Something Good at McDonald's," which highlighted McDonald's as a place to get something edifying, suggesting that this was a special, if not rare experience in black communities. One advertisement in the series, entitled "Carver Day Camp Gettin' Down," featured black adults and children enjoying McDonald's foods as they participated in the type of urban social programs that by the early 1970s were fading from black life. Clearly referring to black scientist George Washington Carver, the day campers are seated outside of a van as they enjoy their lunch with a camp counselor. The use of "gettin'" and "eatin'" versus "getting" and "eating" in the ad copy were deliberate choices to engage black vernacular. The advertisement's text also used slang, telling customers, "on the real side, kids can really dig" a stop at McDonald's.

The use of black vernacular and slang were risky tactics in advertising, but the presence of attractive, dignified black adults and cute children in the depiction signaled that the dropped g's were gestures of recognition, not ridicule. The ad introduced two of the most prevalent tropes in the Burrell projects of the 1970s: the importance of male authority in the black community and home life, and blacks living in modest and working-class communities. Burrell's intentions were transparent. He believed in the corrective possibility of advertising. Chambers argues that "beyond changing McDonald's slogan for the black community, Burrell also created ads that conveyed his vision of black life."[30]

Black media professionals concerned with the portrayal of black families were countering negative depictions in popular media, in academia, and in government policy. The Burrell goal of framing the black family as valuable and black men as responsible citizens evoked the generalizations of the oft-referenced government study *The Negro Family: The Case for National Action*, which was colloquially known as the Moynihan Report. Coordinated by then–Assistant Secretary of Labor, sociologist, and future New York Senator Daniel Patrick Moynihan, the Report provided confirmation for those who were inclined to believe that black poverty and rage were the result of family disorganization and a crisis of manhood. Moynihan encouraged a type of commonsense thinking that supported regressive ideas that black women emasculated their male partners, black families invested too much in their daughters at the expense of their sons, and that in order to restore black America, black men should either enlist in the military or receive preference over black women for jobs. The Report, which was supported by policy shapers of all races, led to a sort of Moynihan logic, in which black families were believed to be so deficient that they needed constant instruction on how to be a family.[31] This logic ignored the devastating impact of racism on people and blamed blacks for being unable to stabilize their families, while ignoring the ways that race and poverty truncated possibilities for advancement. Although Burrell disagreed there was anything wrong with black people and families, by presenting ads featuring black men as model fathers, he reflected the intense pressure black cultural producers felt to use advertisement to not only sell products, but to salvage images also. In the agency's focus on "featuring images of strong and capable black men," they inadvertently gave weight to Moynihan logic, which argued that every problem was caused by and could only be solved by patriarchs. Despite the role of women workers in the service industry or the real experiences of female-headed households, many of Burrell's ads from the 1970s and 1980s focused on black men and the families they ruled over.[32]

The 1971 "She Deserves a Break Today" campaign, a play on "You Deserve a Break Today," portrayed a nuclear family that Burrell hoped could illustrate their efforts to counter stereotypes about black family dysfunction, which was supposedly rooted in black women's dominance and black men's incompetence. The ad featured a middle-class family in a dining room. The father brings home McDonald's so the mother does not have to worry about the family's evening meal. The assumption is that the mother has been home all day, and the father is going above and beyond his patriarchal duties by having worked a full day and "made dinner" by bringing home McDonald's. The convenience of the fast food restaurant allowed this black family to enjoy time together, and in turn, maintain the equilibrium of the father's role as breadwinner and the mother's as homemaker.

Market research in the 1970s recommended that McDonald's advertise more directly to black women, and Burrell eventually created more advertisements that centered black women in the storytelling. A 1979 McDonald's television commercial promoted its breakfast service with an entirely black cast and recognized the value of black matriarchs by featuring a middle-class family comprising a professional, working mother, a father, children, and a grandmother. The black grandmother waited for her children to wake up and expected the woman of the house to cook breakfast before church, but the tired and busy family was able to barely make it out the door in their Sunday best. In a time crunch to eat before church, they stopped at McDonald's before services. The commercial was set to the tune of a Gospel-style song that is sung from the mother's perspective: "After working hard all week, I'd like to get some rest." The song speeds up as the family enjoys their breakfast; each member of the family ordered a different offering, from Egg McMuffins to hotcakes. The song closes with the lead singer's vocals accompanied by a clapping, tambourine-shaking gospel choir: "Since we are going to get to church on time, mama is proud of me," and the campaign tagline "McDonald's, we do it all for you."[33] McDonald's, according to the advertisements, showed how they allowed black families to be their very best. Market research confirmed that their investment in Burrell was a smart one. A market assessment from 1977 outlined that "the image of McDonald's is very positive in the minds of many [blacks surveyed]. McDonald's is seen as a company with quality products at a reasonable price . . . [and people are] aware of McDonald's involvement in the black Community."[34]

An array of classic black McDonald's ads have been pilloried or criticized in recent years as silly or racist. Some of the ads, despite their place in the genre's history, do not age well, and frequently bloggers and writers circulate the now-vintage appeals to castigate either the advertising agency or the corporation itself. A 1979 advertisement that supported McDonald's "We do it all for you" campaign has been relitigated in the pages of *The Atlantic* and on National Public Radio, among other media outlets.[35] The ad copy reads: "Dinnertimin' at McDonald's" and it sells diners on the McDonald's experience by stating: "You don't have to get dressed up" and "there's no tipping." The twenty-first-century commentary on this, and similar ads, immediately registers the absence of the *g* in "timing" and the presence of racist stereotypes about black diners being poor tippers and unable to understand how to dress for polite society. This analysis offers valid concern about racial affectation in advertising, but if this and other ads are understood from the long view of blacks and dining, then another perspective is possible and essential. In ViewPoint's research, blacks indicated a preference for restaurants that didn't require dressing up, and the ads may have been designed to recognize and confirm that.[36] In light of the conflicts around access to restaurants as physical spaces, as well as their exemplification of sites of resistance and violent, racist intimidation during the civil rights movement, including the early McDonald's drive-ins throughout the South, the advertisement's directives about tipping and dress also recognize and alleviate historical anxieties. The ads speak to a troubled relationship between the black consumer and private-establishment dining. Another ad reinforces these ideas with the promise that "At McDonald's dinner is a good deal, not a big one." The ad reassures the black family on their way to McDonald's that they can "come as you are, and you don't have to come far, since McDonald's is right in your neighborhood." Years after the passage of the Civil Rights Act, the memory of the way things used to be, as well as the knowledge of the things that still remained after the Act, loomed large over black customers. These were wounds that needed healing. Burrell and his creative team knew about the fears that followed blacks when they took a seat in a booth or made a left turn into their favorite drive-thru.

Due to the importance of individual franchisees in black consumer markets, some advertisements also gestured toward black customers' relationship with franchisees, rather than food. Two 1984 advertisements in *Ebony* magazine attempted to communicate McDonald's proximity to the secondary goals of black capitalism: the elevation of a black managerial, as well as entrepreneurial, class. "At which $8 billion corporation do Black executives help call the shots?" Accompanying the answer was a small photograph that captured a partial image of a man's fist, but it was not the Black Power salute of the Portland Panthers or a hand clenched in anger during an uprising in Chicago. The man's fist rested on a telephone and was outfitted with a McDonald's ring, presumably the type of corporate appreciation gift given to franchise owners. The advertisement, part of the "Good Neighbors . . . Together, McDonald's and You" campaign, claimed that "black executives are helping shape the future of McDonald's." Citing the hiring of black lawyers, accountants, engineers, and marketing directors, McDonald's positioned itself as a socially responsible brand not only because of the way it treated diners, but because it also elevated the black middle class. The advertisement claimed that these leaders within McDonald's corporate structure began "as crew employees and worked their way up."[37] The second *Ebony* advertisement posed another question: "Who's the largest employer of Black youth in America?" The associated photograph depicted a young black man arranging a paper McDonald's hat atop his head like a soldier with a garrison cap. The ad proudly claimed that "almost 6,000 McDonald's restaurants in neighborhoods across the country employ thousands of Black men and women." Many of these workers earned low wages as they tended griddles and wiped plastic trays, but McDonald's reminded that "since most of the employees live in neighborhoods where they work, their wages have a very positive impact on businesses in their community."[38] The trickle-down reasoning of the advertisements suggested a dollar earned at a fast food joint traveled across the community, but these claims were refuted by researchers. One think tank estimated that a McDonald's in Washington, D.C., that generated "sales of $750,000 a year, and earned $50,000 in profit before taxes," sent more than $500,000 out of the area.[39]

As Burrell's ads continued to evolve and match the type of television programs that featured blacks, McDonald's advertising moved closer to reflecting the ringed executive and away from the young man who took orders at the counter. The growing numbers of upwardly mobile blacks in the 1980s contributed to a move to reflect this change in black marketing, causing a bifurcation of so-called ethnic advertising. Agencies began to devise marketing plans that created content targeting middle-class and lower-income blacks separately. While advertising successfully expanded the markets, television programming like the 1980s hits *The Cosby Show* and spin-off *A Different World* represented aspirational scenarios involving black professionals and middle-class family life.[40] The late-1980s McDonald's commercial entitled "Fraternity Chant" re-created a common scene on college campuses that housed historically black fraternities and sororities. This ad, which resonated with African Americans who attended college, featured a fictional Sigma Delta Phi. A group of black fraternity members lined up at attention awaiting instructions from their pledge master to perform a coordinated routine of step dancing and chanting. "Want to be in my frat? Do the McDonald's menu chant," the pledge master demanded. Actual black fraternities and sororities pair stepping with rapid fire recitations of their Greek organization's history or principles.

In the commercial the men recite the McDonald's menu while performing a synchronized routine featuring precise footwork and clapping. "Fraternity Chant," like the Double Dutch ads of the preceding decade, again brought black dance to a national audience through a McDonald's commercial. Breakdancing, rap music, and hip-hop beats would be added to future campaigns to maintain the brand's requisite level of cool to attract black customers, and as these cultural forms dominated mainstream popularity, these ads engendered familiarity for Americans of all racial and ethnic backgrounds.[41]

By the 1990s, McDonald's continued to find new ways to talk to black America about its preferences and projections in ways that seemed realistic and, more important, would get them to go to McDonald's. Advertisements targeting black customers were shaped around the inedible parts of the fast food experience, from black franchise ownership to the nature of McDonald's work. Two types of work-scenario–based ads emphasized the company's insistence that the person preparing French fries could one day become a franchise owner. Debuting in 1990, the "Calvin" ads were shaped by a synthesis of the two previous periods. Viewers initially met Calvin, a teenager in the inner city, and his appearance was peak cool in his time, with a backward cap, baggy clothes, and high-top sneakers. Soon you learn that Calvin, who passes a basketball court, a group of idle black men hanging out on a street corner, and an elderly woman hauling her groceries home, is on his way to a job at McDonald's. The commercial ends with Calvin flipping his cap and kindly saying, "Welcome to McDonald's. May I help you?" Over the course of the television spot, Calvin is transformed from a stereotype of a menacing black youth to an ambitious and responsible one. The "Calvin" series continued to include his promotion to manager and neighborhood chatter suggesting that Calvin becomes a franchisee, to which he responds "not yet." In a matter of time, the ad suggested, Calvin will join the Cosby class of high-earning black professionals.

Robert Jackson, a consultant on the Calvin ads, said the campaign was as much about getting customers through the doors as it was about rehabilitating the image of a McDonald's job.[42] In the early days of black advertising, working at the Golden Arches was presented as a stepping-stone, but by the late 1980s the image of a fast food job was far from appealing. The term McJob, coined by sociologist Amitai Etzioni, characterized fast food employment as inherently dead-end work that provided no educational value to youth. With McDonald's expansion still strong at the dawn of the 1990s, the company believed it needed to revamp the perception of their jobs, especially as it boasted that it was one of the largest employers of youth.[43] In his meditation on class politics, scholar Robin Kelley reflected on his own time working at a McDonald's in Pasadena in the late 1970s. As a pre–Calvin era worker, Kelley described the various ways that his McJob was the site of irritation, as well as a place for mischief, pleasure, and everyday acts of rebellion within the workplace. Kelley recalled:

> Like virtually all of my fellow workers, I liberated McDonaldland cookies by the boxful, volunteered to clean "lots and lobbies" in order to talk to my friends, and accidentally cooked too many Quarter Pounders and apple pies near closing time, knowing fully well that we could take home whatever was left over.[44]

The complicated nature of fast food work could never be fully represented in a Burrell Communications ad, but for black viewers who were proximate to the experience of working fast food, Calvin's smile and enthusiasm may have been the subject of skepticism, and for white audiences, the disruption of stereotype may have been instructive. Targeted advertisements are not in the business of selling hard truths even when they are designed to refute ugly vestiges of racism, but the lens through which viewers read them provide a challenge to advertisers who must speak with many voices through a singular mouthpiece. Burrell's advertisements did not shy away from referring to the urgency of black America's need for jobs or pathways to professional careers, but each reminder of the obstacles to black equality led to an assurance that McDonald's was lighting the way.

* * *

McDonald's advertising to black consumers seemed more concerned with the heart and soul than with the stomach, but as more black consumers entered the category the industry calls "super heavy users," McDonald's knew that it was worthwhile and advantageous to develop products that catered specifically to this population. In a 1977 report, the distinctions between a heavy and light fast food user showed how race and class informed market segmentation. Heavy users represented 48% of their customers and tended to be "younger, male and blue collar occupationally," and on the whole heavy users were "non-white, principally black, but also other racial minorities." Light users by contrast were "substantially older, female, white and somewhat better educated."[45] The initial fast food staples of hamburgers, hot dogs, fried chicken, and tacos were bestsellers in the consumer market. But companies knew that in order to increase their market share they needed to continually improve and expand their menus, while still maintaining strong profits and keeping prices low. Although McDonald's was a leader in the fast food space, it was particularly timid in its expansion of its menu. Most of the popular revisions to the menu boards were introduced by franchisees. From the Filet-O-Fish to the Shamrock Shake, local operators used regional tastes to pitch additions to the national roster of selections. This was a point of pride for Kroc, who was not as adept at identifying and cultivating culinary trends for the restaurant as he was at selling billions of burgers.[46] For every successful product or concept, such as the Big Mac and the McMuffin, there were more false starts, including the east European pastry kolache and a roast beef sandwich.[47] When McDonald's unveiled new products, they did so with considerable attention to the customers that would be most drawn to them. As Burrell Communications created vibrant images of "real" black life for McDonald's, ViewPoint helped them strategize on how to please black palates. Creating foods for the black consumer market required insights into how blacks perceived and consumed foods for reasons other than sustenance. In the landmark study of black consumer behaviors, D. Parke Gibson's *$70 Billion in the Black,* researchers advised the food industry to pay special attention to black women's attitudes on how to properly feed children. In emphasizing the care black mothers took in choosing their children's food, he may have also wanted to counter the growing and pervasive stereotypes of black maternal carelessness and inadequacy. The report advised:

> Black mothers are more concerned about nutrition. They have less faith in the lunches their children get at school. They put more emphasis on breakfast. While proportionately more black mothers work and would seem good prospects for instant or easy-to-prepare foods, there is a counteracting factor. Black mothers will not sacrifice nutrition or taste . . . Black mothers use meals to a much greater extent as a reward system and as a means of keeping the family together. They put more of themselves into food.[48]

In contrast, white mothers were believed to be moving away from time-consuming food preparation and embracing just-add-water cake mixes, mashed potatoes whipped together from powdered flakes and cups of milk, and aluminum-foil–wrapped trays of Salisbury steak. In 1969, trade magazine *Chain Store Age* predicted that "the clamor for convenience" was permanent.[49]

While the manufactured foods market noted this racial difference in black women's cooking habits, the fast food industry also noticed racial disparities in consumption. When black women chose not to cook, they were willing to spend money on fast food. In the late 1970s, blacks spent an average of 13 cents more per visit than whites on McDonald's. A market research firm discovered that between 1970 and 1976, the number of black female-headed households had increased more than 40%. This rapid increase in women out-earning male partners or not having one at all meant that Burrell's ads couldn't speak only to black men and black fathers. In 1977, consultants told McDonald's to focus more on the 36% of black families being led by women. They also recommended that more advertisements target black tweens and black women by purchasing commercial time during the hit music television show *Soul Train*, sponsoring concerts by talents like singer Natalie Cole, and donating to agencies devoted to sickle cell anemia.[50]

When new products were developed, sometimes McDonald's offered something first and collected feedback later, often to their own peril. Two products illustrated the ways that fast food viewed "urban" consumers as crucial targets of new food items: the fried chicken sandwich and the ill-fated Chopped Beefsteak. Both products, McDonald's reasoned, would be appealing to African Americans. ViewPoint conducted ethnographic research, taste tests, surveys, and focus group interviews to assess how blacks thought about and interacted with new and existing products for various fast food restaurants. McDonald's was well aware of the success of fried chicken in the fast food market, and product development conversations about whether to offer it led nowhere. In 1980, the McChicken sandwich and the Beefsteak, which was to be served with a side of Onion Nuggets, were first introduced. The logic behind these products was to create something that black adults would enjoy when they took their children to McDonald's. Although McDonald's performed well with blacks on the whole, their data from the late 1970s suggested that as consumers aged, they were less interested in the menu. By investing in chicken and steak sandwiches, McDonald's believed they could retain black adults as diners long after their children grew up.

The consumer research offers a window into the modern era of race-conscious marketing. These products required carefully crafted messaging due to their histories as well as the way McDonald's wanted to position them. The McChicken, associated with a highly popular and racially laden dish, fried chicken, needed to taste good and be sold without too much regard to race. The Beefsteak, offered as part of a dinner menu available between 4 and 9 P.M., was advertised as an economical treat for a working-class person who could not afford steak. ViewPoint had experience surveying blacks about other parts of the McDonald's menu, having coordinated studies on the Filet-O-Fish and McRib sandwiches. In 1979, ViewPoint reported that "onion nuggets are faring poorly in black stores" and dispatched in-store surveyors to ask why people were avoiding the product. In the memo instructing field researchers on how to talk to customers, ViewPoint directed them to "probe for purchase of onion nuggets for carry-out purposes"; blacks were more likely to eat fast food at home than in the restaurant. Then, if possible, researchers were to find "a tactful way [to] probe for gas giving nature of product. Try to determine if this is indeed a problem." In a survey of people who had tried the onion side dish, analysts were to "be on the lookout" for the following negatives about the product: "Greasiness, lack of 'real' onion taste, gets cold faster than French Fries," and whether the onion nuggets were delivered "too crisp" or "overdone." [51] It didn't take very long for ViewPoint to realize what the corporation was also discovering from its in-house product development team; the nuggets didn't taste very good. McDonald's lacked a single supplier for the onions, and the lack of consistency flew in the face of what the restaurant prided itself on. The Onion Nugget soon went the way of the McDonald's Hula Burger and strawberry shortcake. [52]

Regardless of race, very few people liked the onion nuggets. But the other products assigned to ViewPoint offered up revelatory insights about what McDonald's was up against if it wanted of maintain its share of urban eaters. ViewPoint sometimes asked interviewees about who they would connect a particular product with, and then assess if these associations were positive or negative. The Filet-O-Fish, created as an alternative for observant Catholics during Lenten Fridays, was a poor performer among blacks. [53] The battered cod sandwich may have seemed like a strange choice for southern-born blacks accustomed to the cornmeal-crusted catfish available at most soul food restaurants. Black diners were less concerned about prohibitions against eating meat before the Easter holiday, and respondents believed the sandwich to be overwhelmingly white in its sensibilities. In one focus group, researchers asked which celebrities, careers, and activities aligned with the Filet-O-Fish. Respondents offered that the sandwich was like comedian Paul Lynde, television sitcom star Mary Tyler Moore, and Secretary of State Henry Kissinger. They believed it to be the meal of choice for suburban housewives who played tennis, Chinese flower arrangers, and others "who did not embody the boldness of McDonald's beef product."[54] It was clear that the Filet-O-Fish had no soul.

Message received. McDonald's believed there was no product bolder than the new Chopped Beefsteak sandwich, and they asked ViewPoint to provide insight on how to sell an ostensibly more refined sandwich than a hamburger to black consumers. A storyboard for a Beefsteak ad alerted black commercial viewers that consuming fast food was nothing to be ashamed of, and that it could be elevated into an economical, yet pleasant treat. In the illustration for a potential Beefsteak ad, a couple is seen riding a city bus together. The "well-dressed black man and woman" are deciding on dinner. The woman asked, "What'd you want for dinner, honey? Hmm, I've got a taste for something special." The man didn't lose a bit of his confidence when he admitted, "Well, I've got a hamburger wallet, and a beefsteak appetite." The bus driver, ostensibly a trusted member of the community, or at the very least an appropriate commenter, suggests: "Try a chopped beef steak sandwich."

The man's dress belied his financial status, an outward sign of a piece of marketing common sense that often was applied to black people: appearance is everything and overcompensation was critical. Market research designed to tap into the hearts and minds of black America assumed that black consumer self-consciousness was central to how blacks interacted with buying toothpaste, choosing a burger, or signing a lease on a luxury car. An article in *Sales Management* magazine advised, "The black traveler is one example of how wrestling with self-perception shapes consumption habits." Citing the 1971 book *The Black American Travel Guide*, the trade journal noted that while on holiday, blacks were likely to spend 30% more on accommodations and food than their fellow white vacationers. The travel guide reasoned that the black consumer spent more "because he doesn't want others to think he can't afford the best." It also offered that travel—and by extension retail spending—was based on "the need to get away from depressing ghettoes."[55] Market researchers also found that blacks, regardless of their economic station, used their clothing as a means of garnering respect. The disparity between what the man in the ad wore and the cash in his pocket was one way of marketing an inexpensive dining option as appealing even to those who looked like they could afford better.

The helpful bus driver went on to describe the virtues of the sandwich. "Pure chopped beefsteak, through and through, on a French roll with onions! And steak sauce too!" The commercial spot followed another adage of how to market to blacks; a touch of slang went a long way. The bus driver assures the pair that "the taste is outta sight!" The duo punctuates his description with a hearty "Alright!" After background singers crooned that the "Chopped beefsteak sandwich is served from four to nine," the man was sold on taking his date to McDonald's. "Right on time!" The man finished the statement started by the singers, "Chopped Beefsteak Sandwich, the taste is . . ." with a "mighty fine," and adds that "It's not just another steak sandwich. It's made to please a man." His companion added, "And his lady. Nobody can do it like McDonald's can."[56]

Based on the available archive of McDonald's commercials that promoted the Beefsteak sandwich, this ad may have never taken shape beyond the storyboards. When compared to other advertisements of this product, when whites were sold the Beefsteak, there was no emphasis on its price or its ability to serve as a prelude to a romantic evening. Ads that were broadcast on television featured white leads or an interracial cast, emphasized the Beefsteak's size, ability to quench an adult's hunger, and convenience after a long and frustrating day at work. Beefsteak lovers were upper-class white-collar employees, mailmen, and construction workers of all races who needed to eat something delicious and filling in the evening. McDonald's reasoned that they could combat the lagging sales of the late 1970s by introducing a time-limited product that would, hopefully, boost the numbers of "dinner-hour customers," who would ordinarily patronize McDonald's during the brisk breakfast and lunch times.[57]

ViewPoint's research files indicate that there was far less concern about the black reception of the Beefsteak sandwich because blacks did not have strong feelings about how steak should taste or look. Perhaps due to the high price of steak, blacks were less likely to consume it on a regular basis. Chicken was an entirely different story. After regional testing of the chicken sandwich, McDonald's made it available to all stores in mid-1980. The chicken sandwich, described in the *Wall Street Journal* as a "sort of chicken burger," was one of the first large-scale commercial attempts to serve what had long been made in the South, a piece of fried chicken between two slices of white bread. Fried chicken, known by some as holy bird or the Gospel bird, was both ubiquitous and special in the African-American communities that would populate the Great Migration destinations of urban America. Often served on Sundays in the South after one's spiritual hunger was satiated, this dish was rendered an everyday food in northern cafés and luncheonettes, which helped popularize southern foods more broadly. Fried chicken and its careful preparation from slaughtering the bird, to sectioning it, to the proper brining or seasoning process, and then the eventual moment when the poultry met the lard or Crisco or oil, is a deceptively difficult dish in that it masks the levels of mastery and care necessary to make it delicious, perfectly crisped, juicy, and appetizing. So to make a chicken patty—a condensed, salty but generally flavorless slab—appealing among the people who perfected the dish in the United States was a formidable challenge.[58] The participants in a McChicken taste test offered an earful for the facilitators. "I never would guess it was chicken . . . you got to have the skin on it." Another offered: "You go there thinking you'll get chicken—you'll get a piece of chicken and . . . when you get there the effect is completely different and it sort of blows your mind . . . expecting chicken dripping or something and it's like . . . looks like a hamburger out there . . . It sort of pulls you apart from . . . what you went there for." One respondent thought the condiments on the sandwich were out of place. "You don't usually eat chicken with mayonnaise . . . you eat chicken with hot sauce."[59]

The taste testers in the ViewPoint study would have probably preferred the Georgia-based Chick-fil-A, which grew from S. Truett Cathy's Dwarf Grill, and began franchising its concept in 1967. After establishing Dwarf and renaming it to focus on chicken, the franchise specialized in opening in mall food courts over the following two decades. The outlet didn't begin building drive-thru–accessible locations until 1986. Today, Chick-fil-A's signature pressure-cooked breaded-chicken-and-pickle sandwiches have attracted a wide following outside of the South, but the sandwich is as emblematic of southern foodways as it is of race. The fried chicken sandwich was the basis of black women's small-scale business life throughout the late nineteenth and twentieth centuries as "waiter-carriers," who sold food to stopped train passengers along train tracks.[60] The sandwiches were a delicious treat for travelers of all colors, and the sandwiches' golden-fried chicken and fresh-tasting bread could never be fully replicated by a frozen chicken patty and shelf-stable hamburger bun. But changes in travel—from greater highway access to the expansion of airline routes—made long-distance train travel less efficient and less popular. In addition to shifts in black women's employment opportunities and more stringent regulations on the sale of food in public places, fewer black women sold their once sought-after chicken sandwiches. The mass-produced disk of chicken would eventually be understood as a fried-chicken sandwich. That conversion would take some tweaking in the advertising strategy to make it more enticing, as well as in the recipe to make it taste more edible.

"Black consumers are heavy chicken eaters, particularly fried chicken," opened ViewPoint's statement on the McChicken sandwich. "As such, blacks were overwhelmingly disappointed with the McChicken sandwich." A number of factors inhibited immediate acceptance of the product. First of all, despite its status as a sandwich, respondents in the study still associated a chicken with "whole chicken on the bone." ViewPoint concluded that the "product therefore did not meet their expectations given their reference point." The accoutrements couldn't help the sandwich either. "Fried chicken with lettuce and mayonnaise-type sauce appears to be an unfamiliar combination which is not appreciated by these black consumers." As Gibson noted, "A meal without gravy or sauce doesn't look appetizing."[61]

The McChicken sandwich did not have to be a total flop, argued ViewPoint. The new menu item did not need better-tasting chicken or different condiments. Rather, ViewPoint saw the McChicken as a matter of reeducating blacks on how they felt about fried chicken and how they could feel about the sandwich. The research team recommended that McDonald's merely take the "perceived negative product attribute—its boneless feature—and highlighting it in such a way as to develop and encourage a more attractive and alluring product." This could be achieved by describing the sandwich as "a unique and delectable piece of boneless chicken that is served in an enticing, unusual sandwich form." Blacks would forget about "proper" fried chicken by simply associating the sandwich with a different way to consume poultry. ViewPoint's excitement increased with each suggestion in the memo: "The McChicken sandwich would be cast as a new and savory approach to fried chicken designed expressly for ardent chicken lovers. It would be removed from the ordinary fried chicken position and advertised as a boneless chicken delicacy." By framing it as an "easy-to-eat, filling, and economical fried chicken delicacy that was created especially for them," blacks would feel catered to and appreciate McDonald's for "offering them a whole new way to love chicken." The new marketing campaign would just need better "definition," and they suggested that black men could help usher in McChicken success. While black men indicated that they "generally disliked McDonald's food and only went to McDonald's because their families like it," ViewPoint found that the men "felt that the McChicken sandwich would be the least objectionable item to purchase for themselves." In order to prevent a mass exodus of these men from McDonald's—especially when their children outgrew the restaurant—the chicken sandwich had to be "substantially improved," in hopes that they "might become heavy McChicken users and would thus remain within the McDonald's consumer franchise." Another recommendation was just to rechristen the sandwich. The researchers reasoned that "since the respondents associate the name 'McChicken' with real chicken on the bone, some consideration should be given to toning down the product name to possibly 'McChicken Steak,' or 'McChicken Patty.' By avoiding the words "chicken" and "sandwich" in the same name, they would avoid the "disappointment with the McChicken." They recommended research that would "secure a name that provides a better understanding of this product offering prior to purchase."[62]

The first McChicken did not have enough market, or internal, support to continue on, and the product was pulled soon after its debut. The Chicken Nugget, however, went on to great fame. McDonald's decided to give the chicken sandwich a second life in 1988, nearly a decade after reintroducing a fried chicken product that was cut into boneless chunks and was evocative of, but never fully resembled, proper fried chicken. By the late 1980s, consumers welcomed a chicken sandwich, and despite a temporary retirement of the McChicken, it continues to live on in fast food menus across the industry. The McChicken taught McDonald's that after their food became a staple, familiarity was more important than taste.

* * *

Burrell's advertising and ViewPoint's insights hammered home that McDonald's could use the icons and symbols of black life and culture to their advantage. Considering the ways that Martin Luther King Jr.'s death loomed large in the way McDonald's and the NBMOA described their journey into black communities, black franchisees and McDonald's national office were leaders in celebrating the Martin Luther King Jr. holiday. The utility of King the icon—versus King the iconoclast—is that his diluted characterizations could be manipulated and recalled for an array of purposes. With each year that passed since his death in 1968, King transformed from a radical, Communist threat to democracy to a man who simply wanted all people to be friends. Fast food franchises are not responsible for the accurate accounting of civil rights history, but their reliance on a flattened image of King allowed them to ingratiate themselves to black communities without having to amend a chicken recipe, reconsider their inner-city market saturation strategies, or raise a wage. Black franchisees, who believed themselves indebted to King's sacrifice, took steps to honor him before it was clear that the nation wanted him remembered as a hero of the people, not as a heretic against democracy. Coretta Scott King hoped that the King holiday would provide workers with a day off and properly commemorate her husband's commitment to labor struggle. Instead, the King holiday became a prime opportunity to sell apolitical ideals like color blindness, which obscures the vicious impacts of racism on people's lives and livelihood.[63] The further the nation moved from King's death and the aftermath, the more King and the movements he led became uncontroversial markers of the past. The profits of the urban market were so high that even Kroc, a staunch conservative, declared himself a supporter of "social change of the late sixties," made evident in his company's recruitment of black franchisees.[64]

Eleven years after King's death, the movement to create a federal holiday to honor the leader took root. Historian David Chappell argues that the concerted four-year effort was one that implicitly conceded that "if substantive gains were no longer feasible, symbols were still important."[65] President Jimmy Carter—at the time desperately trying to stave off Ted Kennedy as the anointed presidential candidate of black America—declared his support for a King national holiday in his 1980 State of the Union address. Carter did not linger on the topic for too long, simply stating:

> Dr. Martin Luther King, Jr. led this Nation's effort to provide all its citizens with civil rights and equal opportunities. His commitment to human rights, peace and non-violence stands as a monument to his humanity and courage. As one of our Nation's most outstanding leaders, it is appropriate that his birthday be commemorated as a national holiday, and I will continue to work with the Congress to enact legislation that will achieve this goal.[66]

While the Congressional Black Caucus, Coretta Scott King, and King's former colleagues were lobbying the halls of Congress, at local McDonald's restaurants the King holiday was being commemorated. Some franchisees ordered tray liners printed with facts about King. Local stores sponsored essay contests about King's legacy. Other franchises displayed widely circulated photos of King at the 1963 March on Washington for Jobs and Freedom in restaurant lobbies.

The federalization of the holiday in 1983 led McDonald's corporate office to buttress the local franchisee efforts, leading to more public programs and commemorations. In 1986, McDonald's restaurants across the country displayed posters with an image of King looking stoically into the distance. His candlelit visage was accompanied with text that explained, "His Light Still Shines, a celebration of the life and message of Dr. Martin Luther King, Jr." Underneath the description was a pair of Golden Arches. "His Light Still Shines" was then the nation's "largest traveling exhibit highlighting the civil rights movement" and King's work. After it toured twenty-two cities and informed and inspired more than a million visitors, the exhibit became part of the permanent collection of the Atlanta Hartsfield (now Hartsfield-Jackson) Airport. Edward Rensi, then–president and chief operating officer of McDonald's, said "it was created for the world's children. Now it will continue to be viewed by millions."[67] At these events, no speaker ever raised the issue that McDonald's would open the year celebrating a fervent anticapitalist, and close it with more than $4 billion in revenue and $480 million in profits.[68] Perhaps, it was easier to evoke the grief of his loss than the substance of his message. For those who were most challenged by King's declaration that America faced "the inevitable choice between materialism and humanism" and his assertion that "capitalism was built on the exploitation and suffering of black slaves and continues to thrive on the exploitation of the poor—both black and white, both here and abroad," the entanglement of a fast food giant and King's legacy may have felt uncomfortable at the very least.[69] But negotiation was nothing new for black people who supported movements for racial and economic justice. With every showing of "His Light Still Shines," or every time a black franchisee sponsored a Black History Month celebration or donated to a historically black college, McDonald's was writing itself into an accessible, sanitized story about civil rights, in which the ability to own a franchise was tantamount to leading a movement for racial and economic justice.

The King holiday experienced a slow start in national acceptance and corporate investment, and McDonald's was unique in its hearty show of support for the remembrance in the 1980s. The Hartsfield Airport commemoration may have come as a relief after a disappointing response to the call to support the country's first official King Day celebration in 1986. The Martin Luther King Jr. Federal Holiday Commission, which included such luminaries as former Ambassador to the United Nations Andrew Young and former franchisee Julian Bond, was unable to raise their projected $1.5 million for various events. Their efforts yielded a war chest of $300,000 from private donors and an additional $100,000 in federal and state funds. The City of Atlanta had to bail out the national King Day grand parade after the event was forced to slash its budget and reduce its number of marching bands able to participate. In addition to the exhibit, which included memorabilia and photographs from the King Center for Nonviolent Social Change, McDonald's commissioned black artist Richard Hunt to create a sculpture entitled "The Altar of Freedom," for the King exhibit. Commissions to and patronage of black artists were also part of McDonald's cultural work in the 1980s.[70] The Black McDonald's Operators Association of Chicago and Northwest Indiana underwrote a musical performance to honor King entitled "If I Can Help Somebody," and the show aired on the home of the Chicago Cubs, WGN-TV.[71]

In areas where the King Day activities were less than robust, observers could check their local listings and watch a McDonald's-funded short film entitled *Happy Birthday, Dr. King: A Celebration of His Life and Times*. Burrell Communications helped with the production and content for the twenty-six-minute tribute, which was a decidedly uncomplicated retrospective, but supporting the King holiday was not without concerns for corporate sponsors. Albert Davis, a former Coca-Cola vice president, admitted that he was advised by some that "it was politically unwise to give this [the holiday] major support."[72] McDonald's, with its history of the franchise transfers and prominent black spokespeople, could not distance itself from the King celebration. In embracing the holiday, they may have made it easier for other corporations to make King work for them.[73] In the decades since the first King holiday, King has been memorialized in volunteer projects, community performances, a thirty-foot granite memorial on an edge of Washington, D.C.'s Tidal Basin, and, in January, inside of fast food restaurants. Although the irony of linking King's message and the practices of the fast food industry remains, the passage of time has further buried these contradictions under piles of advertisements for King Day, buy-one-get-one-free coupons, and circulars promoting sales at shopping malls.

As the National Black McDonald's Operators Association network grew, McDonald's franchisees were able to maintain their enthusiasm for black history and culture beyond the wintertime King activities and Black History Month. Present at the "His Light" ceremony was gospel music star Shirley Caesar. Caesar won a Grammy in 1986 for her tribute to King, and her presence was particularly fitting because of the relationship between black McDonald's franchisees and the spiritual music circuit. Gospel music—the electrification of black, sacred song—and the fast food sector came together previously when Mahalia Jackson debuted Glori-Fried. After her chain closed, fast food companies seeking to connect with black consumers sponsored a series of Gospel music endeavors, from concerts to battle-of-the-choirs performances and songwriting competitions.[74]

Black arts and artists also benefited from the black franchisee turn toward supporting cultural production. The McDonald's Literary Achievement Awards of the 1980s honored poets and essayists who captured the "black experience in America." Under the auspices of the Negro Ensemble Company, a groundbreaking theater troupe based in Harlem, the organization was integral to launching the careers of major black dramatists and actors. Up-and-coming writers could compete for the McDonald's-sponsored Lorraine Hansberry Award, an honor for college students who best portrayed black life on stage. Winners were invited to participate in a feedback session in New York, and the revised screenplay was table-read by professional actors. The partnership among McDonald's, the American College Theater Festival, the American Theatre Association, and the Kennedy Center opened doors for young dramatists, and listed actors Denzel Washington and Phylicia Rashad among the program's mentors.[75]

In the 2000s, appeals to black consumers have used hip-hop aesthetics, social media lingo, and continued sponsorship of black organizations to remain relevant and legible to consumers, but now all of their competitors have learned their secret, which has expanded the fast food industry's imprint on black cultural life. Since 2003, McDonald's has used the 365Black.com website as an online portal to cultural content and directed marketing campaigns. The associated recognition and awards program has honored figures as varied as Herman Petty and other NBMOA founders, the Reverend Jesse Jackson, Congresswoman Maxine Waters, and Harvard University scholar Henry Louis Gates Jr.

* * *

Fast food is about more than just food. Consumers make marketplace choices based on a constellation of emotions, past experiences, memories, desires, and actual hunger. At any moment, one of these impulses can dictate whether a person drives south to a Hardee's or north to a Wendy's or home to cook. The fast food industry invests millions upon millions of dollars each year to better understand how this psychology of buying works, to create business models that convince customers that their burritos, chicken tenders, and hot fudge sundaes can meet whatever needs that propel a person to their restaurant. In the case of black consumers in the United States, these motivations are also shaped by racism and its hold over nearly every aspect of life—housing, education, health, wealth, and socialization. Thus, fast food is as much about the spice levels on a fried chicken sandwich as it is about a franchisee paying for your child's cash-strapped school to go to a museum. Fast food marketing promises authentic experiences in places that are designed to be inauthentic. But, knowing the first name of the owner of your local Burger King and appreciating the touches of black history on her store's wall can mediate the reality that the food sold at that restaurant is no different than the food at the airport terminal or the outlet on the other side of your town. Even if you are skeptical about the fast food industry as a whole, you may appreciate the band of franchisees who contributed to your favorite King exhibit, because you wonder if anyone else would have paid for it. A black college graduate may adopt a vegan diet as an adult but remain grateful for her NBMOA-sponsored tuition scholarship.

The diligence required to cultivate the black McDonald's market in the 1970s and 1980s not only enriched the company and allowed it to wrap itself around so many aspects of black cultural life, but it also provided a model for its competitors to do the same. The industry used similar strategies to enter other communities of color. By the late 1980s, affinity groups for black, Latino, and Asian-American/Pacific Islander franchisees were formed to expand into other market segments. White fast food customers may also know the good works of their local franchisees or read with interest about donations to a Ronald McDonald House— which provides housing for families with children being treated in hospitals—but, on the whole, black consumers' proximity to franchises and franchising is far closer and more dependent because of their distance from economic stability.

The close ties between a black franchisee and the surrounding community is best illustrated in the 1988 film *Coming to America*, and the movie's delightful sight gag, McDowell's, a clear rip-off of a black-franchised McDonald's.[76] The film's protagonist—Eddie Murphy in the role of African royal Akeem Joffer—is a prince who searches for his future queen in the borough of Queens, New York. In an attempt to shield his identity as the heir to the throne of the fictional nation of Zamunda, Murphy goes to work in a regular American job—a fast food restaurant. Owned by the sly Cleo McDowell (played by actor John Amos from the 1971 McDonald's commercial), McDowell's is subject to investigation by McDonald's for trademark infringement and operating a copycat business.

Despite his clear poaching of the burger giant's many concepts, Cleo vehemently defends his business and suggests he came up with the distinctive Golden Arcs and the Big Mic sandwich. Although the McDowell's Restaurant is merely a backdrop for Murphy's budding romance with Lisa, Cleo's daughter, Amos's portrayal of a social-climbing yet community-minded businessman adeptly captures aspects of the culture of black entrepreneurship in the fast food sector in the 1980s. Cleo's presence in his store mirrors the ways that black franchise owners were often present in their restaurants to not only oversee their businesses, but because they also tended to operate fewer restaurants than their white peers. Cleo's sponsorship of a "Black Awareness Rally," a combination beauty pageant and talent show, emceed by a local pastor, was a comedic sendup of the types of community engagements often financed and catered by NBMOA members. Cleo's management of a store constantly being targeted by a neighborhood robber, played by relative newcomer Samuel L. Jackson, also matched the experiences of many franchisees whose businesses were often in areas with high crime. In the film, McDowell's does not have to sort through the challenges and responsibilities of being a black-owned fast food establishment. In real life, frustrated black franchisees could not ignore the inequalities they faced as operators, and as was done in the past, the first step in seeking redress was to call on the civil rights establishment to lend a hand.

CHAPTER SIX

A Fair Share of the Pie

Jesse Jackson's Operation PUSH and Reverend Al Sharpton's National Action Network led national boycotts of corporations throughout the 1980s and 1990s. These boycotts led to aggressive expansion plans that brought more fast food outlets to black neighborhoods across the country. New York Post Archives / Getty Images.

MCDONALD'S BLACK OWNERS ARE IMPRISONED IN THE GHETTO!

The protest signs greeted the visitors to the spring 1984 McDonald's national operators' meeting in Los Angeles. The demonstration was sponsored by the city's chapter of the National Association for the Advancement of Colored People, and at seventy-five years old, the NAACP was taking up the cause of a different kind of victim of racial discrimination than it had become accustomed to representing.[1] The protest was not about a miscarriage of justice in which a black defendant was wrongly sentenced to death. Nor did this moment pivot upon the promise of a child seeking access to a well-funded school district. This action centered on Charles Griffis, a black McDonald's franchisee who had made millions on his Los Angeles locations, and the issue at hand was his access to still greater fortunes in the fast food business. As the signs intimated, the NAACP accused McDonald's of relegating black franchisees to doing business in the most economically depressed, most dangerous, and most expensive-to-insure communities of Los Angeles and other cities. In the fourteen years that lapsed since Herman Petty's grand opening in Woodlawn, McDonald's had franchised restaurants to 137 black, and mostly male, operators. Black women were slowly entering the franchise system as spouses and co-owners of restaurants, and they would grow in numbers over the following decades. With fewer than 150 black franchisees in a system of nearly 8,000 franchise locations across the United States at the time and with many of their white counterparts able to franchise multiple locations, black franchisees wondered why the numbers of black-owned restaurants was still so low. The unquestionable profitability of black-franchised locations, in their view, should have caused McDonald's to clamor for black franchisees to acquire more stores, but expansion was limited. While a McDonald's grand opening happened every seventeen hours in 1984, including an opening in Finland for the first time, few were presided over by a black businessperson.

Experienced black franchisees, as well as franchise applicants, had long appealed to the National Black McDonald's Operators Association to raise this issue with the corporate offices. Some NBMOA members believed that McDonald's was using techniques akin to "redlining," the practice of branding black residential maps with red marks to demarcate them as undesirable. NBMOA members who operated McDonald's in black neighborhoods long maintained that despite profiting from a captive market that wanted to buy affordable food, they shouldered a disproportionate burden because they were presiding over dilapidated stores and protecting employees and patrons from crime. Among those in the know, there were rumors circulating that regional franchising managers maintained black lists and white lists for franchise assignments. These speculations may have conjured up memories of the racism blacks sometimes encountered when trying to buy homes. Even after the practice was deemed unconstitutional, residential redlining continued to shape black community building and economic opportunities. Similarly, despite their economic prosperity as a group, African-American McDonald's franchisees often found themselves in an uneasy position as both models of racial progress and victims of racial discrimination.

Black franchisees may have been reluctant to speak out about their struggles with McDonald's, knowing well that biting the hand that fed millions of people burgers may do more harm than good. Yet racial disparities among franchisees evolved into an attractive civil rights issue for the NAACP and its peers as these organizations sharpened their focus on aligning with corporations that profited handily from black customers and could not risk public accusations of racism and discrimination. The events leading to the Convention Center protest reveal that the success of black franchisees was not a simple tale of how time, legislation, and activism could eradicate racism. Two racial discrimination lawsuits filed by black franchisees against McDonald's led to a rather public exposure of their discontent. The lawsuits evoked the pervasive racial problem of equal access, and showed that wealth did not provide relief from the impact of racial discrimination. The public exchanges between McDonald's corporate and its black franchisees fueled the redlining accusations, and called into question what racial progress actually looked like in the world of franchising.

Los Angeles was among the first cities after Chicago to debut a black franchisee in the local system. In 1969, Bert Willis and Henry Clark franchised a McDonald's in the Crenshaw neighborhood. The duo branded their restaurants the "Willis-Clark McDonald's" in advertisements in the *Los Angeles Sentinel* newspaper so that readers were clear that their franchise was different than the white-owned locations in other parts of the city.[2] Willis-Clark newspaper advertisements emphasized that their McDonald's provided more than food to local communities—it also provided much-wanted jobs and training. Willis-Clark ads featured teen employees testifying to how much McDonald's prepared them to take on life's challenges. In one ad, employee Emma Rayfield's "on and off the job" attitude was consistent with the "Willis-Clark customer service motto of enthusiasm, courtesy and friendliness to all customers."[3] In addition to providing teens like Emma their first jobs, Los Angeles black franchisees used their restaurants as part-time community meeting places and senior citizen centers, while also sponsoring youth sports and college scholarships.[4]

For political candidates and others looking to capture the attention of black audiences, McDonald's was the place to initiate outreach. In 1974, a newly elected Mayor Tom Bradley attended the grand reopening of Ed Lewis's Crenshaw-area McDonald's on South La Brea Avenue, and he continued to take calls from black franchisees as their presence and influence grew throughout Los Angeles.[5] Bradley also delivered the opening address of the 1979 annual meeting of the NBMOA, held at the Century Plaza Center.[6] As the NBMOA grew in size and wealth, members could find a friend in the cohort of history-making black elective officeholders. Black mayors provided immeasurable hope for voters who saw local-level leadership as a means to alleviate their day-to-day struggle: earning well-paying jobs, the enforcement of fair housing laws, and access to good public schools for their children. Carl Stokes in Cleveland, Richard Hatcher in Gary, Coleman Young in Detroit, Maynard Jackson in Atlanta, Harold Washington in Chicago, and Bradley formed a far-flung fraternity of city leaders who had to balance the racial allegiances that earned them support with the watchful and critical eyes of white power brokers. These mayors mostly ran campaigns that united black voters and white progressives with a vision of shared governance for the city and the expansion of equal opportunity, but often led with a moderate, probusiness style that did not challenge the status quo in favor of catering to economic interests among wealthier citizens. Therefore, many of the mayors aligned with the concerns of the black franchise community, and they were indebted to their assistance in raising campaign funds, facilitating voter registration at their restaurants, and bridging the gap between candidates and the black business community. Historian Tom Adam Davies described these mayors' collective leadership strategy as prioritizing "the interests of middle-class whites and blacks and of downtown elites."[7]

Local NAACP chapters were also important actors in helping both franchisees and mayors achieve success through partnerships that could ascribe a civil rights sensibility to any venture or campaign. The Los Angeles chapter of the NAACP, founded in 1914 by two University of Southern California–trained dentists, contributed to the fight for the civil rights agenda that blossomed in mid-century America—ending employment discrimination, litigating school desegregation, and increasing voter rights.[8] The NAACP stepped into new territory when they were approached by two franchisee applicants who believed they were denied restaurants on the basis of race. The first McDonald's case involved the type of person who could have easily been identified as an ideal plaintiff in any civil rights lawsuit, California sheriff's deputy and narcotics specialist James T. Jones, who decided to pursue a franchise in 1971. The celebrated officer had no desire to rock the boat; he simply wanted in on the business after a McDonald's Regional Licensing Manager approached him during a search for potential franchisees of color.[9] By 1975, Jones had graduated from Hamburger University, submitted notice of his retirement from the Sheriff's Office, and prepared to move to Phoenix, where he believed his new store would be located. Jones shortly discovered, however, that the time, energy, and effort he expended studying the required internal temperature of a beef patty and the intricacies of replacing the nitrogen supply on a soda machine had been a waste. McDonald's informed him that he would not receive the Phoenix store. Jones's disappointment with McDonald's turned into indignation when he learned that Paul Gutierrez, a Mexican-American friend he introduced to the McDonald's program, received a franchisee contract in Lancaster, a desert town forty miles north of Los Angeles. Jones then polled the black friends he recommended as potential franchisees, and he learned that not a single one received approval to franchise.[10] The details of Jones's experience are similar to the failed list of twenty that David Hill claimed he provided McDonald's recruiters in Cleveland, to no avail.

Armed with the survey of his peers, Jones contacted the state's equal employment authority for guidance, and in August 1974 the commission determined that Jones "had the right to bring a civil action."[11] Two years later, his lawyers filed a lawsuit on behalf of Jones against McDonald's in Los Angeles Superior Court.[12] Jones's claim against McDonald's included allegations that the company succumbed to pressure from an all-white network of Phoenix operators "who protested Jones's potential appointment by threatening to withhold monies from the Optional Advertising Fund" if he was assigned the Phoenix store.[13] Jones believed that the operators didn't want a black franchisee in the area, and the handful of blacks who later acquired stores in mostly white areas sometimes experienced cold shoulders from fellow operators when they arrived to start their businesses. Along with the lawsuit, Jones submitted letters promising him the Maricopa County restaurant, which was supposedly under construction, a rarity for a black franchisee, a copy of blueprints, and a note that estimated the completion date for the store, January 10, 1974. Jones's lawyer probably knew he would be outmatched by McDonald's legal team, and he advised that Jones seek out additional expertise from civil rights lawyers to pursue his racial discrimination claim against McDonald's.

The Los Angeles NAACP branch president Dr. H. Claude Hudson, a successful banker and cofounder of the Niagara Movement that led to the creation of the NAACP, placed Jones's case on the agenda of their spring 1976 meeting. The executive body agreed that Jones's claim against the leader in fast food was worthy of their time and resources. The chapter's vice president believed that the case could garner publicity for the NAACP, a particular area of interest for the organization as they redefined their role in the era that ushered in the rise of the political right in the state, and concluded with a Republican winning the White House.[14] After making remarkable strides in the fight for school desegregation with the NAACP Legal Defense and Education Fund's masterful work in the 1954 *Brown v. Board of Education of Topeka, Kansas* case, the NAACP's legal wing continued to fight for school desegregation mechanisms, such as redistricting and busing, in an era in which the backlash against these measures migrated from mob rule to school board manipulation. The 1960s and 1970s brought the NAACP lawyers more cases of protesters denied their freedom of assembly, the racially discriminatory application of the death penalty, and even legal cases that blamed the organization for hurting businesses by supporting boycotting and picketing. By the late 1970s, the NAACP was struggling to get its bearings. The Los Angeles base was in dire straits, and nationwide, local chapters hosted "Save the NAACP events" to help it pay off its debts and reclaim its legitimacy. While Black Power radicals convincingly questioned why integration was a worthy goal, the NAACP did not have an articulate response to a younger generation's probing inquiries into what the organization could do for them.[15] Having survived bankruptcy, and observing the way that Jesse Jackson's Chicago-based Operation PUSH was enriched by its corporate negotiation efforts, the Los Angeles chapter may have seen the McDonald's case as the perfect way to join the conversation about economic development in black communities.

Dr. Hudson's letter to the McDonald's System of California office on Wilshire Boulevard read like Operation Black Unity's pitch to bring black franchisees into Cleveland's East Side. The NAACP leader argued that Jones's case for franchising was inextricably tied to black buying power. Jones's grievance was a matter of economic justice and consumer fairness. "A large volume of McDonald's business is done in the Black Community," he wrote, and it was only reasonable that Jones and other "Black business persons [should be] afforded an opportunity to share in the profits derived from doing business in the Black Community." Hudson's argument that black communities should see a return on investment for their spending was one way that the ties between black franchise contribution and black community went above and beyond the framework of corporations as good neighbors to their customers. McDonald's was likened to a wealthy citizen of black America, and in the same ways that wealthy blacks consolidated their power over poorer black people by leveraging their wealth in exchange for loyalty or access to privilege, McDonald's was expected to do the same.

News of Jones's lawsuit led other Los Angeles black franchisees to weigh in on what they viewed as similar problems with McDonald's, namely having their businesses receive inadequate attention from the parent company. "They do these things [discrimination] to black dealers and then they come back and cover it up. They are some treacherous people . . . They are tricky . . ."[16] The "tricks" that frustrated the operator became a subject of an investigation by the California Assembly's Finance, Insurance, and Commerce Ad Hoc Subcommittee, which opened an investigation of allegations of racial discrimination in the franchising sector. Henry Clark, of the Willis-Clark partnership, corroborated Jones's claims: "We are specifically limited to, in our case, Black operators to Black areas of the city which have the maximum problems, minimum income, [and] minimum opportunity for social-economic growth . . ."[17]

Ultimately, a court ruled in favor of McDonald's in the fall of 1975, but Jones's challenge and the issue of black franchisee dissatisfaction would remain a point of interest for the NAACP in the following decades. The news of the problems on the West Coast traveled to Chicago, where PUSH entered the conversation on black franchisees as early as 1979. In 1982, PUSH sent a letter to McDonald's inquiring about accusations that black operators were "being subjected to a double standard" in their ability to access franchises. The next black franchisee dispute, while far more complicated because it involved a less-than-ideal plaintiff, benefited from a more mature Los Angeles NAACP, which was better equipped to confront racial disparity in corporate America. This racial discrimination challenge attracted the necessary press coverage and public concern to force McDonald's to publicly defend its practices and philosophy on black business.

Los Angeles transplant and franchisee Charles Griffis shared many similarities with Herman Petty and the other NBMOA founders. Griffis saw himself as a "race man," a prosperous African American whose greatest weapon in his personal arsenal to fight racism were his bootstraps and his steely focus. "I was twelve years old before I ever saw the inside of a schoolhouse," he reminisced. The former Tennessee sharecropper eventually graduated high school, and following in the footsteps of many African

Americans of his generation, he enlisted in the military in order to widen his career prospects. After serving in the Air Force, Griffis earned a degree from the Northern Michigan University.[18] The budding entrepreneur was operating a gas station in Detroit when he learned of the opportunities available to African Americans to franchise McDonald's restaurants.[19] In 1977, Griffis enthusiastically accepted an offer to purchase a Santa Barbara McDonald's, which he assumed was located in the posh coastal city north of Los Angeles. Griffis claimed his trek from Michigan to California ended with a shocking discovery: Griffis had actually invested in a McDonald's restaurant "on Santa Barbara Street [Martin Luther King Jr. Boulevard as of 1983]," which he described as "right in the middle of the ghetto." An irritated Griffis proceeded with the deal despite being the new owner of "an old store in real bad shape." He managed the Santa Barbara Street restaurant expertly, generated substantial profits, and expanded his McDonald's portfolio to include three more restaurants in South Los Angeles within four years of his heading West. Griffis was a bona fide McDonald's success story with annual sales receipts "ranging from $1.2 million to $1.7 million." His stores met or exceeded the national sales averages in 1982. The man who survived poverty in the South and military service became a business owner with two Rolls-Royces in the driveway of his home in affluent Bel-Air.[20]

Griffis's relationship with McDonald's may have continued unremarkably well if his wife, Patricia—perhaps inspired by her husband's success and encouraged by efforts devoted to recruit women into franchising—did not set out to become a franchisee also. Instead of burgers, Patricia Griffis decided that her destiny awaited her in chicken; she entered a franchise agreement for two Popeyes Chicken and Biscuit shops in Crenshaw in 1982.[21] As Mr. and Mrs. Griffis prepared to become a franchising power couple, McDonald's promptly sued Charles for breach of contract in 1983, citing his franchise agreement which stipulated that profits from Big Macs and Chicken McNuggets could not be used toward the purchase of a competing franchise. Charles Griffis would not allow McDonald's to have the last word on his wife's forays into franchising, and he responded with his own legal action. Griffis filed a lawsuit claiming McDonald's engaged in racial discrimination in the assignment of franchises, which ultimately hampered his capacity to acquire more restaurants.[22] By 1984, when Griffis claimed that he was "systematically kept from buying stores in white neighborhoods," the Los Angeles NAACP chapter had become practiced in deliberating with corporations. The NAACP local eagerly joined Griffis in his public divulgence of his problems with McDonald's and provided a survey they conducted of black franchise locations that supported the conclusion that McDonald's purposely kept black operators out of white areas.

McDonald's was also savvier, having survived Operation Black Unity, Black Panthers, the Ogontz Neighbors Association, and other challengers. They justified their franchisee placement strategy by asserting that they were merely respecting black business owners' stated desire to serve their own communities. If black franchisees wanted to cater to black customers and employ black people, then of course they would be in predominately black locations, McDonald's reasoned. But Griffis's position as a wealthy McDonald's man who lived in the predominately white Bel-Air raised an important question about race and social mobility: where was his community exactly?[23]

Soon the fight over local McDonald's franchises became a topic of national debate. The intersecting issues of race, wealth, and the definition of ownership sparked a series of heated and dramatic conversations between Griffis and McDonald's executives and attorneys. Both sides of the conflict used the language of civil rights to litigate their respective cases in the court of public opinion. Griffis, the Los Angeles NAACP, and two Oakland-based lawyers aggressively attacked McDonald's for betraying the stories of limitless black entrepreneurship featured in advertorials purchased in *Black Enterprise* and *Jet* magazines. The Griffis camp declared that McDonald's treatment of black franchisees was akin to the devastatingly unequal employer-employee relationships of the Jim Crow era when the apparatus of white supremacy suppressed black autonomy at home and at work. Los Angeles NAACP head John

T. MacDonald also evoked the language of housing and mortgage loan discrimination. "We are very concerned about what seems to be McDonald's redlining in the Los Angeles area, and we are collecting information nationwide." The legal pair accused McDonald's of engaging in "unreasonable restraint of trade through racial discrimination and other unreasonable measures to deny free access to the marketplace" in violation of the California Fair Dealership Law and the Civil Rights Act of 1964, because black and white franchise candidates were allegedly placed on separate waiting lists for stores.[24] A former Los Angeles franchisee told the *Sentinel* that he also believed McDonald's kept "two lists of available stores . . . one is for blacks and the other list is for non-blacks."[25]

After news of the lawsuit circulated among major news outlets, Griffis used his newly found platform to deflect McDonald's legitimate contract claims against him. Griffis ignored the Popeyes problem and instead focused on the disparity in restaurant quality among the operator community. In direct conflict with the litany of pro-McDonald's testimonials from other black franchisees, Griffis refused to attribute his high earnings to McDonald's over his own business acumen and hard work. He described his four profitable restaurants to the *New York Times* as being located "in hellholes." Griffis continued: "[My stores] get robbed once or twice a month, and I pay $20,000 a month in security services . . . we had a murder in one and we still get the windows smashed and the bathrooms vandalized. I've upgraded my stores a lot and I don't see why I shouldn't have a shot at a store in a good neighborhood."[26] The day after Griffis shared his story with the *Times*, the *Sentinel* reported that his 1800 South Western Avenue store was the stage for a gun battle between a would-be robber and the store manager.[27] Griffis's characterization of doing business in South Los Angeles required that he make a claim about McDonald's limiting his opportunity while stereotyping the predominately black and brown communities that made him so wealthy. Undoubtedly, some of Griffis's customers felt uncomfortable reading his broad generalizations, while also agreeing with the nature of his challenge. Fair was fair, and why shouldn't black people be allowed to profit off of whites?

McDonald's was not interested in indulging any of Griffis's claims and countered that what Griffis called racism was in fact an enlightened attitude toward race. In placing black franchisees in black communities, McDonald's was simply listening to black consumers and black activists. Borrowing the language of Black Power adherents, black capitalism devotees, and probusiness black mayors, McDonald's stated that where some saw redlining, they were actually being "sensitive to black leaders' requests" by placing "black businesspeople into inner-city neighborhoods."[28] A McDonald's attorney argued that it was Griffis who was duplicitous toward a benevolent company that had given the poor southerner the opportunity to amass a fortune.[29]

The Griffis family held fast to the portrayal of McDonald's as the meddling overseer interfering in their family affairs. Griffis's lawyers adroitly drew upon a long history of African-American economic subjugation, familial disruption, and anxieties about the ways that racism emasculated men in their pithy reply to McDonald's challenge to Patricia's franchise dreams. Griffis's attorney argued that McDonald's could not interfere in "what a member of a man's family does in order to make a living." They offered a simple explanation: Patricia saved her own money and sought an opportunity. They balked at McDonald's actions because the franchise did not "have the right to tell a man how his wife . . . must or must not spend their own money." By restricting Patricia's entrepreneurial drive and independence, McDonald's had intervened in a black man's home in order to "create a virtual monopoly on how far a man can go in business if he is a part of the McDonald's chain."[30] The notion that McDonald's impeded Griffis's ability to establish his patriarchal authority at home and be a businessman resonated with anyone sensitive to the black struggle for personal and professional freedom. The Griffis narrative harkened to the days in which blacks were beholden to white authority at every waking hour. Griffis wanted to make it clear that he was a sharecropper no longer.[31] Griffis enjoyed an early victory in his war on Ronald McDonald. A month after Griffis filed his lawsuit in January 1984, a district court judge refused to grant

McDonald's an injunction that would force Griffis to relinquish his McDonald's franchises. The judge did not believe that Griffis caused McDonald's "any great loss" and "that the matter was for another court."[32]

As each legal team waited for their next day in court, the NAACP invited McDonald's to a meeting about franchise redlining; Mayor Bradley agreed to attend. Bradley's intervention in the boycott was consistent with his probusiness, procompromise managerial style. An historian of the "mainstreaming" of Black Power characterizes Bradley as someone who "lamented urban inequality" but "rarely addressed issues affecting the black poor explicitly." When he did speak about economic inequality or more generally about black advancement, it was almost exclusively communicated in terms of community development, minority business support, and affirmative action—approaches that scarcely made a difference and did not threaten to increase either taxes or welfare spending. He was especially keen to enlist business in the effort to solve urban poverty, believing that private enterprise could "teach poverty communities about how the system works, that it can work and to develop a stake in it."[33] The words "black capitalism" were uttered fewer and fewer times by black leaders in the 1980s, but the spirit of the movement was alive and well. Yet Bradley was not entirely compliant in his plans to ensure that city and business resources flowed toward blacks; but his sensibilities about opportunity were often concentrated in the direction of middle-class people. When he asked businesses to sign an affirmative action agreement in order to secure lucrative contracts with the city, local GM, Ford, and Chrysler dealers refused. Using the most powerful weapon in his arsenal—municipal procurement power—Bradley held firm to his provision. Los Angeles found itself without enough cars for police officers, but Bradley remained unmoved, and eventually the companies conceded. This moment probably confirmed Bradley's hunch that economic hardball could yield results, and his thinking was in line with the NAACP chapter's approach to the McDonald's franchisee dispute.[34]

The ghosts of Cleveland may have haunted the meeting as the

parties gathered in Los Angeles City Hall. With the hindsight of fifteen years since the OBU boycott, McDonald's applied a few lessons since learned about black America's complaints about their business. By the early 1980s, the corporation had hired more black management professionals at Oak Brook, had become more fluent in the language of corporate diversity, and now emphasized that their franchisees were a living memorial to their commitments to equity. From the outside, Griffis may have seemed like an outlier, because the majority of news stories and magazine features about blacks in franchising overemphasized the personal wealth, community impact, and contentment of black franchisees. Frequently featured and quoted in the press, happy black franchise owners emphasized their ability to use the qualities of self-reliance and self-discipline to establish their business. They rejected the idea that McDonald's did anything short of providing spectacular, and equal, opportunity.

While the standard narrative surrounding black franchisees recognized challenges in securing financing or confronting gang activity in and near the stores, black franchisees rarely took McDonald's to task for inequities in restaurant conditions. Nor did they raise their concerns about racially divisive moments endured by franchisees, beginning with Ray Kroc's transgressions. An incident at a franchisee gathering in 1972 illuminated the distance between Kroc's conservative values and the positions of its black operators. In a 1976 exposé about McDonald's entitled *Big Mac: The Unauthorized Story of McDonald's*, writers Max Boas and Steve Chain delved into race relations under the Golden Arches. A chapter opens with the 1972 First International McDonald's Convention in Honolulu. The men described the summit as an opulent affair with no hamburgers in sight at the elegantly catered dinners, but filled with "hamburger millionaires" showing off silk suits and accompanied by wives adorned with diamond jewelry, also financed by Big Macs.[35] The convention was like a fast food world's fair, with new inventions and demonstrations dazzling the participants. McDonald's debuted the Quarter Pounder, screened new advertising campaigns from powerhouse agency Needham, Harper & Steers, and commissioned songs to introduce upgraded store equipment. The convention—and other meetings like it—were designed to unify operators and recommit them to the house that Kroc built. Regardless of where your restaurant was located, you were bound together by your shared interest in providing quality, service, cleanliness, and value. Yet for black operators, these calls for unity were always tempered by the reality that they were superminorities, and often their stores needed more resources than their white counterparts. When Kroc invited newsman Paul Harvey to deliver remarks to the crowd, the fragile unity of the McDonald's System shattered with Harvey's ode to the kind of American myths that extolled meritocracy and ignored discrimination, which easily devolved into racist attacks on communities of color. Boas and Chain described the speech as a "paean to free enterprise mixed with hoary clichés." Harvey decried rioters, those "too lazy to work," and anyone who expected "something for nothing." The speech may have been the final straw for a subset of black operators, who knew that they were running highly profitable, and largely unsupported, restaurants. After the convention, McDonald's executives received a protest letter from black operators in New York, Cleveland, and Chicago; the letter's signatories included the only woman to own a franchise. At least one franchisee claimed that the speech sent him on a path to see what Burger King had to offer.[36]

Big Mac suggested that despite successful endeavors like the Better Boys Foundation partnership and the high grosses of the "ghetto stores," McDonald's corporate failed to take heed of the feedback provided by the early NBMOA. They highlighted missteps like the Ronald McDonald character visiting black neighborhoods; the writers speculated that because of "the new ghetto militancy" the children rejected a white clown. Black labor organizations rallied to get McDonald's to underwrite college scholarships for its workers, an initiative that would later be partially fulfilled by NBMOA partnerships with the United Negro College Fund. During an attempt to counter rumors that McDonald's was selling bad meat at its restaurants in the center of black Chicago, the Oak Brook outfit was unable to maintain a veneer of good public relations to effectively argue its case. McDonald's invited black news reporters to their headquarters to tour the offices and a local meat-processing plant, and then meet with the man himself, Ray Kroc. Instead of assuaging concerns about the food quality, the famously exacting Kroc instead fixated on Lu Palmer, a radio host and writer for the *Black X-Press* newspaper, and his decision to not wear a tie to the event. Palmer said that Kroc told him, "If you let a guy take his tie off, then next he'll want to take off his shirt, and where do you stop?" As tempers flared in the meeting, Kroc decided to simply depart, confirming or exacerbating reporters' suspicions about McDonald's racism. Palmer wrote about his experience the next day, noting that as he left Oak Brook's "fantastic monument to hamburger power," he thought about the "countless blacks who helped build it with their quarters and dimes and pennies."[37]

McDonald's executives were willing to learn more about franchise concerns, but they would not demur from the fight. Representation did not always build trust. Frustrated black operators resented McDonald's bringing black executives to the confab in order to deflect charges of racism. Black executives, including West Coast regional manager Reginald Webb, believed that his employer was being "unfairly castigated and attacked." Webb defended McDonald's, pointing to the statistic that "eight percent of all McDonald's franchise owners are black." The NAACP rebutted that over the course of twelve years, "out of 137 black franchise operators nationwide, only one is in a white area."[38] Webb evoked ideas of racial pride to match the redlining accusations: "I don't see anything wrong with doing business in a minority area . . . Mr. Griffis seems to think there is something particularly wrong with it . . . Every black community is not a ghetto."[39] This was correct, but most black communities where McDonald's stood were disproportionately affected by higher operation costs, and few of the restaurants were in solid condition. Webb suggested that critics look at the big picture. "There isn't a more successful group of black entrepreneurs in America." Webb took umbrage at Griffis's assault on "the very system that had provided him with seven years of such professional and financial success."[40] Griffis retorted by attacking one of the key advertising angles articulated by McDonald's in its targeted marketing toward blacks—McDonald's as a major source of work for youth. "When McDonald's says it is the largest employer of black youth, who are they kidding? I'm the one that hired the 600 employees who work for me."[41]

In addition to deploying black executives to defend McDonald's, the corporation relied on stories of prosperous black franchisees who claimed they saw nothing unfair or restrictive in McDonald's practices. In a feature on Lonear Heard, a Southern California franchise owner, *Black Enterprise* dubbed her the "McQueen of the Golden Arches." As black women were stereotyped as welfare queens—a racist characterization of lazy and unethical recipients that shaped public opinion and public policy—the coronation of a black woman as the queen of the franchise was a routine flourish in black business publications. These feature stories often used the impressive personal narratives and the sizable financial portfolios of upper-income blacks to contest negative depictions of the race.[42] The black press often highlighted the modest backgrounds of the franchise owners, their role as job creators in black communities, and their proximity to community efforts. Heard, the vice president of the Los Angeles chapter of the NBMOA, and her husband relocated to California to manage a McDonald's restaurant. After his death in 1981, she took the helm of her family's multifranchise business. She operated stores in Compton, Los Angeles, and Long Beach. In 1987, her six outlets grossed $11.9 million. Heard said she didn't "buy the argument that black franchisees are intentionally discriminated against by McDonald's and given unprofitable inner-city franchises." *Black Enterprise* reported that "her inner-city restaurants, where the clientele is 80% black, are more profitable than her suburban outlets where the clientele is 60% white." Perhaps inadvertently, she actually confirmed part of Griffis's claims; the article also mentioned that she hired security guards to stand post at all her restaurants.[43]

The problem of fast food in black communities was one of safety and limited institutional commercial choices as much as it was a symbol of unprecedented black success and economic progress.

Griffis's refusal to present his relationship with McDonald's in this way was novel and revelatory, proving that money and class mobility could not trump racism's deceitfulness. The NAACP leadership left their city hall meeting undeterred by the failure to come to a middle ground on Griffis's case. The group decided to escalate its efforts. At a March 6, 1984, press conference, John T. MacDonald asked black Angelenos to "buy with . . . conscience," and indicated that solutions to McDonald's racial disparity problems had to be resolved and realized in the offices of their corporate headquarters, as well as among the ranks of franchisees. He chastised McDonald's for a lack of black management and business leadership, particularly on its board of directors, as well as its lack of contracts with black manufacturers, contractors, and suppliers. In a press conference outside of one of Griffis's stores nearly a month later, the NAACP president declared the start of a selective buying campaign—essentially, a partial boycott that asked the public to *only* patronize black-owned McDonald's restaurants. The NAACP leader shared the organization's collection of damning statistics on how few blacks were in the operator corps. Between 1977 and 1984, McDonald's built 115 new restaurants, and a black franchisee operated only one of them. Although buttressed by compelling data, the campaign subverted the logic of the boycott as a means of economic starvation and illustrated just how much the franchise model obscured the issue of ownership. Although black consumers were asked to refrain from patronizing white-owned franchises, ultimately, McDonald's still benefited from profits generated at black-owned restaurants. The NAACP did not bother drafting and sharing a list of stores to support and which ones to avoid: "It's really pretty simple. Minorities don't own ones in white neighborhoods."[44]

McDonald's may have thought that they didn't need outsiders telling them how to connect to black America. In addition to employing franchisees who provided jobs in black communities, McDonald's devised a strategy for spreading their wealth on their terms. At the close of 1983, McDonald's announced it would provide more than $108 million in contracts to black insurance firms. The black insurance business—which grew from black mutual aid societies established as early as the nineteenth century—was far from its apex in the 1980s. Black insurance companies began to decline in the 1960s, when larger companies were able to expand their already dominant role among black consumers.[45] As part of the McDonald's agreement, black-owned companies—Atlanta Life Insurance Company, Los Angeles's Golden State Mutual Life, the North Carolina Mutual company in Raleigh, and the Chicago Metropolitan Mutual Assurance Company—would capture what accounted for 17.5% of McDonald's life insurance business. Yet, as in many matters involving the expansion of black opportunity, there were white powerbrokers involved. This scheme was facilitated by recommendations from insurance giant Travelers Insurance, which McDonald's contacted for the suggestions.[46] These may have been preventive steps for McDonald's as they saw other companies become more vulnerable to PUSH boycotts, especially in major actions against the beer industry.

McDonald's knew it had to remain vigilant after Operation PUSH launched a national boycott of Anheuser-Busch in the fall of 1982. Operation PUSH was reshaping the landscape of boycotts and would influence how the NAACP proceeded in the Griffis matter. In a feat of expertly synchronized organizing, thirty-three PUSH partners announced plans of the beer boycott on the afternoon of September 4. PUSH emphasized that despite the beer company's popularity in the black alcohol-buying market, Anheuser-Busch had only one black-owned distributor, only 2% of its subsidiaries were black, and blacks were often trapped in the lowest-rung jobs in the company. Company head August A. Busch III refused to meet with Jackson about the issue, and Jackson claimed that Anheuser-Busch not only tried to discredit him and his efforts, but offered support to other black organizations as a way to tamp down on the growth of the boycott.[47] The boycott continued into 1983, and PUSH attracted the support of the National Association of Black Promoters, who were also concerned about the lack of black contractors hired to support the popular Bud Fest concert series, which was favored by black audiences with musical headliners Frankie

Beverly, Kool & the Gang, and Ashford & Simpson. The promoters association sought a negotiation with Anheuser-Busch years before the boycott but were unhappy with Anheuser-Busch's offer, which they described as a "sharecropping or 'colonial' arrangement." The events, PUSH claimed, "attract a significant Black audience, using a large number of Black acts," but shut out black contractors and vendors from the festivals. There were no excuses for the poor record of black hiring, considering the festivals were hosted at venues like the Forum in Inglewood, California, and the Omni in Atlanta. Initially, in Jackson's signature style, he called on blacks to participate in a boycott by declaring, "Bud is a dud, don't drink those suds."[48] Busch, the maker of the "dud" beer, realized that Jackson's rhyming directives like "Dump Those Suds in the Mud" and "Demonstration without Hesitation" were persuasive, and it settled with PUSH a year after the first call to boycott.[49] The settlement carried promises to hire blacks and Latinos at rates that would yield employment statistics inside the company that matched the nation's population percentages. The beer producer also agreed to earmark $23 million in supplier contracts for minority-owned businesses, another $10 million to construction companies, and $8 million in business with advertising firms, such as Burrell Communications. In an attempt to infuse capital into the black banks that began disappearing over the preceding decades, Anheuser-Busch devoted $8 million to certificates of deposit and payroll checks. They also looked to recruit more distributors of color to add to the existing six in their network of hundreds.[50]

Operation PUSH was unabashed in its belief that black power was a matter of politics and the purse. At a 1983 commemoration of King's death, Jackson repeated the well-worn phrase at a rally in Anderson, Indiana: "We have our civil rights, now we're fighting for our silver rights." Jackson continued, "We're not fighting for social generosity, we're not marching for welfare, we're marching for jobs."[51] In the 1980s, even a King disciple like Jackson saw social welfare as an enemy, rather than a friend, to the poor. In the span of a few days, Jackson could be found pontificating to white Republicans about breaking bread with black voters, chastising black nationalists to disavow themselves of "ghetto habits" in order to succeed, and pitching a corporate reparations plan to business executives.[52] Regardless of the audience, Jackson's message about economics castigated companies for failing to do right by black America in the form of jobs and wealth-building opportunities, while also blaming black Americans for failing to capitalize on few jobs and even fewer routes to joining the ownership class. The black capitalists of the 1980s linked the inability of blacks to connect civil rights with the pursuit of silver rights to their own pathological failings, even as they sought structural redress from businesses in the form of employment and economic development. This befuddling mix of rhetoric that simultaneously blamed victims and oppressors melded into a vague call for more black-owned businesses and for blacks to ally with the private sector, with no regards to the negative implications of seeking relief in structures built on inequality. While the advice was sometimes confusing, the financial stakes were crystal-clear. Over the course of a decade, PUSH was able to receive corporate donations and consultation fees that exceeded $15 million. The money that flowed into PUSH supported community-based programming for blacks, as well as buttress the organization and its leadership's influence.

The NAACP was taking notes. In early April of 1984, the Los Angeles NAACP ended a successful five-day boycott of the Coors Brewing Company after gaining concessions on minority hiring. The Coors action, spurred by racist remarks made by sales division head Peter Coors about the transatlantic slave trade being a cosmic favor to blacks, yielded promises for minority hiring and contracting.[53] Years of cultivating internal black talent and support for the NBMOA did not, and could not, provide cover for McDonald's. Black organizations, due in large part to Jackson's example, reimagined what a community demand looked like. The community was not the customer or the barber around the corner who may want to one day have a franchise. The community meant the professionals and professional societies with the talents, skills, and social capital to be included in the wealth that was being made off the backs of working and middle-income people. The franchise dispute highlighted that blacks at every rung of society contended with some form of exclusion and racial barrier to achievement and self-sufficiency. But as the boycott became an extension of securing business for well-positioned blacks, the poor and struggling received programs and coupons instead of substantive work and more choices.

* * *

In May of 1984, a month after the operators' meeting boycott, the NAACP turned up the heat with a message to black Los Angeles via the pages of the *Sentinel*. "You Need to Know!!! The McDonald's Corporation has no respect for Los Angeles Mayor Tom Bradley, the NAACP, or the black community!"[54] At a meeting regarding McDonald's "hiring, franchising and purchasing policies, claims which spoke of overt racial discrimination," McDonald's vice president Richard Starmann, probably cognizant of the Coors concessions, held his ground and he told the NAACP, "We'll be happy to discuss anything . . . but we're not in any way conducting negotiations or bargaining with them."[55] The advertisement made clear that the NAACP would accept nothing less than *negotiations and bargaining*. The ad continued: "The McDonald's Corporation owes the black community through the NAACP a total commitment to reinvest a Fair Share of the $1.6 billion Black people spend on their products to show the proper respect to an organization which has spent over 75 years fighting for full and equal rights for all Americans."[56] The rules and terms of engagement were now in the hands of the NAACP and their vision of economic progress— reinvestment through corporate employment, promotion, and contracts—was going to dictate any further conversation. The presenting issue was expanding black franchising, but focusing on white-collar employment and contracting was grafted onto the call to hold McDonald's accountable to black communities.

By the time a Los Angeles jury finally heard *McDonald's Corp. v. Griffis* in 1984, the melee over burgers had shifted. The NAACP was poised to initiate another action if necessary, and McDonald's abandoned its defensive stance in the charges of franchise redlining.

Instead, spokespeople took a laudatory tone about the special gifts that black franchise owners brought to service counters and drive-thru windows in predominately black neighborhoods. McDonald's gushed about the "exceptional skill of black franchisees" and claimed that they enlisted their talents because it "was a matter of good business" to cultivate an affinity between owners and communities. One spokesperson explained, "The fact that problems of operating certain locations in the inner-city, predominately black areas, require a person with particular abilities and that persons having these abilities have, in many instances, been black, involves no act of racial discrimination."[57] Black franchising began because of white hesitancy in doing business in black neighborhoods, a fact that McDonald's openly discussed in the late 1960s and 1970s. In 1984, McDonald's presented the issue of blacks in black communities as both a concerted effort to respect racial solidarity, and a coincidental fact that blacks tend to have the ability to do business well in black areas. Although the logic wasn't the most cohesive, McDonald's may have believed that it was in their best interest for the suit to resolve itself quickly before Griffis gave another one of his press interviews. Griffis and McDonald's eventually settled the lawsuit in 1985.[58] McDonald's paid Griffis $4.7 million in the settlement, but they stressed that the payment was unrelated to charges of racial discrimination. A McDonald's attorney stated that they had simply offered to "buy back Mr. Griffis's four restaurants." He added that Griffis was not given "15 cents for those bogus racial discrimination claims."[59] Griffis collected his millions and continued in the restaurant business. In 1987, the Griffis family opened a small soul food chain named Chicken Charlie, which specialized in "truly down home style fried chicken." Griffis used his experiences with McDonald's to convince black customers to support a "real" black-owned business. "We've eaten everybody else's food for centuries; indeed, our food is a composite of other ethnic dishes, so why not a chain featuring the improved version of soul?" Griffis rehearsed arguments that echoed the sometime castigating tones of other black capitalism missives suggesting that buying black was a way of expressing racial authenticity and solidarity. They argued that to not buy black was to betray one's people. Griffis argued, "Every other racial extraction has pride in their heritage and cultural background that includes their food, so why not Black Americans?"[60]

The NAACP was also asking McDonald's "Why not black Americans?" after they settled with Griffis. Fair Share, however, could never address or repair the foundational problems that triggered McDonald's push for black franchising in the first place, including the loss of capital into and within inner cities and commercial white flight, and it did not guarantee employment for more black, low-wage workers. To be sure, the NAACP and its legal branch did not abandon housing, education, and employment justice broadly, but their pivot toward corporations did mean that fewer resources were available to address the economic calamities concentrated in black America. The NAACP became a major beneficiary of lucrative financial sponsorships from McDonald's corporate coffers. Franchise ownership could not and would not effectively expand the power of African Americans within McDonald's, so the Fair Share and hiring approaches to equity would provide another means of turning the tide, if only a bit. While wages and conditions were not focal point issues about people of color and the fast food giant, the distribution of contracts was the closest to a trickling down of any economic benefit from the wealthy, franchisee elite to communities.

Even with Griffis out of the picture, the organization still believed that their relatively small boycott could yield large returns. The issue of franchisee redlining was never sufficiently addressed, but the NAACP did not need Griffis's claims to leverage a Fair Share plan with McDonald's, having already tested the waters with executives in meetings for months. Weeks after the Griffis case was settled, the national NAACP announced a historic agreement with McDonald's that "reaffirmed a commitment to economic development for blacks and other minorities." Bob Beavers, then McDonald's only black senior vice president, called the five-year agreement "good business and . . . good corporate citizenship." McDonald's promised to "employ the same percentage of minorities and females as the nation's workforce, increase the number of minority suppliers, strengthen its minority insurance program, and hire more minority construction companies."[61] The plan included a provision that McDonald's would "establish 100 new black-owned restaurants" over a four-year period, hire more black managers, and offer more contracts to black businesses—from food suppliers to attorneys.

With an estimated $100 million worth of business on the table, the Los Angeles chapter wanted to make sure that some of those dollars returned home where the campaign began. The NAACP chapter estimated that 10 percent of the contracts and new business generated from the agreement would come to Los Angeles and offered to help McDonald's identify potential black contractors and franchisees.[62] The McDonald's victory represented a key moment in how the franchise operated among African-American communities across a broad spectrum—from the low-income diners who frequented the restaurant multiple times a week to black businesspeople to civil rights establishment leaders. The campaigns deconstructed the layered and enmeshed ways community resources were made available or limited due to race, and it determined what was a "fair share."

In the late 1980s and into the 1990s, the black franchise community multiplied throughout Southern California, and the legacy of the Griffis boycott allowed for more franchisees of color to enter the McDonald's System and black professionals to blaze trails in the McDonald's headquarters. When the NBMOA met in Long Beach in 1989 for its annual convention, executive board members emphasized that the franchisee was a leader in the issue of opening opportunities for black professionals. NBMOA president Kendrick Ross proclaimed that their "restaurants provide business opportunities for numerous minority suppliers, as well as meaningful jobs and career options in the food service industry for Black youth." Like Herman Petty's donation of his profits to Martin Luther King Jr.'s right-hand man twenty years earlier, Ross's speech placed McDonald's franchising squarely in the history of black freedom movements. "After years of marching, protesting and civil rights gains, the next step for many adults is to enter into the economic mainstream." Ross reflected that with 220 black franchise owners nationwide, the uptick in the black franchisee corps proved "that dreams come true."[63] Not all dreams are found at the end of a lawsuit or part of a Fair Share plan. But, in the 1980s, the expansion of black franchising further placed businesses in the position of not only setting the agenda for individuals in industry, but also setting the priorities of black civil rights organizations.

Silver rights were winning. Black unemployment and poverty in the 1980s were still pervasive reminders of how little had changed since the sweeping legal changes of the 1960s, so fast food may have seemed like a sensible industry to appeal to for the economic opportunities that the government did not care to support. It is difficult to fault organizations like the NAACP and Operation PUSH entirely for being lured by the financial promises of the fast food industry, especially if their respective leaders believed that concessions were the only way to keep civil rights struggles alive. Constrained choices yield constrained possibilities. Yet, it may be also possible that considering the power of the boycott in areas in which fast food was so wildly popular, the NAACP could have brought corporations to the negotiation table with other demands, more in line with the people the organization struggled to reach in the 1970s and '80s. The same strategy of consumer abstinence and business disruption could have been used for the purpose of organizing workers to raise wages, improve scheduling practices, or provide workers with child care facilities or transportation subsidies. Maybe the fast food industry could have bent under the pressure of an Operation PUSH call for health care rights alongside silver rights? Would today's urban landscape have been different if the Griffis case had not only exposed the discrimination franchisees experienced, but also the extent to which black and brown taxpayers subsidized his operations and turned consumer attention on the federal government's corporate welfare to the inner city? It is easy to speculate what could have happened in this moment and others. As the 1990s approached, civil rights organizations, the federal government, and everyday people would continue to turn to the fast food industry to deliver on the very thing it could never prepare, sell, market, or deliver—justice.

CHAPTER SEVEN

The Miracle of the Golden Arches

After the 1992 Los Angeles riots, McDonald's claimed that its restaurants in the epicenter of the violence remained untouched because of the company's deep connection with black consumers. John T. Barr / Getty Images.

Getting back to normal was going to take a while. Los Angeles had been on fire for five days. On April 29, 1992, a not-guilty verdict had been delivered in the Rodney King police brutality case. As it had been in other moments in years past and in places near and far from Los Angeles, the denial of justice for a black person beaten by the police ignited an uprising. The fury was not only about the King decision. A week earlier, a California Court of Appeals upheld the sentence of no jail time for a Korean convenience store owner who shot and killed black teenager Latasha Harlins. These two moments aggravated the same racial and economic tensions that boiled over in Watts in 1965. Over the course of five days, the city endured at least 58 deaths, 2,400 injuries, and property damage totaling a billion dollars.[1] Media from all over the world swarmed Los Angeles. Each night, photographers risked their safety on the streets to capture scenes of pharmacies and convenience stores on fire. Reporters in helicopters accustomed to covering the snail's pace traffic of Southern California's freeways were suddenly capturing shopkeepers armed with handguns and semiautomatic weapons, hell-bent on protecting their stores. At press conferences held after the trial's conclusion was made public, journalists asked why police officials were so lax in dispatching assistance to the heart of the crisis zone, South Los Angeles. On May 4, Mayor Tom Bradley took the first step toward normalcy when he lifted a citywide curfew. After firefighters extinguished the flames of burning buildings, cleanup crews cleared glass and debris off the streets, and shop owners tallied what had been lost and damaged, Los Angeles's most difficult work was still ahead. What could be learned from this latest uprising? Was there some way to prevent it from happening again? Did Los Angeles really want to return to normal?

Twenty-seven years of hindsight hadn't changed much in the approach to solving the American dilemma of racism; businesses were expected to save the day, again. Although the King beating raised serious concerns about racial violence and the Los Angeles Police Department, businesses also occupied the center of the story of what went awry when the chaos broke. The Korean-owned supermarket—like the one where Harlins was shot and killed because store owner Soon Ja Du saw a bottle of orange juice in the girl's backpack and did not see the money in her hands as she approached the checkout counter—represented the life-or-death tensions in the multiethnic inner city. News pundits provided commentary over live footage of looters carrying everything from loafers to portable CD players to gallons of milk out of vandalized stores. When Los Angeles finally quieted down, some op-eds in national newspapers and talking heads on cable news programs seemed to mourn the loss of commerce more than the loss of life. On that fragile Monday the curfew ended, when Los Angeles was to ready itself for healing and rebuilding, the city looked to business to lead the effort to get back on track. In future retellings of how Los Angeles made it through the upheaval, McDonald's would emerge as one of the strongest leaders throughout. When a school couldn't get its lunch shipments delivered, black franchisee Harold Patrick donated Happy Meals. When fatigued National Guardsmen and police officers who had been dispatched to the crisis at the height of the unrest needed something to eat, they could take their meal vouchers to McDonald's.[2] When business interests needed to make a case for their role in Los Angeles's recovery, they also looked to McDonald's.

McDonald's provided no comment about state-sanctioned violence or the recklessness of the Los Angeles Police Department, but it had plenty to say about the uprising. McDonald's proudly proclaimed that their South Los Angeles restaurants were spared the ire of the angriest and most disaffected Americans who took to the streets that spring. The fast food chain declared itself inoculated from the virus of urban anger and suggested that its vaccine was injected after the Holy Week uprising in 1968. A business magazine suggested that McDonald's survival was "the vindication of enlightened social policies begun more than three decades ago." McDonald's CEO Edward Rensi theorized: "Our businesses [in Los Angeles] are owned by African-American entrepreneurs who hired African-American managers who hired African-American employees who served everybody in the community." Rensi's claims were the basis of a *Financial Week* article, which quoted Leighton Hull, a black franchisee from Lynwood, a town north of Compton. Hull posited that McDonald's "involvement in the neighborhoods it serves" was a defense mechanism tested but not pierced by the Los Angeles rebellion. *Financial Week* mused, "It has evolved, at least in the inner cities, as a plan for peaceful and prosperous coexistence between the corporation and its occasionally fractious environment."[3] In the same ways that the spray-painting of SOUL BROTHER or SOUL BUSINESS on the exterior windows of businesses was considered a prophylactic at the height of the 1960s uprisings, the declaration that a business was black-owned was believed to be a survival strategy during the Los Angeles crisis. In addition to this measure, historian Brenda Stevenson found that "some Korean shop owners who were known to have employed blacks found themselves immune from attack or were protected by the employees who lived in the neighborhood."[4] After more than two decades, Ronald McDonald had finally become a naturalized citizen of black America.

Whether McDonald's was protected due to trust, good luck, or the efforts of police to protect its restaurants is hard to assess. There is little mention of activity near McDonald's restaurants in the official accounting of the uprising by the Los Angeles Webster Commission, the body assembled to study what went wrong in the lead-up to and during the event. From the existing records, it is difficult to corroborate Rensi's claim. In some reports, McDonald's only suffered minor damage and was able to reopen quickly. In other tellings, the restaurant was protected by police, community members, and employees. The *Orange County Register* reported that the McDonald's at 18th Street and Western Avenue was spared the ruinous fate of neighboring "restaurants and a supermarket, which was cleaned out by looters," including a Winchell's Donut House and a J. J. Newberry's discount store. The location was operated by African-American franchisee Harold Patrick beginning in 1983, and he reasoned that he was saved because the staff were "close with our customers." "We know them." He told the *Minneapolis Star Tribune* that his patrons saved the day. "Our customers stood outside and talked to those from outside the neighborhood . . . they told them this is their restaurant."[5] He may have also benefited from the National Guardsmen dispatched to the area on the afternoon of April 30.[6] Perhaps in gratitude or out of fear, Patrick later planned to create a police substation inside the restaurant. The *Orlando Sun-Sentinel* published a picture of a

McDonald's with the words BLACK OWNED spray-painted on the window.[7] Another McDonald's location hung a perhaps redundant sign: DUE TO CURRENT PROBLEMS, WE ARE CLOSED.[8] *Time* magazine reported that McDonald's "suffered the least damage," with the loss of a few windows, but "Burger Kings and Taco Bells in the same neighborhood took it on the chin." A franchisee figured that the community believed that "these are the good guys; let's not do this to them."[9] In a National Black McDonald's Operators Association video, franchisee Larry Tripplett reiterated his version of what happened in Los Angeles:

> When they had the Rodney King incident, one of my stores is African American . . . I was there that evening, and this is the Bay Area, not Los Angeles, they burned down . . . and trashed the Kentucky Fried Chicken, it's out of business now, they trashed a post office, they burned down a market . . . My store was open, did not get touched, had nothing but high volume sales that day. Now that was because . . . we had given back to the community, we knew everybody in the community, and quite frankly, that community to this day is very proud of this McDonald's . . .[10]

Whether or not this moment for McDonald's—this Miracle of the Golden Arches—is a fact or a convenient truth is unimportant. That it could be believed and that McDonald's suggested that it was so familiar, important, and precious to communities that had been distanced from institutions, equity, and justice speaks volumes about a process that started decades earlier. McDonald's was a citizen of black Los Angeles, and despite the calamity of 1992, it wasn't going anywhere. The testimonies about the Miracle of the Golden Arches revealed how constrained choices can lead to forgetting, on the local and national level, about the other kinds of conflicts that surrounded all-American meals. The Los Angeles uprising's emergence almost twenty-five years after King's assassination made some reflective about what, if anything, had actually changed over two and a half decades of continued struggle. More blacks were in elected office. Colleges and universities were starting to see the effects of affirmative action policies that not only diversified student bodies, but also brought well-trained doctors, lawyers, and educators in service to underresourced communities. If fast food franchising was a metric for progress, franchisees were expanding their small empires, donating vast sums of money, and continuing to employ a large swath of black America. But honest accounting cannot allow the most positive stories to hold the most weight, and the issues of continued racial discrimination, poverty, health disparities, and unemployment continued to torment black America. A quarter of a century after the entry of blacks into franchising, the problems of the 1960s continued to plague inner-city America.

While the fast food industry had created growth opportunities for individual franchisees and corporate executives, the success of a few black elites had little impact on the life of those languishing in the very communities that housed and staffed their businesses. As the language of black capitalism transformed into the rhetoric of black empowerment, the fast food industry made more aggressive promises to help rebuild the inner city. No longer pursuing the piecemeal recruitment efforts of the 1960s and 1970s, the Fair Share and voluntary affirmative action agreements of the 1980s and early 1990s pursued corporations with as much gusto as movement activists of the past. Fast food franchises sought powerful holding companies and partnerships to open their restaurants in multiple locations and territories to capture the black dollars that were still up for grabs, as supermarkets and large retailers still ignored pockets of working-class and poor black America. This transitional period was grounded in the certainty that fast food was an accepted and welcomed presence in black communities. Franchisees of color, in their own self-evaluation and in the eyes of government lenders, the hearts of chambers of commerce, and the minds of probusiness politicians, could be trusted to not only feed black America, but also lead black America. For decades, black publications had celebrated franchisees for massing sizable assets and donating generously to black causes, while also staying connected to poor and working-class blacks through their employees, customers, and beneficiaries of their community outreach. After the

Miracle of the Golden Arches was widely distributed in the press, an audience of white business consultants, government aides, and philanthropists learned about the multiple roles that black franchisees played in their communities. So, they thought, more franchises could solve more complex problems.

Initiating conversations about what black America has to do to get better has always been a popular American pastime. Unlike the questions about black opportunity and black economic independence in the previous decades, the conversation in the 1990s did not wonder about the potential of black franchising. The decade's musings on what black America needed began with a sense of certainty that black franchises were viable solutions, it was only a matter of how many and how fast they could open.

Two black franchisees whose businesses were built in the period before and after the Los Angeles uprising capture the transition in franchising from the late 1980s to the 1990s. Ted Holmes's Chicken George was one of the last black franchises that was baptized by the spirit of black capitalism in the 1960s and survived to see the late 1980s. Blacks would establish franchises after the last Chicken George closed its doors, but the ways that Holmes's restaurant venture reshaped the fried chicken market is illustrative of why it was difficult for black capitalism's boosters to implement their own advice after the major fast food companies saturated inner-city markets with black-franchised outlets that could make a case to consumers who wanted to "buy black." Holmes's Baltimore-based Chicken George franchise modeled itself in the ways of Champ-Burger and Mahalia's Glori-Fried in its claim to be authentically black. It was so genuine that it took its name from *Roots*, the book and film fictionalization of author Alex Haley's genealogy. Chicken George's early success pushed major fast food restaurants to think about its appeal to African Americans, and then they were able to use their massive resources to overtake Chicken George.

After Holmes's Chicken George faded into obscurity, La-Van Hawkins became the talk of the fast-food world with aggressive franchising deals that demonstrated the ways that access to franchises provided vast amounts of power to few people in urban

America. Hawkins's story also explains how the policies of the 1990s, as well as the racial tensions of the period, reinforced hope that fast food would pave the way forward for black communities. Hawkins, the P. T. Barnum of black empowerment, was a larger-than-life black franchisee who peddled everything from burgers to chicken to pizza. Supported by a plethora of Fair Share–style initiatives and federal assistance, Hawkins's forays into D.C., Philadelphia, and Detroit epitomized how franchises sought to claim every commercial inch of the food landscape. Hawkins, who had entanglements with a number of major companies, and created his own franchise concepts, provides a cautionary tale about the limits of black capitalism as a sustainable economic investment strategy and pathway to racial reconciliation. In both instances, Hawkins's enterprises and Chicken George illustrated how fast food no longer relied on small-scale franchisees to make their restaurants black, and in the ongoing use of franchises to equalize racial opportunity, black franchisees continued to find themselves at the margins.

Ted Holmes, a Congress of Racial Equality alum from York, Pennsylvania, first entered business in 1969, when he founded a personnel services company. Holmes was well aware of the opportunities available from the Office of Minority Business Enterprise and Small Business Administration, and after handling government contracts, he realized the lucrative nature of food service agreements.[11] Holmes found the post–King-uprising climate for business rife with tokenism, and despite invitations to apply for lucrative financial grants, he did not know if the black capitalism moment was making much of a difference. When asked if segregation was a good thing for black business, he answered, "Yes, but I would qualify that by saying that the word 'segregation' may be a little harsh. I think 'community-minded' might be a better term. There were, all across this country, flourishing black shopping areas prior to desegregation laws in the '50s and '60s. Once we started shopping everywhere those businesses just melted away."[12] In the post–Civil Rights Act world, the question of segregation and integration weighed heavily on black consumers and business owners. If segregation stalled black progress, what did integration do to black communities? In trying to resolve the question, black businesses often overemphasized their authentic blackness, and nothing screamed authenticity like Alex Haley's *Roots*.[13] Chicken George, the restaurant, debuted in 1979 and capitalized on the popularity of the character Chicken George from the 1976 book and the television miniseries that premiered the next year. Portrayed by actor Ben Vereen, Chicken George was the clever grandson of Haley's fictitious patriarch Kunta Kinte. George gets his name after participating in the cockfighting racket on his master's plantation. Costumed with a feathered bowler hat and a green scarf, George's charisma grants him an opportunity to travel to England, secure his freedom, and return to the states on the eve of the Civil War. The eight-part series drew an average of 32 million viewers per evening, and for years after its airing, Haley's representation of black familial bonds and connections to Africa resonated with black America. McDonald's even sponsored a sweepstakes in which winners could travel to West Africa and meet members of the Haley family. Curiously, Haley and broadcaster ABC held no trademark on the name Chicken George, and Holmes cleverly used the moniker to squeeze himself into the fast food chicken market.

As Holmes entered franchising, he studied up on why other black-owned enterprises failed, and he believed that a lack of capital held black people back. He set the restaurant's entry fee at $25,000, a more accessible amount for black businesspeople. Soon he was able to sell restaurants in more than a dozen locations. The entry fee wasn't the only distinction for the restaurant; unlike Mahalia's and ChampBurger, which drew mixed reviews for the quality of its food, Chicken George was known for its outstanding fare. In a feature on the business, the *Baltimore Sun* wrote:

> Unlike other fast-food operators, Chicken George's served up its spicy chicken with the appetites and pocketbooks of middle-class blacks in mind. In an industry conspicuously lacking in minority ownership, this company established itself—setting sales records unequaled by the industry at large—by going to the roots of the black community.[14]

Holmes was particularly proud of his ability to make Chicken George authentic. "No one had collard greens in the fast-food concept . . . Popeyes, that had biscuits and rice, but that was out of the Louisiana experience." Chicken George didn't take its cues from Popeyes, and the restaurant was not afraid of offending the tastes of nonblack consumers.[15] By opening its first location at the Mondawmin Mall, which then served a mostly middle-class area of Baltimore, Holmes prepared and priced his foods for a slightly more discriminating consumer. Market segmentation among racial lines was proving a smart strategy for major retailers and companies in the 1970s, but the secondary segmentation of blacks across class lines was still emerging as a viable avenue to maximize profits. While other chains imagined their black consumers as mostly low-income even as their advertisements signaled their desire to depict black, middle-class life, Chicken George believed it could capture a slightly more affluent market. In its franchise recruitment materials, Chicken George talked about a desire to appeal to the "untapped market" and believed that "the black community was just waiting for a business that wouldn't take them, their tastes or their dollars for granted."[16]

In the model of the traditional black franchises, Chicken George was also seen as a sound investment for community programs. In Camden, New Jersey, the Black People's Unity Movement—a one-time radical collective—had incorporated into a community development group, BPUM Impact Corp., which tried its hand at a Chicken George franchise.[17] Chicken George was a runaway hit. Within four years of opening, it was number 64 on *Black Enterprise*'s annual list of black-owned businesses, with a gross of $13 million.[18] Although Holmes struggled with self-promotion and granting media interviews for the business, the company eventually hired black advertising firm Lockhart & Pettus to create a campaign for them from their new Atlanta branch, and they called upon Image Advertising in Chicago to develop ads in 1984.[19] In the winter of 1983, a Houston real estate development team announced plans to develop up to 600 locations in Texas, Oklahoma, Louisiana, and New Mexico, with a plan for the Chicken George headquarters to add another 300 franchises.[20]

Chicken George's low-budget television commercials captured diners eating their products inside a restaurant and declaring the chicken better than a wife's and a mother's recipe. The tagline of the campaign, "Say good bye to ho hum chicken, say hello to Chicken George" was sung by a throaty blues singer and depicted an interracial customer base. With little money spent on advertising and only eight locations in the 1980s, Chicken George's success was unprecedented for a new restaurant franchise. With average sales per outlet exceeding a million dollars, Chicken George was even able to put a nearby Popeyes restaurant out of business, and a Kentucky Fried Chicken representative conceded that the business was like "a house on fire," with its long line of customers and repeat business. Chicken Georges in Baltimore and Philadelphia lured larger and better-financed Popeyes and Kentucky Fried Chicken to compete in the market more aggressively. With so many failures in the franchise market, Chicken George's resilience shocked the major chicken outlets in the Northeast. Kentucky Fried Chicken, which had yet to make a splash in the region, decided to commit to an extensive market penetration strategy. They began a plan to enter Baltimore and its suburbs with sixty new restaurants over a four-year period between 1984 and 1988.[21]

Chicken George may have had authenticity and flavor on its side, but it could not compete in terms of capital. While its franchise expansion plan was hampered by a lack of headquarters leadership and by sparsely supported franchisees, its competitors could pour more resources into developing products and could bear the losses on failed stores. Chicken George's business model, a news article reported, collapsed when "the competition was realizing the black community is an entity and was going after them with coupons, which effectively lowered the price of their product to the consumer."[22] When the company started to waver due to stronger competition and Big Chicken's ability to provide more product discounts, the founder became more withdrawn from Chicken George and its processes. Few could get ahold of Holmes, who had turned his attention overseas. Holmes befriended African businessmen, who were determining how to leverage "American corporate assets in South Africa to pass on to black entrepreneurs in that country."[23] Holmes had moved on.

The void left by Chicken George was filled by an amended Kentucky Fried Chicken chain that targeted inner-city locations. In the early 1990s, Kentucky Fried Chicken unveiled twenty-seven "Neighborhood" stores, which appears to have been a code for "black." Diners could decide among the Colonel's traditional recipe chicken and biscuits or "red beans and rice, mean greens, macaroni and cheese," and finish off lunch or dinner with southern favorites "peach cobbler or sweet potato pie." In Detroit, the newly renamed KFC presented restaurants that offered the locally made Mr. FoFo's sweet potato pie. A press release explained that the "new crew uniforms" would include African kufis (hats) and "kente cloth–accented dashikis." KFC explained, "The uniforms evoke the proud heritage of African-Americans to whom Neighborhood KFCs are targeted." While eating Honey BBQ Wings or Hot 'n Spicy Chicken in Baltimore, Atlanta, Boston, Chicago, New York, Detroit, and Philadelphia, customers could listen to "tunes likely to be found on local urban radio stations."[24] The greens were test-marketed in the early 1980s, and some speculated it was a response to the popularity of Chicken George's collards side dish.[25] KFC had traditionally tested well with black consumers, but the Neighborhood concept was the most explicit adoption of foods and reconfiguring of the in-store dining experience in the direction of black customers. Had Holmes decided to use his experiences in business to simply franchise one of Chicken George's competitors, his story may have ended much differently.

In 1986, after filing bankruptcy, Holmes's interest in franchising collapsed and he was now invested in using his strengths in the fight against apartheid. He was still willing to share the hard lessons he learned after the end of Chicken George, a cautionary tale about businesses' missteps for the next generation of entrepreneurs.[26] Chicken George, and Holmes's experiment, could not survive the outgrowths of the very movement, black capitalism, that brought him to the food business. Holmes retreated from the public eye, and another black businessman's attempt to reopen

Chicken George in Baltimore failed. By the 1990s, the fast food industry realized how to be attentive to black consumer preferences and present in black communities, and by relying on franchisees to assume the liabilities of the risky restaurant business, they could stay the course when upstart competitors challenged their positions. In the fast food franchise world, making a good product or simply being black-owned was not enough. The name of the fast food game was capital, and without it, a new restaurant could disappear as quickly as a two-piece chicken meal.

* * *

"Come on La-Van!"

A voiceover's soulful command—a cross between Anita Baker and Gladys Knight—introduced the star of the television commercial: the one and only La-Van Hawkins. "You got to twist and dip," the voice crooned. An all-female dance team comprised of uniformed Pizza Hut employees began a choreographed number. "My new twisted crust pizza is lavish," said the Pizza Hut franchisee, a tall, broad man outfitted with an apron and dark-rimmed glasses. Hawkins, much larger than the dancers and the background performers jamming to the Pizza Hut song, awkwardly bounced to the song. As the identified creator of this innovation that married a pizza with several servings of breadsticks, Hawkins looked straight into the camera and provided a bizarre description of the new dish as both "luscious" and "lusty," in addition to being "crusty." Hawkins's voice boomed: "It's pizza and breadsticks in one hardworking bite!" Throughout the 1990s and early 2000s, Hawkins was also hard at work, having spent the better part of nearly two decades inking deal after deal to franchise hundreds of inner-city fast food restaurants in succession and concurrently.[27] Detroiters in the 1990s craving a Whopper, carrying out a Twisted Crust Pizza, or even dining on a plate of haute-cuisine chicken and waffles, knew Hawkins, fast food's greatest hypeman.

Hawkins's persona and approach was an amalgam of all the black business rhetoric from the late 1960s up to the 2000s; his recipe for success included a bootstraps-heavy personal narrative, a charismatic presence in urban centers, and friends in high places with access to investment dollars. Hawkins moved from city to city, from franchise to franchise, offering some of the most blighted black and brown corners of America unparalleled opportunities for jobs and advancement in the franchise system. When he would exit those same cities after complications with his businesses emerged, he often left behind broken promises and bad debts. Somehow, although his enterprises often fell short, he managed to find a way to acquire more franchise opportunities. The revival of the myth that black businesses could deliver the black poor from economic isolation had no better representative than Hawkins. Hawkins's run with and through the fast food industry exemplified the limits of fast food as an answer to complex social problems.

A striking man more than six feet tall, Hawkins had a compelling, albeit sometimes hard-to-corroborate rags-to-riches story that began with a childhood in poverty. Hawkins recounted that his father died when he was in high school, compelling him to drop out of private school and go to work to support his mother. The mix of youthful independence and a paycheck may have contributed to his troubled adolescence in a Chicago street gang, and he claimed that he developed a costly drug addiction before his sixteenth birthday. Hawkins credited his working at an uncle's McDonald's franchise as salvific, giving him the requisite knowledge of the industry that would change his life. Determined to make something of himself, Hawkins left behind the vagaries of street life and immersed himself in the whirlwind of fast food. His first stop was Kentucky Fried Chicken, where he rose through the ranks to work with the franchise on its minority recruitment efforts. Kentucky Fried Chicken had long boasted its partnership with All-Pro Chicken founder Brady Keys, who sold his franchise to Kentucky Fried Chicken and acquired his own four locations in 1970.[28] In the late 1980s, Hawkins departed Kentucky Fried Chicken to enter franchising himself. He was part of a financial development group, contracted to build a dozen Bojangles' Famous Chicken 'n Biscuits restaurants in the Northeast. Many of the outlets of the North Carolina–based chicken franchise went under, but Hawkins exited Bojangles without any major financial losses. He then returned to his roots: burgers.[29]

Between 1991 and 1996, Hawkins introduced Checkers on the East Coast, with locations in Washington, D.C., Baltimore, and Philadelphia. Checkers was a relative newcomer to the fast food family system, and its merger with Rally's, founded a year earlier in 1985, brought the drive-thru concept to cities on both coasts and points in the middle. Hawkins's deal with Checkers was one of the first major moves for the La-Van Hawkins Inner City Foods company. For his goal of making black millionaires via franchising, Hawkins was lauded in the press for establishing Checkers in some of the most economically devastated communities and providing well-paying jobs to local youth. He boasted to *Nation's Restaurant News*: "I'm in the unique position to take people off welfare, give them job training, and educate and motivate them."[30] Taking people off of welfare was an oft-repeated goal of CEOs and politicians. President Bill Clinton's historic Personal Responsibility and Work Opportunity Reconciliation Act of 1996 limited the length of time a person could receive state-funded public assistance and often required workforce participation to receive benefits. This shift funneled many former aid recipients into fast food and other service sector jobs.[31] These efforts definitely employed people, but education and motivation may have been scarce.

Hawkins's promises were in the same vein of the black franchisees who converted gang members into crew members in the early 1970s and brought much-needed jobs to Chicago, Detroit, and Los Angeles after the uprisings of the 1960s. But job creation in black communities in the 1990s was contending with conditions even more vexing than those of 1968. New fast food restaurants were settling in and around neighborhoods devastated by the introduction of crack cocaine into the urban drug market and greater efforts to police and incarcerate blacks in an ongoing War on Drugs. The war created casualties in black America.[32] The urgency of providing relief to neighborhoods eviscerated by decades of poverty may have inspired so much hope and relief that Hawkins's promises did not meet scrutiny from the private investors, public officials, and community partners who entrusted Hawkins with so many millions and millions of dollars.

While most cities rolled out the red carpet for Hawkins's Checkers, Hawkins's return to Philadelphia was not welcomed. Fresh memories of the abandoned Bojangles experiment from the 1980s summoned more fury than fanfare. When locals learned that Hawkins had leased a location (complete with a sign that alerted: "Another La-Van Hawkins Checkers Coming Soon") at the intersection of Broad and Girard Streets, the community made its feelings clear. Members of the Girard and Broad Business Association repeated some of the concerns voiced by Ogontz decades earlier. In addition to the usual worries about saturation and public safety, Hawkins's involvement was a major point of contention. He didn't meet with the association prior to seeking approval for the Checkers, known for its double drive-thru architecture, making it a greater traffic generator than traditional fast food places. Checkers officials entrusted Hawkins to deal with the opposition without them, and they were unmoved by the arguments against Hawkins's leadership and the neighborhood's existing goals. To add insult to Hawkins's history of injuries, residents initially believed that Checkers was black-owned, a common misconception due to Hawkins's profile and the chain's inner-city locations. The misunderstanding may have also emerged from the way Hawkins indicated, or misrepresented, his franchise leases as ownership. In 1993, Hawkins's actual ownership stake was 25% of three Atlanta locations and another 25% claim on five locations in Philadelphia.[33] Hawkins opened a Washington, D.C., location with a far warmer welcome, but his promise to add ten more stores to the area never materialized. His investments were not the only issue that raised eyebrows. With every interview he granted to the press, and every contact he made in the industry, Hawkins's backstory changed ever so slightly. Was he really the youngest McDonald's manager ever? Was he 16 or 11 when he started working at McDonald's? Hawkins's claims were inconsistent at best, but the most important question was, would he really help black America as much as he said he would?

At the start of 1996, Hawkins was preparing to move again,

this time leaving behind a sinking Checkers brand and selling his franchises back to the parent company and whoever wanted the dozens of store locations Hawkins acquired in the South and the East. Hawkins was on to higher climes with a new fast food company, and he was making friends. Hawkins was meeting with fellow fast food enthusiast President Bill Clinton. In a ceremony celebrating Clinton's rendition of the federal Empowerment Zone program, a collection of initiatives to fight unemployment, business loss, and other critical needs in blighted areas. Cities—via economic development councils and community-development corporations—submitted proposals based on the neediness of sections of their cities and towns, and "winners" could offer tax breaks, job-training programs, and other enticements to business to move into the zone. Competitions in 1994, 1998, and 2001 brought hundreds of millions of dollars into the cities, and a later program extension allowed for additional funding schemes until the program formally ended in 2013.[34] Hawkins joined the CEO of Burger King to announce their commitment to open 25 outlets in black neighborhoods, which would be the start of something even bigger for Hawkins. Hawkins claimed that he would eventually build 225 restaurants in the inner city. For the second-largest fast food burger chain, the ceremony was part of a *mea culpa* of sorts, forced from the corporation as part of an Operation PUSH settlement to bring more business to black suppliers and contractors, as well as boost the number of minority franchisees.

While Clinton offered the nation a series of programs aimed at reducing the number of welfare recipients, he presented the private sector with an expanse of tax breaks and subsidies.

> The solutions to America's real challenges, economic and social challenges, have got to be community driven. The private sector has got to be an integral part. The Government—it's not like the Depression—the Government is broke. We have some money to invest in education and training, to invest in environmental protection, to invest in new technologies, to invest in infrastructure, but we got to get rid of this deficit. So we can't go out and just hire

everybody that doesn't have a job. The private sector has got to do that. And we have to have the right kind of partnership to get them involved . . . [35]

The Empowerment Zones included the same geographic areas that were studied by riot commissions in 1968, received Fair Share–brokered businesses in 1984, and became the new magnets for federal dollars and tax breaks under the Empowerment Zone program, which resided in the Department of Housing and Urban Development (HUD). As historian Chin Jou has noted in her research on the relationship between the federal government and the fast food industry, the Empowerment Zones "were a recycled initiative under a new name."[36] The 1994 "winners" included economically depressed areas of Atlanta, Baltimore, Chicago, Detroit, New York, and the Philadelphia-Camden metro area as well as rural locales such as the Kentucky Highlands, the Mid-Delta in Mississippi, and the Rio Grande Valley. The secondary competition program offered funds to Los Angeles and Cleveland.[37] A 2005 yearbook of successful Empowerment Zone projects included a roster of fast food favorites. The report heralded a grant of more than $230,000 for a Popeyes franchise's rehabilitation project and tax subsidies for the thirty-five local people employed at the restaurant. A black-franchised Wendy's in Columbus, Ohio, also enjoyed the tax credit provision for employing local people. The list of franchises benefiting from additional funding included a Cold Stone Creamery, a Moe's Southwest Grill, a Pizzeria Uno, a Chili's Bar & Grill in the "economically distressed" Overtown neighborhood of Miami, and a Gary, Indiana, Bennigan's pub.[38] Fast food seized on the moment and focused on building its own power rather than changing the features of its industry. Taxpayer subsidies helped establish and maintain fast food restaurants, and welfare reform helped supply applicants for low-wage jobs. Communities, in theory, would be able to determine what they needed and wanted, but in practice the investments were determined by the types of businesses that saw the poor, urban community as a viable consumer market.

At the White House ceremony featuring Hawkins and announcing his partnership with Burger King, Clinton complimented HUD Secretary Henry Cisneros for making ends meet with a shrinking budget and then pledged $3.5 billion in federal monies and tax breaks to the private sector. In a statement about the event, Burger King called the partnership a renewal of its "commitment to minority development."[39] The Burger King deal drew an even brighter spotlight onto Hawkins. A *Newsweek* profile highlighted his "half-million-dollar grants to church foundations and school programs" and his appearance on the dais of the Million Man March, where he "preached his personal gospel of black self-help." Hawkins believed himself to be modern-day black America's great benefactor and statesman in the mold of Booker T. Washington. He underwrote Cirque du Soul, the popular black circus that toured throughout the country in the late 1990s and early 2000s. His wealth made him a minor celebrity and he socialized with a higher-profile crowd each year. In the spring of 1997, he joined Louis Farrakhan to assist in negotiating a ceasefire after the murder of rapper Biggie Smalls in Los Angeles.[40] La-Van Hawkins was indeed everywhere.

Burger King gave Hawkins critical latitude with his locations and his business development company, allowing him to make changes as he saw fit and acquire other franchises while holding the leases on more than two dozen Burger King locations. Burger King said nothing about Hawkins displaying a portrait of himself on his outdoor drive-thru menus. Or perhaps Hawkins merely acted first and asked permission later. What was clear was that a Hawkins-franchised restaurant was different, and it resonated with black customers. The Hawkins touch on a Burger King was the embodiment of decades of fast food's investment on how to reach black consumers. At Hawkins's franchises you could think you were buying authentically black, you were supporting jobs in your community, and you were eating food tailored for you. Hawkins introduced Cajun fries and banana milkshakes to his Burger King menus and got rid of onion rings and salads. Burger King later amended his changes, but they claimed only "to improve the ideas." Over the course of a year between 1996 and 1997, Hawkins built 25 Burger Kings, many of them Express locations designed to do only drive-thru business, a measure believed to protect staff from crime and serve areas where residents relied on cars. He was making changes at his other places, too. For the 60 Perkins Family Restaurants he claimed he would bring into his portfolio, Hawkins wanted to infuse a little soul into the chain founded in Cincinnati in 1958 to serve up hot pancakes and coffee. Hawkins promised to add "ribs, pork chops, Southern-fried chicken, macaroni-and-cheese, and black-eyed peas" to the menu.[41] In 1998, Hawkins established Wolverine Pizza, LLC, and moved his operation from Baltimore to Detroit so that he could take possession of 8 Pizza Huts, in a deal that was the beginning of his acquisition of 89 Pizza Hut restaurants across the state of Michigan. In typical Hawkins fashion he left the Charm City with no fewer than 12 lawsuits for "unpaid services and breach of contract . . . in monetary claims from $31,000 to $14 million."[42]

While Hawkins was presiding over grand openings and reopenings across Detroit, the question of equity in the fast food industry persisted among potential franchisee and civil rights groups. Although the NAACP, PUSH, and other organizations that facilitated the recruitment of black franchisees were sometimes on retainer as consultants, the process was not seamless. Questions remained across the franchise industry. In the summer of 1997, a group of black franchisees took their concerns public and asked why, among the more than 5,000 KFC stores in the United States, did only 70 belong to African Americans? After Popeyes acquired Church's Chicken, why did the parent company put more resources into promoting Church's at the expense of its black Popeyes franchisees? While racial discrimination issues regarding Denny's, where Secret Service members were refused service, captured most headlines, the franchise world was embroiled in a less public debate.[43] Kentucky Fried Chicken's Office of Minority and Governmental Affairs claimed that it was difficult to convince people to invest in the inner city. He pointed to "an African American owner in Detroit" who cashed out and reestablished his business elsewhere.

In Detroit, the Wayne County executive said companies such as KFC used crime statistics as a smoke screen. Businesses were doing just fine. "According to the FBI reports, crime is down in Detroit. But all you have to do is look at La-Van Hawkins Burger Kings and McDonald's and you can see that fast food franchises are operating well."[44]

While large-scale programs were able to help franchise companies meet their aggressive goals sooner, they still needed the traditional franchise recruitment and development that helped build their consumer base in the urban market. In the 1990s, the Kentucky Fried Chicken minority financing program offered "95% of the total cost of the franchise" and exempted applicants from the personal finance requirement of possessing a net worth of $400,000 and $150,000 of liquid cash. Applicants of color only needed to prove that they could front 10% of the fees, between $65,000 and $75,000.[45] Twelve years after the Fair Share agreement, KFC was still struggling to make good on its promises. A national boycott was planned for late November 1994. Louis Coleman Jr., a leader with the Justice Resource Center of Kentucky, listed the issues he heard from franchisees: rundown restaurants, pay disparities between blacks and whites, repercussions for hiring too many employees of color, few store managers of color, and problems with PepsiCo, the owner of KFC. Employees accused a manager of telling them that suburban stores paid their employees more for the same work because "kids in the suburbs don't have to work."

On the other side of the issue were members of the Executive Leadership Council, an organization of senior-level executives from different corporations, who sided with PepsiCo. Coleman's earlier negotiation with KFC indicated that food quality and nutrition were slowly entering the conversation about the industry's responsibilities to communities. "We met with Walt Simon (KFC's vice president–minority business development) and he made a commitment that 35% African Americans would be placed in management positions in inner city stores in Louisville and promised salad bars in inner city stores," stated Reverend Coleman. "Nothing has been done." He also said that the minority franchising schemes ensnared optimistic franchisees and they were often "set up to fail." Attorneys for a group of KFC franchisees in Yuba City, California, who filed a grievance against the chicken chain argued that "the whole thing could have been resolved at the cost of the chicken they throw out every week."[46]

While Kentucky Fried Chicken was struggling to use franchising as an inroad into the inner city, Hawkins was working his magic in Detroit. With the Checkers issue behind him, Hawkins became a local hero with his Burger King outlets. His connections to the city's mayors, religious leaders, and business communities could have protected him from questions about what happened in Philadelphia, Baltimore, Washington, D.C., Atlanta, where the loathed name La-Van Hawkins was associated with checks bounced, drive-thrus closed suddenly, or entire staffs left unemployed. Locals didn't care what happened on the East Coast, they knew what was happening in Detroit, and the promise of two hundred more La-Van Hawkins stores coupled with his Pizza Hut franchises made Hawkins a top employer of black youth in a city that had suffered the worst of deindustrialization and depopulation. In true Hawkins fashion, his relationship with Burger King eventually began to sour. Bills weren't being paid, and Burger King wanted their stores back. Burger King argued that Hawkins had falsely represented their expansion agreement and refuted his claim that they had entrusted him with developing hundreds of new stores. Citing the expiration of his franchise leases due to failure to pay rent, Burger King announced that Hawkins was in violation of trademark laws in continuing the operation of his locations. Burger King was in the process of seeking new franchisees for his locations, and they had to figure out how to take care of the hundreds of employees still working at his stores.[47] This was a matter of money.

Hawkins was not accustomed to backing down without a spectacular fight, and he matched Burger King's lawsuit with his own. Hawkins countersued for nearly $2 billion, claiming that Burger King had used him "as a pawn to make them look good to black people and black leaders," and then retaliated when he became too successful.[48] The allegations hurled from the two camps read like fodder more suited for a gossip column than for the business pages. Hawkins had shored up the urban market for Burger King, and they didn't appreciate that he did the very thing that they had asked him to do: connect with his consumer base, a loyal base for the fast food industry. The customizations may have been "too ethnic" for Burger King, but they resonated with black Detroiters. He flew black, green, and red black-liberation flags over American flags at the store. He hired Nation of Islam members—decked in their signature black sunglasses and shirts advertising that they were F.O.I. or Fruit of Islam—as security. The R&B hits that replaced the Muzak in the restaurant was sometimes piped outside and inside. What was wrong with that? He charged that Burger King's racially discriminatory practices were limiting his ability to expand his own franchise kingdom.[49] Unlike Charles Griffis and the other franchisees before him, Hawkins's claims to be on his way to building hundreds of more franchises made his argument unconvincing. Yet, Hawkins's case provided the opening for civil rights groups to insert themselves in a dispute with Burger King again, which cemented more opportunity for their members and associates to enter franchising.

Boycott and protest are critical actions to expanding opportunities for marginalized groups. Yet, by the 2000s, the fast food industry knew that these measures would yield concessions that ultimately benefited them in that they brought more franchisees of color into the parts of the country that were the riskiest and most profitable. If fast food companies could withstand the sting of a little bad press, agreements like the ones that brought Hawkins to Burger King franchising were not too bad after all. It was as if there were two keys that opened the door to opportunity for blacks. One of them was the uprising and the other, the national boycott. On the other side of that door, however, was a plethora of low-wage jobs and a few people able to get rich.

With the lawsuits filed and the accusations flying, Hawkins made himself available for press interviews so he could take his case to the American public. A 2000 profile on Hawkins's struggle with Burger King described him as a "folk hero in the inner cities," who treated his customers to "thumping hip hop and Motown music, inside and out." He added: "I've proven I know how to create jobs and opportunities for them," he said. "They trust me."[50] Hawkins may have had questionable business acumen, but there was no uncertainty that he was a consummate entertainer. When Burger King filed suit against Hawkins, he enlisted the equally charismatic and verbose attorney Johnnie Cochran, of the O. J. Simpson murder trial, and National Action Network's Al Sharpton for assistance. Sharpton's siding with Hawkins may have initially seemed a low-stakes gesture considering the good Reverend had long been involved in boycotts of corporations, police departments, and U.S. government policy. Boycott was second nature to the New Yorker, whose reputation loomed large over organizations nervous about their record on minority hiring or embroiled in racial scandal. Evoking Sharpton conjured up an image of picketing, followed by dealmaking. Corporations did not want to have to give into Sharpton, but they knew he had a platform, and so did he. Sharpton called for a regional boycott of Burger King in September of 2000 based on Hawkins's claims, and he organized pickets of New York franchise locations that October.[51]

The Burger King issue actually put Sharpton at odds with his friend and colleague Jesse Jackson, who had negotiated a Fair Share plan with Burger King in the 1980s. Jackson argued that Hawkins was the one who had acted in bad faith, and even if that Reverend saw merits in Hawkins's case, he could not betray Burger King. The path of corporate negotiation for civil rights groups may have expanded the field of possibilities for black businesspeople, banks, insurance companies, and advertising agencies, as well as minimum-wage employees, but it ultimately bound up the ways that these organizations deployed their activism while settlements and deals were being implemented. The rift not only put Hawkins at odds with Burger King, but it also triangulated black America's Three Kings of Black Empowerment: La-Van Hawkins, Jesse Jackson, and Al Sharpton. The fight, intensified by their own feelings about how much access they had to the Clinton White House, led both Jackson and Sharpton to spend a year taking jabs at each other.

Sharpton believed this was a matter of where they existed in the civil rights leadership orbit. "Our conflict is also definitely generational," Sharpton, who is thirteen years Jackson's junior, said. "There is a younger voter that Jesse can't reach, that I can. Poor folks in the projects. The hip-hop generation . . . Jesse doesn't have the defiance I have."[52]

Sharpton's defiance-fueled boycott, supported by the Nation of Islam, didn't get too far, nor did Hawkins's lawsuit. A few months after talk of a boycott, a judge dismissed Hawkins's $1.9 billion lawsuit against Burger King. In the winter of 2000, the New York State Supreme Court had the final say, ruling that Hawkins and his business entities owed Burger King's affiliated entity, Franchise Acceptance Corporation, the company's lending arm, $8.4 million.[53] At the start of the new year in 2001, Burger King settled with Hawkins, who initially estimated his debts at $6.5 million in unpaid fees, rent, and supplier invoices. Burger King agreed to take back twenty-three of his twenty-five franchise locations. Apologies were also exchanged between the two clergymen that year. Burger King's battle with Hawkins exemplified the way that franchising had become so imbricated in black life and culture that his defenders ranged from Sharpton to fruitarian Dick Gregory and other black leaders beholden to Hawkins's commitment to black charities, especially for children and education.[54] After agreeing to an undisclosed payout, an only slightly chastened Hawkins told the press, "Burger King and I have shaken hands, and I wish them all the best of luck. I'm still spending their money and enjoying my luck."[55] But Hawkins's luck ran out rather quickly, and he eventually lost his Pizza Hut franchises, fine-dining restaurants in downtown Detroit, and his jazz club.

In the years following the Burger King debacle, Hawkins was inexplicably able to acquire more franchises, and each came with higher risk, few community rewards, and more legal trouble. As he did in the Motor City, Hawkins promised that his ventures would bring jobs and dollars to black communities, and with each agreement executed, he reified the idea that fast food not only had a special place in black America, but could do the work of transformation. In 2004, he returned to court to respond to corruption charges stemming from serving as a go-between for fraudulent activity between a Philadelphia attorney and Detroit's city treasurer. The indictment revealed that Hawkins was part of a scheme to purchase one hundred Church's Chicken locations, then resell them back to the parent company.[56] For his role in the plot, Hawkins received a sentence of nearly three years in jail and was ordered to pay $25,000 in restitution. As he arranged to report to a Duluth, Minnesota, correctional facility, he was served a separate set of papers from a Chicago-based Italian beef and pizza franchise for bouncing checks and failing to pay vendors.[57] After serving eighteen months of his jail term, Hawkins was embroiled in yet another municipal scandal; this time it involved Detroit's "hip-hop mayor," Kwame Kilpatrick, who was forced to resign from office after pleading guilty to obstruction-of-justice charges.[58] In August of 2007, Hawkins was found guilty of wire fraud and perjury and received a twenty-two-month prison sentence for his role in a Detroit bribery and conspiracy case involving local businessmen.[59]

After disappointing and imperiling his employees and charities, serving multiple prison sentences for fraud, and having been exposed as untrustworthy, Hawkins maintained that ultimately black indifference sunk his enterprises. Hawkins traded in the specious, but well-worn, claim that the economic problems of black America stemmed from its failure to invest in itself. When newspapers interviewed black business owners who could not match the high discounts that major retailers could offer, they blamed black customers for not supporting their own. Rarely did these reports explore why black customers had to be so price-conscious. If a black business was destroyed in an uprising, then the conclusion was that blacks don't value their own people's businesses. Few of the conversations lingered on why people were so upset. When La-Van Hawkins deceived scores of people in the nation's most vulnerable neighborhoods, few asked how in the world he had the power to do this. When times were good and cash was flush, Hawkins had the solution to what afflicted black America—jobs at his franchise restaurants. But, after he was held accountable for the financial mismanagement of his stores, he argued that it was franchising itself that was the problem, and that blacks on the whole did not know how to achieve financial freedom because they were tethered to the white benevolence of the industry. In a postprison interview with a local Detroit television show *American Entrepreneur*, Hawkins claimed that he had finally seen the light. From his telling, his newfound independence from franchising represented his greater commitment to empowering black communities. "We give away 95 cents of every dollar . . . the shackles have been put on our mind . . . We allow every dollar . . . to leave our community."[60] Hawkins hinted that he had spent his prison term dreaming up new franchise concepts that could ensure that the black dollar didn't go anywhere. Using this "common sense" diagnosis of the black condition and echoing the sentiments expressed by Charles Griffis after he left McDonald's franchising, Hawkins offered that his new franchise concept, Sweet Georgia Brown restaurants, was not only going to provide black economic freedom, but would also decolonize the black consumer mind. The critiques of these franchises as falling short of authentically allowing customers to "buy black" still swirled, but those voices were dampened by the praise for the industry from civil rights organizations, local economic development councils, and the White House. Soon after he did the interview on liberating black consciousness, Hawkins was convicted of tax evasion, and the court gave him a ten-month sentence and an order to pay back $5.7 million.[61] Despite the jail time and the declining reputation, Hawkins—the king of reinvention—hadn't turned his back on franchising entirely.[62] In 2018, a company associated with Hawkins had applied to bring twenty Habit Burger Grill franchises to the Midwest. Hawkins did not live to see the plan emerge; he died on April 6, 2019. *Crain's Detroit Business* described him as "a one-time fast food franchise mogul, restaurateur and controversial figure."[63]

Decades of failed attempts to use capitalism as a balm, a shield, or an antidote to the sting, force, and toxicity of racism has failed to change the narrative that what ailing communities need most are fast-food restaurants. On the whole, black franchisees have tried to provide stop-gap measures to employ people, provide them with peripheral community programs, and leverage their influence for broader black achievement. There is no doubt that some difference has been made. For black women like Janice Baker, a McDonald's manager in Dallas, Texas, her time working for a former NBMOA chairman allowed her to create a stable, middle-class life after her husband died. Baker takes pride in hiring people who would not otherwise have access to employment because of prior felony convictions or a lack of experience. The longtime McDonald's manager also appreciates the opportunity to work for a black boss, franchisee Roland Parrish, after experiencing racism in the workplace. Parrish has given generously to Fisk University and his alma mater Purdue University, local youth sports programs, and has employed thousands at his more than twenty McDonald's restaurants. To ignore the positive impacts of franchise networks among communities of color that appreciate their contributions would be shortsighted. It is equally shortsighted to ignore the government subsidies, civil rights organization endorsements, limited community resources, and economic desperation that supports the dubious idea that fast food—and business on the whole—can solely, or even substantively or singularly, breathe life into an underdeveloped community.

If the fast food industry was concerned that hucksters like La-Van Hawkins would endanger their rapid-growth strategies and the fulfillment of lingering Fair Share–style deals, then they may have elevated the vetting process for new franchisees, or simply returned to their roots in recruiting high-profile, and ostensibly cash-rich, celebrities to enter multiunit franchising contracts. Founded by the Los Angeles Lakers star in 1987, Magic Johnson Enterprises began after he made relatively modest investments in retail stores and a couple of radio stations. A few years later, he partnered with *Black Enterprise* founder Earl G. Graves to acquire a Pepsi-Cola distribution outfit, a franchise opportunity that was slower to expand to African Americans than fast food. Graves and Johnson's purchase of a Washington, D.C., area bottler in 1990 was believed to be a first for investors of color for Pepsi. The men were receiving a more lucrative financial opportunity than a franchisee.[64] Johnson Enterprises expanded over the following decades with cobranded outlets of movie theatres created by the Johnson Development Corporation, hundreds of Starbucks coffee stores, TGI Fridays restaurants, dozens of Burger Kings, and Fatburger locations.[65] Johnson's franchises were located in diverse communities from South Los Angeles to Harlem, but whether he was selling movie tickets or milkshakes, the promise of bringing jobs to where they were needed made these massive, and often Empowerment Zone–funded, projects welcomed additions to blocks that may have already had more than their fill of fast-food joints but where jobs were always needed. Yet, like the business owners who bristled at the Small Business Administration programs that promised to rebuild Watts in the 1960s and failed to even communicate with Watts, not every community felt these initiatives were indeed magic. Johnson argued he was bringing "retail justice" to people long denied the opportunity to keep their black dollars inside of black neighborhoods, but one observer believed that in South Los Angeles—and by extension all the places that Johnson set up shop and sometimes closed the shops when they were deemed too difficult to operate or not as profitable as he had hoped—people wanted "real justice."[66]

While some people wondered if retail justice was a worthy goal, growing concerns about food justice were also emerging among public conversations about the wealth and health of black America. By the time Hawkins was singing the praises of a pizza and breadstick combo and Magic Johnson's name was on everything from fries to Frappuccinos in the inner city, the nation was well aware of the long-term impacts of a diet filled with food rich in fats. In 1988, Surgeon General of the United States C. Everett Koop published the results of his office's first study of the relationship between diet and chronic disease. The report highlighted that "Black Americans, for example, have higher rates of high blood pressure, strokes, diabetes, and other diseases associated with obesity . . . than the general population."[67] Subsequent research studies and surgeons general would discourage overindulgence in fast food, and public health practitioners would provide suggestions on modifying fast food–dependent diets. These interventions were important in helping the nation to make more discerning choices about what to eat. In the constant evaluation of black health as jeopardized, many public health advocates fixated on food choices and acknowledged the disproportionate numbers of fast food locations in black neighborhoods. But, few made the connection with the federal government's concentrated, sustained efforts to bring more and more fast food into the inner city, nor did they see the handiwork of the civil rights authorities in sanctioning the process.

While accusations that racist, corporate greed fueled fast food's proliferation in the inner city were not inaccurate, the other actors that could be appealed to for catalyzing the corporation were rarely made visible. Rallying against fast food companies for endangering black health was a start. The campaigns organized on behalf of fast food workers that materialized as the Fight for $15 to raise the minimum wage were another way of taking up the problems created by fast food in poor communities. In 2012, the same year that Fight for $15 commenced, the National Labor Relations Board determined that fast food companies are coemployers with fast food franchisees, and therefore they share the responsibility in adjudicating wage disputes. This decision came after labor activists in the Fight for $15 movement alleged workers were fired and intimidated for their organizing activities. Six years later, in 2018, the NLRB allowed McDonald's to settle the issue and the company admitted no wrongdoing. Overseas, McDonald's workers have organized unions, but the fast food industry relied on the franchise issue to keep collective groups out of their restaurants. The transition from a Democrat to a Republican in the White House endangered the ruling, and activists are concerned that settlements further obscure the problem of wages and workers' rights.[68]

Perhaps the most vexing work may come in reconciling fast food's nonfood, nonwork properties, namely its very association with feelings of black pride, belief in community investment, and response in times of crisis. As historian Bethany Moreton has discovered in her research on Wal-Mart and its ability to fuse fervent Christianity with ferocious, free-market capitalism, Wal-Mart does not explicitly call itself a Christian company. Rather, Moreton effectively proves, Wal-Mart provided the terrain in which a "particular strain of "family values" Christianity . . . met mass consumption . . ."[69] By no means is McDonald's a "black" company per se, but its ability to use the tropes of blackness skillfully and to leverage its black franchisees in the service of proximity to black communities provides a worthy, and insightful, entry point into thinking about racialized health disparities in the service of eradicating them. The affective is effective, and there is no way of staving off the influence of fast food in vulnerable communities without recognizing this poignant and unsettling fact.

* * *

Twenty years after the Los Angeles uprising, residents near South Van Ness Avenue celebrated the opening of a Food 4 Less. The store opened less than a mile from the intersection where truck driver Reginal Denny was beaten by a group of young men. The crowds that gathered to check out the discount grocer may have thought about Denny that day before they perused the produce section or evaluated the bakery's offerings. One appreciative shopper said the store and the accompanying projects in the Chesterfield Square Plaza "provided jobs, a lot of jobs, for our youngsters to keep them off the street . . . Some of them are minimum wage, but that's better than nothing."[70] At present, there are two McDonald's restaurants within a mile of the grocery store, as well as a Wingstop, Pizza Hut, Taco Bell, and KFC. This was not what was promised in 1992, but it was appreciated in 2012. South Los Angeles, like the other sections of U.S. cities of the 1960s and '70s that were noticed only after their businesses and community centers disappeared, had waited and waited for change to come. In its wake, they got more fast food and fewer options.

Below the surface of the energetic conversations about rebuilding Los Angeles and the swelling of the Miracle of the Golden Arches, there were doubts and questions. A former Korean business owner who left Los Angeles after the uprising believed that the focus of the recovery was misguided. The head of the Korean American Grocers Association observed: "The rich and poor gap is getting bigger. That is the reason for riots. The job is not done with getting a McDonald's there. It is the unemployment."[71] Even the restaurant industry was willing to concede that it was a fallacy to rely on service sector jobs to lead the way forward. *Nation's Restaurant News* warned: "No one expects the restaurant industry to pioneer an economic renaissance of our inner cities. After all, only so many service businesses can hope to exist in locales where disposable income so often consists of welfare checks, food stamps and the limited rewards of dead-end jobs." One of Los Angeles's few independent black restaurant owners agreed. Multigenerational poverty would only be solved through "jobs for the upcoming generation that will be meaningful, so that they can educate their kids properly."

Despite the critiques, the magazine also presented its own version of the Golden Arches miracle with an anecdote about "the survival of a franchised Denny's under construction in Watts" that was "protected from looters and arsonists by residents who recognized the restaurant and its surrounding shopping center as a nucleus of opportunity for the long-blighted neighborhood."[72] No matter how many times the Miracle was repeated and amplified as the perfect case study in why corporate community investment could pay off, the notion that fast food would save communities was a leap of faith some were unwilling to take. Integral to the post–Los Angeles rebuilding process was a gang truce supplemented with greater economic opportunities, but a new generation of South Los Angeles residents knew that prosperity after peace would require serious investment in an expansion of good employment. As one former gang member put it, "Now that the killing has stopped, there are no jobs." He added: "People are standing around wondering what is next. We have to support our families . . . We need some long-term jobs, not McDonald's," he said.[73] Rebuild L.A., the organization tasked with redeveloping the battered city, fell short of its own lofty goals. Bernard Kinsey, the cochair of Rebuild

L.A., characterized the inner city as littered with "liquor stores and funeral homes," and "every other retail establishment is looking at a potential gold mine in the neglected areas."[74] Another publication put it more simply: "The Crips and Bloods held up their part of the bargain, Rebuild LA did not hold up theirs."[75]

In addition to jobs, the issue of supermarkets became less and less avoidable. The Crenshaw neighborhood mourned the loss of beauty shops in their community after the uprising but hoped the new development plans would not only rebuild the salons, but also bring in badly needed grocers and affordable retailers. "It's not that there's anything wrong with the beauty shops themselves," explained the executive director of the Crenshaw Chamber of Commerce. "What we have is not enough supermarkets."[76] The supermarkets eventually came, in small numbers and of varying quality, to South Los Angeles. They also came to Chicago's South Side, Washington, D.C.'s U Street corridor, and the other centers that were obliterated in the 1960s, and, in some cases, the 1990s. The new supermarkets were at times a sign of gentrification, and in other cases actual attempts to serve the local market. Regardless of the motivations and circumstances surrounding their arrivals, supermarkets could not adequately address the myriad problems that led to the development of retail at the exclusion of public housing and services, the distribution of low-wage jobs, and the subsidizing of tax breaks for business. But at the very least they provided an avenue to improve nutritional choice in communities flooded with fast food restaurants.

With the benefit of more research on fast food, race, and nutrition, as well as the addition of words like "food desert" in the national lexicon of inequality, Los Angeles political and business leaders tried to find creative solutions to health disparities that had worsened since the uprising. In 2007, Los Angeles City Councilwoman Jan Perry proposed a moratorium on new fast food restaurants in South Los Angeles for two years in order to promote better health in the area. Perry framed the issue in terms of the rising health care costs among her residents, who she claimed had "higher incidence of diseases that doctors link to obesity than the rest of the city and the county." Nearly half of all restaurants serving the 700,000 residents of South Los Angeles were fast food outlets. On Los Angeles's richer and whiter West Side, only 12% of dining options fell under the fast food category. The initiative challenged the long-held notion that any business was good business in low-income communities, and while a two-year halt would not eliminate existing restaurants, the failed proposal revealed how much of the fast food problem was linked to individuals with limited choices. An opponent of the plan argued that this was not a matter of market saturation, but of overcoming nutritional ignorance. "We have to teach inner-city kids how to eat or they will find the less healthy foods even at the better restaurants," reifying the notion that better nutritional information could disrupt the deep bonds that the industry had forged with black consumers. In the press coverage of the proposal, newspapers also noted that the dilemma of fast food was also a matter of failed attempts to mediate the problems of the uprising. "After the Rodney King riots in 1992 devastated these neighborhoods," the *Christian Science Monitor* reported, "officials promised more supermarkets and restaurants . . . But for a variety of reasons, that has not happened."[77]

Black capitalism's progeny—public-private partnership and economic empowerment—was welcomed into black communities with the same mix of hopefulness and skepticism as its ancestors. An array of researchers and scholars have examined whether Empowerment Zone (EZ) initiatives paid off in terms of rates of poverty, economic growth, and unemployment. In one of the more sanguine assessments, urban studies scholars found that although "several EZ cities produced improvements in their distressed neighborhoods . . . The gains were modest." They concluded that "none of the local EZ programs fundamentally transformed distressed urban neighborhoods."[78] With varied levels of funding, the federal Empowerment Zone program was geared to engage the private sector and was one of a number of supposedly race-neutral, lean-government, bi-sector ideas that captured the attention of post-1968 political leaders. The language and rhetoric of black capitalism became the framework of empowerment. With the departure from black capitalism came a resounding endorsement of the Empowerment Zone idea. Imported from the United Kingdom in the era of Thatcherism, conservatives from Ronald Reagan to Jack Kemp welcomed this free market solution. "Those who view poverty and unemployment as permanent afflictions of our cities fail to understand how rapidly the poor can move up the ladder of success in our economy," Reagan said during his bid for the White House, "but to move up the ladder, they must first get on it. And this is the concept behind the enterprise zones."[79] As nebulous as black capitalism was as a goal for an earlier generation, empowerment was just as hard to capture. Who was to be empowered? And could power be held by many, not just one? These were the questions that remained unanswered, if uttered at all, as Hawkins and his cadre in fast food found a new way to link federal investment in business with black people's investment in seeing blacks succeed in their communities, sometimes without meditating on the consequences for too long.

The idea of financially sound black institutions is alluring across the ideological spectrum because it allows white conservatives and liberals alike to claim plausible deniability in their role in supporting systems and policies that maintain racial capitalism. Whether it's called black capitalism or empowerment, the politics of black business can serve many interests, except for those of blacks most susceptible to the extremes of capitalism and racism. Historian of black banks Mehrsa Baradaran describes the pull of supporting black economic empowerment as binding unlikely partners. "On the right, the myth that capitalism can fix what racist state policy created . . . on the left, it's the idea that microcredit can fix macro injustices."[80] The label "black-owned" obscures the multiple systems that are not only outside of the hands of people of color, but will never be truly accessible under capitalism.

In some rare instances, chefs and entrepreneurs have tried to "hack" the fast food formula and make healthy fast food.[81] LocoL, the experiment in low-cost, healthy food by Roy Choi, the Korean-American food truck king of Southern California, and double Michelin star holder Daniel Patterson has been lauded for its creative foods and desire to address the challenge of affordability and nutrition. LocoL offered tofu burgers, whole-wheat tortilla sandwiches, and juices alongside quesadillas and burgers, made from carefully sourced ingredients sold by local vendors. Meals were priced to compete with the extra-value-meal crowd. People from the neighborhood were hired.[82] LocoL's multiple locations experienced challenges. The downtown Oakland restaurant closed after thirteen months in business, and the Watts location and a scaled- back Oakland outpost required several tweaks to address the lack of profitability.[83] Choi and Patterson have emphasized that the goal of the initiative is not to make money, but to create a community resource.[84] In a departure from the methods of the Empowerment Zone, LocoL relied on a mix of private investment and crowdfunding, a twenty-first-century way of funneling the public's funds directly to projects (in addition to the tax breaks and incentives still enjoyed by businesses that move to poor areas). LocoL's debut was held on the 2016 celebration of Martin Luther King Jr. Day. Black capitalism's indefatigable advocate Jim Brown was on hand to cut the ribbon. The event's soundtrack featured King's "I Have a Dream" speech and the Black Lives Matter movement's informal anthem, Kendrick Lamar's "Alright." The past was the present. A newspaper report described the grand opening in Watts this way: "Like other economically depressed communities without access to fresh food, its citizens are at increased risk of obesity and its attendant ailments: heart disease, stroke, high-blood pressure, diabetes, cancer." Like other economically depressed communities without access to choices, the people of Watts, still hoping to dissociate their neighborhood's name from racial chaos, held their breaths and hoped that this time, things would be different. The restaurant closed in August of 2018, but some are hopeful that the adjacent catering company will make it.[85]

Bigger than a Hamburger

The Fight for $15 movement has targeted McDonald's and other fast food restaurants for low wages and bad working conditions, including inconsistent scheduling practices and sexual harassment of workers. A protest in Chicago used elements of the civil rights struggles of the 1950s. Photo by Scott Olson / Getty Images.

Eventually, the news cameras, the protesters, and the National Guard cleared out of Ferguson, Missouri. In their place came a few new community programs and some more businesses. The QuikTrip that burned after Michael Brown was killed has been converted into an Urban League Community Empowerment Center and a Salvation Army mission. The Boys and Girls Club of Greater St. Louis broke ground for a new youth center on the former site of a Ponderosa Steakhouse. Over the course of four years, nearly $40 million in investments for new businesses and municipal improvements have flowed into Ferguson; most of it has enriched the historic downtown and predominantly white sections of town.

In 2016, Starbucks CEO Howard Schultz made good on his pledge to open a Ferguson branch of the coffeehouse. Unlike most of the new businesses, the Starbucks is located on West Florissant, across the street from the now-repaired and still-bustling black-franchised McDonald's. Poor and working-class black residents of the apartments and single-family homes near West Florissant Avenue have yet to realize much of the economic benefits of the renewed interest in Ferguson.[1]

This book is concerned with the reasons that places like Ferguson are more likely to get a fast food restaurant rather than direct cash aid to the poor, oversight over the police department, or jobs that pay more than $8.60 per hour after an uprising. This story also explains how fast food became black and why it came to mean so many things to black communities. In order to fully appreciate the origins of our contemporary health crisis, we cannot fixate solely on the food. We have to tell stories about the many functions of capitalism, and its ability to satisfy some of our most personal needs while starving our collective present and future. Government support for fast food franchising has imperiled black health, but our societal vigilance should take us beyond that. In addition to government assistance, the fast food industry relies on indefinable, but palpable, emotional appeals to black consumer citizenship, the extension of the mid-century march for civil rights toward the marketplace, and calls for racial solidarity under the expansive umbrellas of "black capitalism," and later "black empowerment." The origins of the urban food crisis reveal the ways that various actors—politicians, civil rights activists, business executives, advertising agencies, community organizers, and market researchers—aligned to use the symbols, language, and strategies of black freedom movements to sell scores of hamburgers, myriad buckets of fried chicken, and gallons of soda. Studying the hidden history of how fast food and civil rights aligned to change black America, and the ways that black America changed fast food, can lead to more nuanced understandings of our concerns about ensuring that communities that have the least receive the most support to create choices for themselves and for their future generations.

A public that decries fast food as a matter of bad choices is a public that is ignorant to the fact that the meeting of racism and capitalism can only produce demeaning and uncomfortable options.[2] In the ongoing, yet still superficial, public conversation about fast food, race, and health, we have to remember that our catastrophic disparities are a result of a structural indifference to the depth of black hunger for everything from nutritious foods to well-compensated jobs to racial justice. This hunger makes communities without wealth or power vulnerable to the excesses of government and corporate impulses that seek to deprive or overfeed rather than nourish. Social critic Naomi Klein's 2007 book *The Shock Doctrine: The Rise of Disaster Capitalism* is a helpful guide to interrogate the concern about fast food and health. In tracing the ways that natural and political disaster facilitate the arrival of sweeping, and disastrous, market-based policies and processes that exploit the vulnerable and destabilize the distribution of public resources, Klein's framework is instructive for all invested in food justice. Whether it be the reinvigoration of the service-based tourism economy after an earthquake or the elimination of public schools in favor of charter schools after a hurricane, disaster capitalism feeds on destitution and chaos. In Klein's view, the disasters are sometimes dramatic, like a civil war, and in other times, the disaster comes with a seemingly peaceful election of a probusiness politician or a promise to reform public entitlements. Regardless of how rapidly or quickly the shock to citizens is delivered, there are commonalities in its effect. Klein notes: "All these incarnations share a commitment to the policy trinity—the elimination of the public sphere, total liberation for corporations, and skeletal social spending . . ."[3] Since the late 1960s, the fast food industry has similarly capitalized on racial unrest to infiltrate black communities, ingratiate itself with the community's most influential figures, and evoke a complicated set of emotions about the industry by contributing to black cultural and social life but never fully enriching it.

Attempts to legislate food choices, or to provide "healthy alternatives" to food that has been labeled junk, can also confuse and distort the difference between real food and highly processed food. This gesture can also distract us from which people are most subject to eating what is offered rather than choosing what is desired. Although states like California have been successful in banning soft drinks and junk food from school vending machines, food in schools is not necessarily fresh or healthy. Considering black children attend public schools at a rate of more than 90%, their schools also play a role in developing food habits and preferences. Bans on fast food in schools do not mean that children are not consuming products that mimic the taste level, preparation style or nutritional emptiness of fast food. Chicken fingers—the close cousin of the McNugget—and crispy shelled tacos of the kind Glen Bell popularized in the United States are pervasive on school lunch menus. Even if McDonald's or Chick-fil-A is not in a specific school cafeteria, the palates of students are still being set by the fast food industry. Fast food's multivalent definitions—as social scourge, evidence of family decline, a marker of blackness—are contingent upon who is eating it, where they are eating it, and how often. The fare at an earth-toned Panera franchise or a sleekly designed Starbucks are both fast food products, but due to their price points, their claims about sourcing and the locations of these establishments, they are not marked as places where parents should not take their children frequently, nor are they targets of criticism about nutrition.[4]

The castigation of the eating habits of poor people, or the choices they make for their children's meals, obscures the origins of those choices. Judging food selections and indulgences assumes that what we eat only has to do with food. In tackling the problems borne from a faulty food environment for poor African Americans, it is also essential to dispense with romanticized notions of a healthier food past, as this nostalgic rhetoric can often be used to excoriate women for failing to cook healthy meals for their families, or to suggest that there was a time that black communities easily provided food for themselves without need of capital investment. There was a time in the pre–Great Migration era that blacks—concentrated largely in the South—subsisted on a diet that derived from the land they toiled. But often blacks did not own the land they worked, and it is misleading to assert that race did not overdetermine the quality of the black diet in the era before fast food became a fixture in largely black neighborhoods. Blacks may have eaten more freshly harvested vegetables and fewer Whoppers or chicken tenders, for sure, but the quantity and consistency of food has always been a challenge for black people and families in America.

Food writer Michael Pollan has observed that fast food "obscures the histories of the foods it produces by processing them to such an extent that they appear as pure products of culture rather than nature—things made from plants and animals."[5] Similarly, the mainstream discussion about fast food and health in communities of color disguises the intertwined histories of capitalism, racism, and violence that undergirds every part of the nation's existence, and therefore foodways and dining are no exception. The history of blacks in fast food franchising—when integrated into the historical analysis of black capitalism—yields a story of troubling success. The meeting of burgers and black capitalism worked. In fact, one of black capitalism's greatest experiments—to bring fast food within the reach of black communities—went so well that its origins have been underresearched, its impacts masked, and its history largely ignored.

For most Americans, it may be hard to imagine a world without McDonald's or Kentucky Fried Chicken or Taco Bell. Now, in the early adulthood of the twenty-first century, we may not be able to conceive of the United States without some form of cheap and easy food source. The sit-in's descendants—the Black Lives Matter die-in at a mall food court or a Starbucks picket line after a racist incident happens inside the coffee shop or a petition against a restaurant's practices that gets circulated among social media channels—have revealed themselves as of late. They remind us of the effectiveness of litigating social wrongs by taking to the streets, including Main Street. Yet the market cannot dictate opportunity or solely guarantee the well-being of communities. In our contemporary fight to ensure the health and wealth of people relegated to the margins, all does not begin and end with the presence of the drive-thru. In order to combat the outsize, and possibly harmful, impact of that very drive-thru, we must assess the lack shaped by the racist commitments of the state. When resources that create steady infrastructure for well-paying jobs, a multitude of food options, and safe spaces for children and senior citizens to build community are absent, then fast food is able to present itself as capable of providing sustenance rather than simply feeding. Moving forward, food justice movements must interrogate the racist suppositions about poor people's nutritional ignorance of the dangers of fast food and question the assumptions that black people are innately attracted to it.

Attempts to revolutionize the food system must begin with the history of the ways communities have been sold the idea of fast food as a practical solution. We all must remain vigilant in the places that the industry appears: where students go to school, where families worship, where young athletes demonstrate their talents, where the elderly monitor their blood glucose levels, where high school students proudly collect their scholarship checks, where a formerly incarcerated person is able to work, where Martin Luther King Jr.'s legacy is commemorated, and where children play on weekends. In each of these spaces where the funds from the industry flows, food justice activists must imagine a world in which public funds, community investment dollars, and collective energies sustain them. Before another garden bed is prepared or a vegan recipe is shared and demonstrated in the name of food justice, the concerned must have a thorough and deep deliberation on racial capitalism. When McDonald's, or any other corporation, supplants the state in neighborhoods forced to scramble to acquire necessities for life, then we must adjust our focus to understand how this happened and continues to happen. Fortunately, an emergent generation of food justice advocates, based in communities of color, are linking the fight for healthy and nutritious food options to radical critiques of capitalism that are patient and compassionate toward the people they choose to serve.[6]

Activist Ella Baker was especially prescient and prophetic when she argued that the sit-in movement's goal of ending discrimination at lunch counters and other public accommodations was only half of the battle, and that economic justice needed to match the fight for access. In matters of race and capitalism, Baker argued, the struggle is "something much bigger than a hamburger."[7]

ACKNOWLEDGMENTS

If I had to sum up the origins of this project, I'd say it began with my participation in a black-history–themed quiz bowl, *Know Your Heritage*, in my sophomore year at St. Ignatius College Prep in Chicago. Broadcast on a local TV station and hosted by ABC-7 news anchor Jim Rose, *Know Your Heritage* was aired during Black History Month. Each year the competition revolved around a central theme, and watching the show on Saturday mornings always introduced me to something new about African-American life and culture. *Know Your Heritage* led to my first experience of reading about Chicago's Great Migration, my area of study in graduate school and the topic of my first book. Although our team was outmatched by better-prepared squads from across the city, I appreciated the chance to visit a television studio, spend time with the other students on the team, and, more important, travel to the DuSable Museum of African American History for the awards ceremony. The show and our consolation prizes were underwritten by the Black McDonald's Operators Association of Chicago and Northwest Indiana.

Growing up, McDonald's was everywhere. We ate at McDonald's before or after church on Sundays. I hosted my friends at birthday parties there, and no matter how many high-end pastries I sample, the chocolate-banana birthday cake offered at the McDonald's on Western Avenue in Chicago's Rogers Park is my favorite of all time. My friends and I would pool our orders of French fries on the brown trays after school and chat as we enjoyed our growing freedom. In high school, I would go to a McDonald's in downtown Chicago that was decorated with portraits of black history makers and prints from black painters and visual artists before I took an hour-long train-and-bus commute home. In my financially lean days of college and graduate school, McDonald's was a staple of my diet when I was scrambling to finish term papers and dissertation chapters. I frequented other fast food restaurants over the years, but McDonald's was where I grew up, and for most of my life, I have eaten there and enjoyed it. As I have aged and studied, my feelings about fast food have changed, but my gratitude remains for the many memories I have collected over the years sitting in swivel chairs or smashed into a booth catching up with my mom, Mecthilde Boyer, in between her shifts of work. My appreciation for her love and care can never be fully articulated, and it has never been unfelt. My mother's membership among the army of women who work without the protection of unions, the promise of fair compensation, or the possibility of stable retirement has taught me volumes about injustice. My siblings, Regine, Lupita, and Ronald Rousseau have provided me with the support integral to taking risks and charting one's own path. My niece and nephew Emmanuel and Anastasia have brought our family closer together, and I strive to be an aunt that can fill them with pride.

The nourishment I cannot receive from food comes to me through love. My network of aunts, uncles, cousins, kinfolk, fictive kin, and family members in the making have nurtured my ambitions since I was a little girl. My in-laws, Elaine and Fred Yapelli, supported and cared for me from our first introduction in the summer of 2006. Their encouragement—and the love of my now-departed grandmother-in-law Valerie Yapelli—has made me feel like I have always been a member of their family. I am saddened that Elaine passed away five months before the publication of this book. But I am grateful that she was able to receive an advanced copy before she was hospitalized and that she held it in her hands before she was too weak to do so. A great lover of books and a teacher of reading, she appreciated having what she called "such a valuable copy."

This book is as much dedicated to every stranger who has worked to feed me as it is to the people I know and love. When I am eating a plate of Haitian fried pork and plantains at an aunt's house, grabbing a premade salad at an airport concessions kiosk, or on the rare occasions I actually cook in my home, I try to remember the hands—coerced and free—who toil in fields, farms, and factories so others can eat. I'm also grateful to the scores of hotel workers who prepared my rooms, made my breakfasts, retrieved my rental cars, and asked me how my day was going when this book project took me to Los Angeles, Portland, Chicago, Dallas, Charlottesville, New York, Atlanta, and all points in between. In addition to archival research, this book was strengthened by conversations with members of the National Black McDonald's Operators Association and former McDonald's executives, including Roland Parrish, who spent some of his precious time away from his more than twenty franchises to talk to me about history. Roland Jones, Wayne Embry, Albert Okura, Robert Jackson, Janice Baker, Leroy Walker, and Eugene Morris provided me with interviews about their years with and feelings about McDonald's. I am also grateful to Myaisha Hayes for her insights about the work outside of fast food franchises, namely in the Fight for $15 movement, to give me a window into the complexity of worker concerns and worker constraints.

Writing a book is a daunting and often intimidating task, and with each sentence you write, you expose something about yourself and how you look at the world. In turn, the process also invites feedback about how the world looks at you. This process is grueling and can be infuriating without the love and support of friends and community. I'm fortunate to have people in my life who care about my ideas and who help me bear the weight of my internal criticism and fears. While completing this book, I celebrated twenty years of friendship with Elizabeth Pickens, whose book *Your Art Will Save Your Life* did just that for me when I was too overwhelmed and afraid to write and to believe that I had something of value to say. Her care and love for art and artists has changed so many people's creative trajectories, and her humility masks her tremendous impact on arts and activist communities. Writer and artist Ali Liebegott was a virtual companion on many of my research trips, where I could count on her to read my text messages about what true crime television show I was watching, while I decided what I would eat for dinner.

I developed my passion for writing in college at the Missouri School of Journalism and as a student in the Department of Religious Studies. My Missouri family has remained close more than two decades after I showed up for new student orientation with no sense of what I was doing. My mentors Jill Raitt, Laura Hacquard, and Sue Crowley guided my scholarly and activist paths, and their examples are why I decided to pursue the professoriate and a career in higher education. My friends Jamila Wilson, Mark Powell, Michael Watters, Andrew Allan, Brad Paul, Nikole Potulsky, and Michael Lockner supplied the humor and compassion I relied on for years after we graduated to get through my twenties (and thirties, for that matter). Without my selection as a Harry S. Truman Scholar in my junior year of college, I can't imagine how I would have realized my career goals as an academic committed to public service. Fortunately, I had the excellent mentorship and guidance of Andrew Rich, Tara Yglesias, Tonji Wade, the late Diana Aubourg-Millner, and scores of Truman Scholars whose commitment to the greater good always inspires me. I am especially indebted to my Truman Scholar friends Matthew Baugh, Wendi Adelson, Rebecca Buckwalter-Poza, Monica Bell, Nate Watson, and Alex Tyson.

In my graduate school days, I doubted whether I could actually complete a dissertation, let alone two whole books, but my mentors constantly pushed me to sharpen my focus and remember the impact scholarship can have on not only commemorating the past, but also on reimagining the future. My dissertation committee chair Mari Jo Buhle continues to be a model of scholarly discipline and productivity in my transition to a new phase of my career. When I see James Campbell at events, we are now colleagues, but I still remain a student of his flourishes in storytelling on the page and in person. My friendship with Matthew Garcia has steadied me during some of the most difficult and disappointing inflection points in my career. With every twist and turn, I know that I can call Matt and he will remind me that the track is long, and my voice is necessary. I've loved growing up with my friends from those years at Brown, and every time we meet, we are able to mentor each other on our academic paths, as well as provide advice on managing the sometimes crushing realities of aging, parenting, and caring for aging parents. Thank you to Matthew Delmont, Mireya Loza, Mario Sifuentez, Sarah Wald, Angela Mazaris, Angela Howell, Ricardo Howell and the members of my Brown community for getting older with me. And, my "young friends" from Brown, Hentyle Yapp and Izetta Autumn Mobley, thank you for your constant light when I am afraid to venture outside of my head.

My career has taught me that the smartest people are often the kindest ones. The generosity of my colleagues at the University of Oklahoma and Georgetown University can never be repaid, but I will always try to match it when I'm in the world. Julia Ehrhardt, Maurice Jackson, Katherine Benton-Cohen, John Tutino, Chandra Manning, Carol Benedict, Bryan McCann, Judith Tucker, John McNeill, Jim Collins, Michael Kazin, Aviel Roshwald, Ananya Chakravarti, and Joseph McCartin have been incredible advocates for me, and I wish every academic experienced their level of commitment and concern as they navigate their careers. Georgetown has brought incredible people into my life, and by way of my work with Georgetown University's Working Group on Slavery, Memory, and Reconciliation, I was able to see the integrity and intellectual leadership of David Collins, Kevin O'Brien, and Adam Rothman. The generosity of Adam, and the students who have organized the Georgetown Slavery Archive, in helping families stitch together the narrative fibers of their ancestry has inspired me to fight the cynicism that can obscure my perspectives. My friendship with and spiritual guidance from Kevin O'Brien has been a gift, and his introducing me to Ignatian exercises has centered so many parts of my life. My Georgetown community—especially Greg Schenden, Madeline Vitek, Ben Shaw, Colleen Roberts, Aya Waller-Bey, Missy Foy, Corey Stewart, Jason Low, Sarah Johnson, Terrence Johnson, James Benton, and Olivia Lane—has always shown me such grace and appreciation. I am also especially appreciative of the support I have received from Georgetown University's president, John D. DeGioia. At every opportunity, he introduced me as a scholar working on a very important book. Thank you for your vote of confidence, Jack!

Over the years, I have received invaluable funding and research support that allowed me to travel to archives, hire lifesaving assistants, and take the necessary time away from the classroom to finish this book. I owe everything to the librarians and archivists at the various libraries and museums where I collected my research, including libraries at the University of California–Los Angeles, Portland State University, the University of Virginia, Duke University, the University of Southern California, and the Chicago Public Library, the New York Public Library, the Western Reserve Historical Society, the Chicago History Museum, and the Library of Congress. I am thankful for grants from the Ford Foundation Diversity Postdoctoral Fellowship, the New America Eric and Wendy Schmidt Fellowship, the National Endowment for the Humanities Faculty Fellowship, and small research grants from Duke University Libraries and the Summersell Center for the Study of the South, as well as internal Georgetown University faculty grants. I wish I knew all the names of the program officers, reviewers, and office support staff who made sure my applications were logged in, reviewed, and my monies disbursed. Research assistance from Yongle Xue, Khadijah Davis, Esther Olowobi, Cheynee Napier, Alex Vicas, and Sade Bruce were godsends when my office was overrun by photocopies and magazine clippings. I owe special gratitude to Julian St. Reiman who contacted me out of the blue and asked if I needed research help. Without him, I would have never been able to write my proposal. Photographer Francis Shad helped me to look my very best on this book jacket, and I thank him for his creativity. At the eleventh hour when I needed those last few bits of research done, permissions secured, and facts checked, doctoral student Emily Norweg stepped up with such precision and speed. Last but not least, I would have not survived the years between 2015 and 2017 without Nicolette S. Thompson's work as my assistant when there were way too many flights to book, appointments to manage, and urgent emails that needed responses. Nikki's drive and work ethic will be known by many soon enough.

This book has been nurtured by so many brilliant readers and listeners. I presented on this project for the first time in 2013, at the Dark Room Symposium on Race and Visual Culture, and over the past seven years, each audience question and feedback session has challenged and strengthened my ideas. I am deeply indebted to Kimberly Juanita Brown's organization of the Dark Room, as well as her friendship and modeling of how to be a generous academic. Early meetings about this project with editors from other presses helped form the work, and I appreciate the comments that Susan Ferber of Oxford University Press and Mark Simpson-Vos of the University of North Carolina Press offered. Their passion for good historical scholarship has been helpful to so many. I am thankful to the Georgetown University Americas Initiative Seminar, the Johns Hopkins University History Seminar and Center for Medical Humanities and Social Medicine, the University of California-Santa Barbara's Seminar on Work and Labor, the College of William & Mary's Law School, Lewis & Clark College, the University of California-Los Angeles Black Feminist Visions Symposium, the University of Georgia's Dirty History Workshop, the Washington, D.C., Area African American Studies Works-in-Progress Seminar, the Smithsonian National Museum of American History Seminar, the Woodrow Wilson Center for Scholars History Seminar, Princeton Food Studies Conference, New America Fellows Lunch Series, and Yale University's departments of history and African American studies for invitations to share my research and for all of the great advice on improving it. Fellow historians Robert Weems and Carol Anderson were invaluable sounding boards for this book and career matters as I navigated the tenure track. My colleagues at New America—Ted Johnson, Nikole Hannah-Jones, Robin Harris, Janell Ross, Awista Ayub, Veronica Mooney, and Samieleen Lawson—made my time on fellowship there rewarding and welcoming. There were many days I was certain I couldn't read one more newspaper article or sort through one more box of documents, when text messages, phone calls, emails, and happy-hour excursions with Sheyda Jahanbani, Nathan Connolly, Sam Pinto, Nicole Ivy, Christian Hosam, Amira Rose Davis, and Sherie Randolph lifted my spirits and helped lead me back to my computer. A research presentation on this paper led to a friendship with Brandi Thompson Summers, and that made it all worth it.

This book would not exist without Carole Sargent's encouragement. Carole saw me through the publication of my first book, and she was the first person who celebrated when I signed the contract for this one. Carole connected me to Michelle Tessler, who represented me after I overcame my fears and decided to pitch my book with a trade press. Michelle has an uncanny way of investing in an author's project while respecting the author's vision and expertise. As I waited to hear about press interest in my book, I kept my fingers crossed that this project would land with Katie Adams of Liveright Publishing. Katie's warmth toward and encouragement of her writers parallels her intelligence and wit. From our very first conversation, I knew that working with a person of such integrity and one who valued the many dimensions of who I am was exactly what I, and this book, needed. When Katie left her post with Liveright, I was able to transition to the incredibly talented and enthusiastic agenda of Marie Pantojan. And editor Dan Gerstle and associate editor Gina Iaquinta's inheritance of the book after Marie left Liveright was seamless. The patience, dedication, and professionalism of the Liveright and Norton teams allowed my years of research to transform into a book that I can be proud of; for this, I am deeply grateful and humbled. Steve Attardo's beautiful cover design captured the complexity and the sensitivity I hoped to convey with this project. Production manager Julia Druskin and assistant project editor Amy Medeiros made this project's release stress free. Copyeditor Fred Wiemer's diligent review of my manuscript may have cured me of my addiction to commas. Proofreader Susan Goarke and compositors Joe Lops and Ken Hansen carefully managed my many changes during the proofing process, and JoAnne Metsch elegantly designed the interior of the book. Finally, I'm grateful to the marketing and publicity team—Golda Rademacher,

Peter Miller, Cordelia Calvert, and Nick Curley—at Liveright for their hard work promoting my book.

My most ebullient thanks go to my spouse, Mark Yapelli, for living with this project in the best and worst ways. I know that my work does not make our lives easy, but I hope it is always worth it. Even though this journey has ended, I will still point out converted Pizza Huts to you while we are on road trips, and I will still light up when you mention Arthur Treacher's Fish & Chips.

After the 2016 election, I found myself with a heightened sense of despair about the direction of the nation, the future of my students, and the safety of the people I love most. At the end of the academic year, a student asked me, "What's going to happen next?" As a historian, I love pretending that I can actually predict the future because I believe myself to have a grasp on the past. But, I am not so arrogant as to believe that I could do this in such troubling times. So, I told my students the one thing I find myself repeating constantly, because it is not a prediction, but rather a truth I've discovered over the years. "I do not know what will happen, but I know we have each other, and that is worth a lot." The future is uncertain, indeed, but if the present is any indicator, I know I will not face it alone.

NOTES

Preface to the Paperback Edition

1. McDonald's USA, "McDonald's Black and Positively Golden Movement and YWCA USA Join Forces to Close Entrepreneurship Knowledge Gap for Rising Moguls," PR Newswire, September 30, 2019, https://www.prnewswire.com/news -releases/mcdonalds-black--positively-golden-movement--ywca-usa-join-forces -to-close-entrepreneurship-knowledge-gap-for-rising-moguls-300927169.html.

Introduction: From Sit-In to Drive-Thru

1. Radley Balko, *Rise of the Warrior Cop: The Militarization of America's Police Forces* (New York: PublicAffairs, 2014). In a *Newsweek* article from the summer of 2014, Taylor Wofford reported that small towns acquired grenade launchers, Humvees, and mine-resistant, ambush-protected (MRAP) vehicles through this program. Taylor Wofford, "How America's Police Became an Army: The 1033 Program," *Newsweek*, August 13, 2014.

2. Ferguson, Missouri, and St. Louis County have been the topic of a number of scholarly examinations on racial divides among municipalities, as well as the ways that city-county separation has exacerbated social problems. See Colin Gordon, *Mapping Decline: St. Louis and the Fate of the American City* (Philadelphia: University of Pennsylvania Press, 2009), and *Citizen Brown: Race, Democracy, and Inequality in the St. Louis Suburbs* (Chicago: University of Chicago Press, 2019). Keona K. Ervin's *Gateway to Equality: Black Women and the Struggle for Economic Justice in St. Louis* (Lexington: University Press of Kentucky, 2017) explores the role of black women in fighting for improved working and living conditions in the city.

3. On Wednesday, August 13, 2014, *Washington Post* reporter Wesley Lowery and the *Huffington Post*'s Ryan Reilly were arrested by Ferguson police for "trespassing in a McDonald's." St. Louis County later dropped the charges against the journalists. Wesley Lowery, "In Ferguson, Washington Post Reporter Wesley Lowrey Gives Account of His Arrest," *Washington Post*, August 14, 2014, and Niraj Chokshi, "Ferguson-Related Charges Dropped Against *Washington Post* and *Huffington Post* Reporters," *Washington Post*, May 19, 2016.

4. Centers for Disease Control, National Health and Nutrition Examination Survey, 2018, https://www.cdc.gov/nchs/nhanes/index.htm.

5. Cedric Robinson, *Black Marxism: The Making of the Black Radical Tradition* (Chapel Hill: University of North Carolina Press, 1983).

6. Angela Hilmers, David C. Hilmers, and Jayna Dave, "Neighborhood Disparities in Access to Healthy Foods and Their Effect on Environmental Justice," *American Journal of Public Health* 101, no. 9 (September 2012): 1644–54.

7. National Institutes of Health, "Rates of New Diagnosed Cases of Type 1 and Type 2 Diabetes on the Rise Among Children, Teens," April 13, 2017.

8. "Table 58: Normal Weight, Overweight, and Obesity Among Adults Aged 20 and Over, by Selected Characteristics: United States, Selected Years 1998–1994 through 2011–2014," National Center for Health Statistics, With Chartbook on Long-term Trends in Health, Hyattsville, MD, 2017.

9. Pew Charitable Trusts, "The Role of Emergency Savings in Family Financial Security: What Resources Do Families Have for Financial Emergencies?" November 2015, 8.

10. Eric Schlosser, *Fast Food Nation: The Dark Side of the All-American Meal* (New York: Mariner's Press, 2013). Schlosser's text is one of the most important pieces of research about the fast food industry. In *Super Size Me*, filmmaker Morgan Spurlock embarked on a thirty-day diet of only products purchased at McDonald's. During the course of his experiment, Spurlock gained more than twenty pounds, and his doctor reported that his cholesterol levels were significantly raised. Morgan Spurlock, director, *Super Size Me*, Samuel Goldwyn Films, 2004.

11. "America's Epidemic of Youth Obesity," *New York Times*, November 29, 2002. Accessed December, 2018.

12. The research and scholarship on food justice, health equity, and the fast food industry is vast. A few texts have gained considerable attention in their analysis of these issues, but they often fail to take on how race and history intersect with their concerns. Vegan and environmental activist John Robbins, who spurned his family's Baskin-Robbins Ice Cream inheritance, approaches the issue of food justice by challenging the consumption of meat from a moral-ethical as well as a health perspective. John Robbins, *Diet for a New America: How Your Food Choices Affect Your Health, Happiness, and the Future of Life on Earth*, 2nd ed. (San Francisco: HJ Kramer/New World Library, 2012). Nutritionist Marion Nestle's research on food and politics exposes the way that the food industry not only establishes what people want to eat, but she indicts its leaders for using bad science to influence how the federal government sets standards for nutrition and deems products "healthy." Marion Nestle, *Unsavory Truth: How Food Companies Skew the Science of What We Eat* (New York: Basic Books, 2018); *Soda Politics: Taking on Big Soda (and Winning)* (New York: Oxford University Press, 2015); *Food Politics: How the Food Industry Influences Nutrition and Health* (Berkeley: University of California Press, 2013); and *Safe Food: The Politics of Food Safety* (Berkeley: University of California Press, 2010). Michael Pollan's writing on the nature of food, cooking, and advice on what to eat has been quite popular, and his suggestion that people need to "eat food, not too much, mostly plants," emerges from several studies that distinguish between real food and fake food. Michael Pollan, *Cooked: A Natural History of Transformation* (New York: Penguin, 2013); *Food Rules: An*

Eater's Manual (New York: Penguin, 2009); *In Defense of Food: An Eater's Manifesto* (New York: Penguin, 2008); and *The Omnivore's Dilemma: A Natural History of Four Meals* (New York: Penguin, 2006). African-American food studies have provided critical interventions into the food studies field to highlight the importance that race plays in what people cook, consume, and contend with under oppressive systems, from slavery to the era of segregation to contemporary struggles. Jennifer Jensen Wallach's *Every Nation Has Its Dish: Black Bodies and Black Food in Twentieth-Century America* (Chapel Hill: University of North Carolina Press, 2019) emphasizes the way food is an expression of black identity and politics. Jessica B. Harris, *High on the Hog: A Culinary Journey from Africa to America* (New York: Bloomsbury, 2012), provides a wide overview of black foodways. *Black Hunger: Soul Food and America* (Minneapolis: University of Minnesota Press, 2004) by Doris Witt is an excellent exploration of the meaning of food to the black cultural experience. Toni Tipton-Martin, *The Jemima Code: Two Centuries of African American Cookbooks* (Austin: University of Texas Press, 2015), examines the ways that black food writing has been used as a tool of cultural self-fashioning and self-preservation. Similarly, the essays in Rafia Zafar, *Recipes for Respect: African American Meals and Meaning* (Athens: University of Georgia Press, 2019), uncover how black food writing serves as a lens for understanding black politics and cultural life. Most recently, anthropologist Ashanté M. Reese directs attention to the bigger picture of food justice and race in her study of the ways that African Americans in a Washington, D.C., neighborhood navigate food access restraints in a gentrifying city. Ashanté M. Reese, *Black Geographies: Race, Self-Reliance, and Food Access in Washington, D.C.* (Chapel Hill: University of North Carolina Press, 2019).

13. Bart Elmore, *Citizen Coke: The Making of Coca-Cola Capitalism* (New York: W. W. Norton, 2014), 10. Also see Peter M. Birkeland, *Franchising Dreams: The Lure of Entrepreneurship in America* (Chicago: University of Chicago Press, 2002).

14. In James Watson's *Golden Arches East: McDonald's in East Asia*, 2nd ed. (Stanford, CA: Stanford University Press, 2006), he demonstrates how McDonald's has had an influence on how affluent people in Hong Kong, China, Taiwan, South Korea, and Japan relate to a business that is both associated with the United States and adjusted for local consumer market preferences. This process leads to a form of naturalization in which McDonald's is simultaneously foreign and familiar.

15. Andrew Smith, *Hamburger: A Global History* (London: Reaktion Books, 2008), 25.

16. Smith, 31.

17. Smith, 31. Also *White Tower System, Inc. v. White Castle System of Eating Houses Corporation*, May 4, 1937.

18. Burger Chef was founded by Frank and Donald Thomas as an Indianapolis-based franchise restaurant. The men had designed the first flame broiler, which would be used to distinguish Burger King's burger from its competitor McDonald's. Burger Chef expanded throughout the 1960s and 1970s, after General Foods acquired the chain. Often credited with developing a children's meal and toy combination that inspired the McDonald's Happy Meal, Burger Chef mostly disappeared by the early 1980s. See Eric Dodds, "*Mad Men*: A Brief History of the Real-World Burger Chef," *Newsweek*, May 19, 2014.

19. Albert Okura, *Albert Okura: The Chicken Man with a 50 Year Plan* (Author House, 2014), 51.

20. Okura, 60.

21. Stacy Perman, *In-N-Out Burger: A Behind-the-Counter Look at the Fast-Food Chain That Breaks All the Rules* (New York: Harper Business, 2010).

22. Schlosser's *Fast Food Nation* pays particular attention to the stresses felt by franchisees who must meet royalty, advertising, and leasing requirements before they can make any profits.

23. Lizabeth Cohen, *A Consumers' Republic: The Politics of Mass Consumption in Postwar America* (New York: Vintage Books, 2003), 7. See also Traci Parker, *Department Stores and the Black Freedom Movement: Workers, Consumers, and Civil Rights from the 1930s to the 1980s* (Chapel Hill: University of North Carolina Press, 2019).

24. "Speculative Bellyache: Fast Food Franchisers Are Risking a Bout of Indigestion," *Barron's*, August 25, 1969.

25. "Speculative Bellyache."

26. The history of black business illustrates the ways that African-American ingenuity has led to more than just the selling of goods or the opening of stores. African-American businesses secured the freedom of the enslaved, supported institutions in the era of segregation, and funded critical social movements. See Juliet K. Walker, *Free Frank: A Black Pioneer on the Antebellum Frontier* (Lexington: University Press of Kentucky, 1983), and *The History of Black Business in America: Capitalism, Race, Entrepreneurship*, vol. 1, *To 1865* (Chapel Hill: University of North Carolina Press, 2015). John Sibley Butler, *Entrepreneurship and Self-Help Among Black Americans: A Reconsideration of Race and Economics* (Buffalo: SUNY Press, 2005), emphasizes the civic role of black businesses. Some studies look at African-American leadership in specific industries. Quincy T. Mills, *Cutting Along the Color Line: Black Barbers and Barber Shops in America* (Philadelphia: University of Pennsylvania Press, 2013), and Douglas Bristol Jr., *Knights of the Razor: Black Barbers in Slavery and Freedom* (Baltimore: Johns Hopkins University Press, 2015), explore the importance of black barber shops. Tiffany Gill, *Beauty Shop Politics: African American Activism in the Beauty Industry* (Urbana: University of Illinois Press, 2010), and Susannah Walker, *Style and Status: Selling Beauty to African American Women, 1920–1975* (Lexington: University Press of Kentucky, 2007), highlight the ways that beauty salons and the beauty industry at large allowed black women to voice their political concerns, assert their financial independence, and circumvent working for whites. In Shomari Will's profiles of black millionaires, the journalist highlights economic success across sectors, and he highlights the economic gains collected in all-black towns. Shomari Wills, *Black Fortunes: The Story of the First Six African Americans who Escaped Slavery and Became Millionaires* (New York: Amistad, 2018). African-American banks played a critical role in helping businesses grow. See Shennette Garrett-Scott, *Banking on Freedom: Black Women in U.S. Finance Before the New Deal* (New York: Columbia University Press, 2019).

27. For more on the War on Poverty, see Jill Quadagno, *The Color of Welfare: How Racism Undermined the War on Poverty* (Oxford: Oxford University Press, 1996), and Marissa Chappell, *The War on Welfare: Family, Poverty, and Politics in Modern America* (Philadelphia: University of Pennsylvania Press, 2011).

28. Laura Warren Hill and Julia Rabig, "Introduction," in Laura Warren Hill and Julia Rabig, eds., *The Business of Black Power: Community Development, Capitalism, and Corporate Responsibility in Postwar America* (Rochester, NY: University of Rochester Press, 2012), 2.

29. Leah Wright Rigeur, *The Loneliness of the Black Republican: Pragmatic Politics and the Pursuit of Power* (Princeton: Princeton University Press, 2015), is an excellent analysis of black support and critique of Richard Nixon, as well as conservatives broadly, and it presents a nuanced look at how economic issues shaped racial politics for black and white Republicans from 1968 to the 1980s.

30. For more on black capitalism, see Robert L. Allen, *Black Awakening in Capitalist America: An Analytic History* (Trenton, NJ: Africa World Press, 1990).

31. Chin Jou, "Donald Trump Isn't the First President to Give Fast Food His Seal of Approval," *Washington Post*, January 18, 2019.

Chapter One: Fast Food Civil Rights

1. Keeley Webster, "San Bernardino Faces Its Post-Bankruptcy Future," *Bond Buyer*, December 30, 2016, https://www.bondbuyer.com/news/san-bernardino -faces-its-post-bankruptcy-future. Also, Joe Mozingo, "San Bernardino: Broken City," *Los Angeles Times*, June 14, 2015.

2. John F. Love, *McDonald's: Behind the Arches* (New York: Bantam Press, 1995), and *The Founder*, directed by John Lee Hancock (New York: Weinstein Co., 2016), Netflix Streaming.

3. Douglas Flamming, *Bound for Freedom: Black Los Angeles in Jim Crow America* (Berkeley: University of California Press, 2005).

4. Flamming, 88.

5. See Stephen Johnson, *Burnt Cork: Traditions and Legacies of Blackface Minstrelsy* (Amherst: University of Massachusetts Press, 2012), and John Strausbaugh, *Black Like You: Blackface, Whiteface, Insult, and Imitation in American Popular Culture* (New York: Penguin Press, 2006).

6. The literature on race and western United States history has contributed significantly to understanding the African-American experience outside of the confines of the South and the industrial North. Josh Kun and Laura Pulido, eds., *Black and Brown in Los Angeles: Beyond Conflict and Coalition* (Berkeley: University of California Press, 2013); Shana Bernstein, *Bridges of Reform: Interracial Civil Rights Activism in Twentieth-Century Los Angeles* (Oxford: Oxford University Press, 2011); and Kenneth W. Mack, *Representing the Race: The Creation of the Civil Rights Lawyer* (Cambridge: Harvard University Press, 2010), provide an excellent analysis of the Los Angeles NAACP and their leader, attorney Loren Miller.

7. Lisa Napoli, "The Story of How McDonald's First Got Its Start," Smithsonian.com, November 1, 2016.

8. "New Utopia for Negroes," *Los Angeles Times*, December 19, 1904.

9. Jason Kottke, "Early McDonald's Menus," last modified March 18, 2013, https://kottke.org/13/03/early-mcdonalds-menus, and Donna Scanlon, "McDonald's Bar-B-Que," *Library of Congress* (blog), May 15, 2010, https://blogs.loc.gov/inside_adams/2010/05/mcdonald%E2%80%99s-bar-b-que/.

10. Andrew Smith, *Hamburger: A Global History* (London: Reaktion Books, 2008), 10. Smith debunks the urban legend that Delmonico's restaurant in New York City invented the hamburger, as well as the claim that the hamburger debuted in 1904 at the Louisiana Purchase Exposition in St. Louis.

11. Smith, 15.

12. Smith, 20–24.

13. "All-Colored Jury Hears Man's Case in California," *Pittsburgh Courier*, March 27, 1926.

14. See "Guide to the Black History Collection, 1984–1999," Pasadena History Museum, http://pdf.oac.cdlib.org/pdf/phm/blackhis.pdf.

15. Lisa Morehouse, "So Much More than Tacos: San Bernardino's Mitla Café," Eater.com, July 25, 2018. The owners of the Mitla Café claim that Glen Bell, founder of Taco Bell, learned about Mexican food from them. Bell's hot dog stand was located across the street from their café. Opened in 1937, it was a place for Mexicans and Mexican-Americans in San Bernardino to not only eat familiar foods, but to organize politically against segregation and discrimination. See also Gustavo Arellano, *Taco USA: How Fast Food Conquered America* (New York: Simon & Schuster, 2012). For more on Mexican Americans and segregation in California, see Vicki L. Ruiz, "South by Southwest: Mexican Americans and Segregated Schooling, 1900–1950," *OAH Magazine of History* 15, no. 2 (Winter 2001): 23–27.

16. Love, 12.

17. Love, 15, and George Harrison, "Anyone for a Tempting Cheeseburger? This is What the Original McDonald's Menu Looked Like," *The Sun*, December 2, 2016.

18. The Air Material Command Center, later renamed for World War II casualty Leland Francis Norton, became known as Norton Air Force Base. Norton was where a young Morgan Freeman discovered he did not want to become a fighter pilot; rather, he wanted to play the role of a pilot in the movies. See Henry Louis Gates Jr., *In Search of Our Roots: How 19 Extraordinary African Americans Reclaimed Their Past* (New York: Crown, 2009).

19. A. J. Scott, "The Technopoles of Southern California," *Environment and Planning* 22 (1990): 1575–1605.

20. "FEPC Hearing Opens on Railman's Charge," *Los Angeles Times*, January 10, 1961.

21. Thomas J. Sugrue, "Automobile in American Life and Society, Driving While Black: The Car and Race Relations in Modern America," http://www.autolife.umd.umich.edu/.

22. For more on the *Negro Traveler's Green Book*, see Michael Ra-Shon Hall, "The Negro Traveller's Guide to a Jim Crow South: Negotiating Racialized Landscapes

During a Dark Period in United States Cultural History, 1936–1967," *Postcolonial Studies* 19 (January 2015): 1–13, and Erin Krutko Devlin, "Navigating the Green Book (The Negro Travelers' Green Book)," *Journal of American History* 104, no. 1 (2017): 312–13.

23. Ryan Hagen, "Norton Air Force Base Marks 20 Years Since Closure," *San Bernardino Sun*, March 22, 2014.

24. Jean Simon, "San Bernardino Vet Tells Story of Two-Year House Hunt," *Los Angeles Sentinel*, January 15, 1948.

25. Love, 25–26.

26. Raymond Mohl, "Planned Destruction: The Interstates and Central City Housing," in John F. Bauman, Roger Biles, and Kristin Sylvian, eds., *From Tenements to the Taylor Homes: In Search of an Urban Housing Policy in Twentieth Century America* (State College: Pennsylvania State University Press, 2000), 226–45.

27. Mohl, 233–34.

28. The term "food desert" was first used by researchers Steven Cummins and Sally Macintrye in relationship to a study of residents in a Scottish public housing community. Other researchers and food justice activists argue for different terminology to describe the phenomenon of people being unable to access healthy foods close to where they live. Karen Washington offers the term "food apartheid" because it signals a concern about inequality broadly. See Steven Cummins and Sally Macintyre, "Food Deserts—Evidence and Assumption in Health Policy Making," *The BMJ* 325, no. 7631 (August 24, 2002), 436–38, and Karen Washington, "It's Not a Food Desert, It's Food Apartheid," *Guernica*, May 7, 2018.

29. Love, 27–28.

30. Love, 41–44.

31. Love, 192–201. Love estimated in 1995: "If McDonald had not sold his right to the 0.5% of McDonald's sales that was due him and Mac under their ninety-nine-year contract with Kroc, he would have become one of the country's wealthiest men, almost as wealthy as Ray Kroc. Since the brothers sold their rights for $2.7 million in late 1961, McDonald's restaurants have rung up a total of $198 billion in sales. The royalty payments that would have been due the McDonald brothers had they not sold out come to a total of $990 million. Today, the McDonalds would be earning more than $109 million a year." Love, 201.

32. Love, 201.

33. Love, 153.

34. Ray Kroc, *Grinding It Out: The Making of McDonald's* (New York: Bedford/St. Martin's, 1992), 203.

35. "Other People's Business," *Chicago Defender*, June 13, 1959, and "Other People's Business," *Chicago Defender*, April 8, 1957.

36. Untitled display ad, *Chicago Defender*, September 9, 1961.

37. "A Great Decade," *Chicago Defender*, February 24, 1966, and "Opportunity Awaits at McDonald's," *Chicago Defender*, March 12, 1966.

38. Victoria W. Wolcott addresses the struggle for racial integration and places of amusement. Victoria W. Wolcott, *Race, Riots, and Roller Coasters: The Strug-*

gle over Segregated Recreation in America (Philadelphia: University of Pennsylvania Press, 2014).

39. Anne Moody, *Coming of Age in Mississippi* (New York: Dell, 1992), and Melba Patillo-Beals, *Warriors Don't Cry: A Searing Memoir of the Battle to Integrate Little Rock's Central High* (New York: Simon & Schuster, 2007), 21, 66.

40. Renee Romano, "No Diplomatic Immunity: African Diplomats, the State Department, and Civil Rights, 1961–1964," *Journal of American History* 87, no. 2 (September 2000): 546–79.

41. August Meier and Elliot Rudwick, "How CORE Began," *Social Science Quarterly* 49, no. 4 (1969): 789–99.

42. For more on fashion, hair, and protest during the civil rights movement, see Tanisha C. Ford, *Liberated Threads: Black Women, Style, and the Global Politics of Soul* (Chapel Hill: University of North Carolina Press, 2015), and Tiffany Gill, *Beauty Shop Politics: African-American Women's Activism in the Beauty Industry* (Urbana: University of Illinois Press, 2010).

43. Rebecca Cerese and Steven Channing, *February One*, distributed by California Newsreel, aired 2004 on *Independent Lens*, PBS.

44. Aniko Bodroghkozy, *Equal Time: Television and the Civil Rights Movement* (Urbana: University of Illinois Press, 2013).

45. Melissa Clark, "Other People's Food and the Greensboro Four," *Splendid Table*, August 16, 2016. William Henry Chafe, *Civilities and Civil Rights: Greensboro, North Carolina, and the Black Struggle for Freedom* (Oxford: Oxford University Press, 1981).

46. "August 15, 1958 Complaint," Library Integration Collection, Digital Archive of Memphis Public Library, https://memphislibrary.contentdm.oclc.org/digital/collection/p15342coll4/id/88.

47. Wayne Risher, "Golden Arches Paved Way for Memphis Entrepreneur Saul Kaplan," *Memphis Commercial Appeal*, February 26, 2016.

48. "List of Memphis Businesses Willing to Desegregate," Maxine A. Smith NAACP Collection, Box 4, Folder 2, Civil Rights Digital Library, http://crdl.usg.edu/export/html/tnmpl/smithnaacp/crdl_tnmpl_smithnaacp_000210.html?Welcome.

49. Jerry Bledsoe, "The Story of Hardees," May 27, 2011, https://www.ourstate.com/hardees/. See also "Greensboro, North Carolina, 1963," Assistant Director's File, 1942–1965, Box 3, Folder 12, Congress of Racial Equality (CORE) Records, 1941–1967, Wisconsin Historical Society, Madison, Wisconsin. The arrival of the thrifty meal had been a hit, and the restaurant would later inspire Navy veteran-turned-restaurateur-and-innkeeper Wilber Hardee to create his namesake burger franchise a year later in Greenville.

50. Eugene E. Pfaff Jr., oral history interview with Lewis A. Brandon III, Greensboro Voices/Greensboro Public Library Oral History Project, Tape 1 transcript, http://libcdm1.uncg.edu/cdm/ref/collection/CivilRights/id/807.

51. "Memorandum," dated May 10, 1963, Departments and Related Organizations Memoranda, 1963–1965, Box 48, Folder 9, CORE Records, 1941–1967, Wisconsin Historical Society.

52. "McDonald's Store #433 Sign," National Register of Historic Places Registration

Form, http://www.arkansaspreservation.com/national-register-listings/mcdonald -39-s-store-433-sign. Accessed January 26, 2018.

53. Randy Findley, "Crossing the White Line: SNCC in Three Delta Towns, 1963–1967," in Jennifer Jensen Wallach and John A. Kirk, eds., *Arsnick: The Student Nonviolent Coordinating Committee in Arkansas* (Fayetteville: University of Arkansas Press, 2011), 68, and Vivian Carroll Jones, "The Civil Rights Movement in Pine Bluff" in Wallach and Kirk, eds., 170–71. "Students Attacked with Ammonia Acid in Pine Bluff, Ark.," *Atlanta Daily World,* August 4, 1963.

54. "Students Attacked with Ammonia."

55. "Students Attacked with Ammonia."

56. "In Arkansas: McDonald's Boycott Called; Helena Police Arrest Three," *Student Voice,* December 9, 1963.

57. "SNCC Annual Report, 1964," in Jensen et al., *Arsnick.*

58. Angela Jill Cooley, "A Helping of Gravy: Golden Arches & White Spaces," *Gravy* 53, (December 3, 2014), and *To Live and Dine in Dixie: The Evolution of Urban Food Culture in the Jim Crow South* (Athens: University of Georgia Press, 2015).

59. United States, *Civil Rights Acts of 1964* (Washington, D.C.: U.S. Government Printing Office, 1969). For more on the journey to the passage of the Civil Rights Act, see Todd S. Purdum, *An Idea Whose Time Has Come: Two Presidents, Two Parties, and the Battle for the Civil Rights Act of 1964* (New York: Henry Holt & Co., 2014), and Clay Risen, *The Bill of The Century: The Epic Battle for the Civil Rights Act* (New York: Bloomsbury, 2014).

60. "Fried Chicken: Whites, $1.75 Negroes $5.25," *Chicago Defender,* September 24, 1964.

61. Whitney Young, "To Be Equal," *Chicago Defender,* October 24, 1964.

62. United States National Advisory Commission on Civil Disorders, *The Kerner Report: The 1968 Report on the National Advisory Commission on Civil Disorders* (New York: Pantheon Books, 1968), 82. See also Thomas J. Hrach, *The Riot Report and the News: How the Kerner Commission Changed Media Coverage of Black America* (Amherst: University of Massachusetts Press, 2016), and Steve Gillon, *Separate and Unequal: The Kerner Commission and the Unraveling of American Liberalism* (New York: Basic Books, 2018).

63. United States National Advisory Commission on Civil Disorders, Report of the National Advisory Commission on Civil Disorders: Summary of Report (Washington, DC: United States Government Printing Office, 1968), 26.

64. "Civil Rights Timeline, August 21, 1959," Civil Rights Collection, Digital Memphis.

65. "Campaign Flyer for Sugarmon, Hooks, Bunton, and Love," George W. Lee Collection, Digital Memphis, https://memphislibrary.contentdm.oclc.org/digital/ collection/p13039coll2/id/170/rec/2. For more on black civil rights in Memphis, see Shirletta Kinchen, *Black Power in the Bluff City: African American Activism in Memphis, 1965–1975* (Knoxville: University of Tennessee Press, 2016); Aram Goudsouzian and Charles W. McKinney Jr., *An Unseen Light: Black Struggles for Freedom in Memphis, Tennessee* (Lexington: University Press of Kentucky, 2018); and Jonathan Chism, *Saints in the Struggle: Church of God in Christ*

Activists in the Memphis Civil Rights Movement, 1954–1968 (New York: Lexington Books, 2019).

66. Martin Luther King Jr., "All Labor Has Dignity," American Federation of State, County, and Municipal Employees (AFSCME) mass meeting, Memphis Sanitation Strike, Bishop Charles Mason Temple, Church of God in Christ, Memphis, Tennessee, March 18, 1968, in Cornel West, *The Radical King* (Boston: Beacon Press, 2015).

67. Martin Luther King Jr., "I've Been to the Mountaintop," April 3, 1968, Memphis, TN, http://kingencyclopedia.stanford.edu/encyclopedia/documentsentry/ive_been_to_the_mountaintop/.

68. Black insurance companies provided life insurance and burial policies to African Americans, and sometimes played the role of lender and investor for blacks unable to access bank services. Walter B. Weare, *Black Business in the New South: A Social History of the North Carolina Mutual Life Insurance Company* (Durham: Duke University Press, 1993).

69. "I've Been to the Mountaintop."

70. For more on the Poor People's Campaign, see Charles Fager, *Uncertain Resurrection: The Poor People's Washington Campaign* (Grand Rapids: Eerdmans, 1969); Hilliard Lawrence Lackey, *Marks, Martin, and the Mule Train: Marks, Mississippi—Martin Luther King, Jr. and the Origin of the 1968 Poor People's Campaign* (Xlibris, 2014); Sylvie Laurent, *King and the Other America: The Poor People's Campaign and the Quest for Economic Equality* (Oakland: University of California Press, 2018); and Gerald D. McKnight, *The Last Crusade: Martin Luther King, Jr., The FBI, and the Poor People's Campaign* (Boulder, CO: Westview Press, 1998).

71. "I've Been to the Mountaintop."

72. "McDonald's Buys Gee Gee Holdings," *Washington Post*, October 25, 1967.

73. Author interview with Roland Jones (former McDonald's executive), March 2018.

74. Martin Luther King Jr., "The Civil Rights Struggle in the United States Today," *Record of the Association of the Bar of the City of New York* 20, no. 5 (April 21, 1965): 20.

Chapter Two: Burgers in the Age of Black Capitalism

1. "Mayor Daley Orders Chicago's Policemen to Shoot Arsonists and Looters," *New York Times,* April 16, 1968.

2. Vincent Harding, *Martin Luther King: The Inconvenient Hero* (Maryknoll, NY: Orbis Books, 2000), 78.

3. Author interview with Roland Jones.

4. Author interview with Roland Jones.

5. Author interview with Roland Jones.

6. The Great Migration radically transformed the racial politics, economic systems, and cultural production of northern and western cities, from New York to Los Angeles. For more on the Great Migration, see James N. Gregory, *The Southern Diaspora: How the Great Migrations of Black and White Southerners Trans-*

formed America (Chapel Hill: University of North Carolina Press, 2005); Isabel Wilkerson, *The Warmth of Other Suns: The Epic Story of America's Great Migration* (New York: Vintage, 2011); and James Grossman, *Land of Hope: Chicago, Black Southerners, and the Great Migration* (Chicago: University of Chicago Press, 1991).

7. For more on black hospitals, see Vanessa Northington Gamble, *Making a Place for Ourselves: The Black Hospital Movement, 1920–1945* (Oxford: Oxford University Press, 1995).

8. Robert McClory, "Unemployment at 30% in Woodlawn," *Chicago Defender*, May 20, 1975.

9. "McLegends in Spotlight: NBMOA Celebrates 25 Years of Progress," *Atlanta Daily World*, October 16, 1997.

10. Herman Petty, Transcript from National Black McDonald's Operators Anniversary Film.

11. Patricia Sowell Harris, *None of Us Is as Good as All of Us: How McDonald's Prospers by Embracing Inclusion and Diversity* (Hoboken, NJ: Wiley, 2009), 31.

12. "Hamburger's Last Stand: Hidden Costs of Fast Food," *East West Journal*, June 1979, 30.

13. Jones, 169–75, and Harris, 33.

14. Perri Small, "City's Black McDonald's Owner Reflects on Career," *Chicago Weekend*, November 13, 1997, and "Black Owners Meet," *Chicago Tribune*, August 25, 1980. Harris, 33.

15. "Rangers to Open Restaurant," *Chicago Tribune*, November 11, 1968, A18.

16. William Jones, "How Blackstone Rangers Helped Scuttle Red Rooster Food Chain," *Chicago Defender*, March 8, 1970.

17. Harris, 32.

18. Tom Brune and James Yliselany, "The Making of Jeff Fort," *Chicago Magazine*, November 1988. Jeff Fort, who migrated to Chicago from Mississippi as a child, was a proponent of black capitalism, so much so that he famously received an invitation to President Richard Nixon's 1968 inauguration. Fort organized his gang into a political group, the Grassroots Independent Voters of Illinois, and received a million dollars in grants and donations, including monies from the Office of Equal Opportunity, to open businesses and provide job training. A month before Petty's McDonald's store opened, in November of 1968, the Rangers debuted their own non-profit, twenty-four-hour restaurant on the site of a former coffeehouse. Funded by a $3,000 loan from the Kenwood-Oakland Community Organization—a local body that drew the funds from another program named Toward Responsible Freedom—the restaurant was supposed to provide job training to local youth. But the restaurant's greatest challenge was Fort's federal indictment over how he secured so much funding for his projects, which provided him with a salary.

19. Harris, 32.

20. Harris, 33.

21. Harris, 33.

22. For more on the 1968 Democratic National Convention, see Michael Schumacher, *The Contest: The 1968 Election and the War for America's Soul* (Minneapolis: University of Minnesota Press, 2018); John Schultz, *No One Was Killed: The Democratic National Convention, August 1968* (Chicago: University of Chicago Press, 2009): and Jan Weiner, *Conspiracy in the Streets: The Extraordinary Trial of the Chicago Eight* (New York: New Press, 2006).

23. Author interview with Wayne Embry.

24. Max Boas and Steve Chain, *Big Mac: The Unauthorized Story of McDonald's* (New York: E.P. Dutton & Co., 1976), 167.

25. ViewPoint, Inc. 1994/04, Subject Files, Box 90-5, SF, Corporate Files, McDonald's, 1975–1977, 90-5, ViewPoint, Virginia G. Harsh Research Collection, Carter G. Woodson Regional Library, Chicago Public Library.

26. ViewPoint, Inc. 1994/04, Subject Files, Box 90-5, SF Corporate Files, McDonald's, 1975–1977, ViewPoint.

27. ViewPoint, Inc. 1994/04, Subject Files, Box 90-5, SF Corporate Files, McDonald's, 1975–1977, ViewPoint.

28. Harris, 39.

29. Graydon Megan, "Robert Beavers, Former McDonald's Executive, Dies at 71," *Chicago Tribune*, June 27, 2018.

30. Harris, 40.

31. Harris, 42.

32. "Birth Pangs of Black Capitalism," *Time*, October 18, 1968, 124–27.

33. Harris, 45.

34. Petty, Transcript, 4. The first efforts to recruit minority franchisees mostly focused on African-Americans but would soon pivot toward Latinos, Asian Americans, and Pacific Islanders. This new interest in being supportive of people of color was embraced by some but for others made the question of racial identity rise to an uncomfortable surface. Outside of McDonald's, the franchising rush was also consuming the thoughts of potential businesspeople. For some, franchising was not as fulfilling as the potential of starting one's own business, and the issue of opening opportunities to minorities drew some people to questions about their own identities. "I always considered myself a normal American," Albert Okura wrote in his self-published autobiography about his life in the chicken business with his small California franchise, Juan Pollo. He said the franchise race led him to think: "But now I am considered a minority. By the time I entered the management ranks of Burger King I was the only non-Anglo manager in the meetings." His survival strategy, as a second-generation American and son of Japanese internees, was to "go with the flow." Okura concluded, "I can tell people I'm a minority when it is convenient and I can tell others I am a red-blooded American when it is convenient." As a manager in the Burger King system in the 1970s, Okura noticed the dizzying pace of store openings and franchise recruitment. "Burger King owned by the deep pockets of Pillsbury Foods was competing with McDonald's to become the largest chain in America . . . Areas and territories were being snapped up left and right. Corporate executives were jumping ship to buy a franchise." See Albert Okura, *Albert Okura: The Chicken Man with a 50 Year Plan* (Author House, 2014), 28.

35. Carol Kramer, "McDonald's Plans TV Specials," *Chicago Tribune*, August 4, 1967.

36. "Most Chicago Land Values Found Higher," *Chicago Tribune*, June 5, 1973.

37. Yla Eason, "They Invest in Themselves for Fun and Profit," *Chicago Tribune*, June 21, 1973.

38. "Better Boys' Burgers, McDonald's Franchise Nets Profits for Chicago Boys Club," *Ebony*, March 1972.

39. "Better Boys' Burgers."

40. For an excellent treatment on business and gender, which looks at the National Negro Business League and other black organizations, see Tiffany Gill, *Beauty Shop Politics: African American Women's Activism in the Beauty Industry* (Urbana: University of Illinois Press, 2010), and Kevern J. Verney, *The Art of the Possible: Booker T. Washington and Black Leadership in the United States, 1881–1925* (New York: Routledge, 2014).

41. Devin Fergus, *Liberalism, Black Power, and the Making of American Politics, 1965–1980* (Athens: University of Georgia Press, 2009), 200.

42. Robert E. Weems Jr. with Lewis A. Randolph, *Business in Black and White: American Presidents and Black Entrepreneurs in the Twentieth Century* (New York: New York University Press, 2009), 115.

43. Weems, 98.

44. Richard Nixon, Remarks on the CBS Radio Network: "Bridges to Human Dignity, The Concept," April 25, 1968, *The American Presidency Project*, http://www.presidency.ucsb.edu/ws/?pid=123905.

45. "Bridges to Human Dignity."

46. Rachel Devlin, *A Girl Stands at the Door: The Generation of Young Women Who Desegregated America's Schools* (New York: Basic Books, 2018). In Devlin's analysis of school desegregation cases, she notes the ways that legal challenges to segregation masked attempts to draw funding to segregated schools. Megan Ming Francis has traced the relationship between donors and the agenda of the NAACP, and she argues that pressure from funders shifted the civil rights organization's attention from racial violence to education in the early twentieth century. Megan Ming Francis, "The Price of Civil Rights: Black Lives, White Funding, and Movement Capture," *Law & Society Review* 53, no. 1 (2019): 275–309.

47. Mehrsa Baradaran, "A Bad Check for Black America," *Boston Review*, November 9, 2017.

48. Frederick Sturdivant, *The Ghetto Marketplace* (New York: Free Press, 1969), ix–x. See also Anne Fleming, *A City of Debtors: A Century of Fringe Finance* (Cambridge: Harvard University Press, 2018).

49. Under the Economic Opportunity Act of 1964's Title IV, the federal government encouraged low-income citizens to "create or expand" businesses. The Office of Economic Opportunity established thirty-nine centers to work with the Small Business Administration to allocate small loans at modest interest rates. With grants up to $25,000 available, the program also provided guidance and mentorship for the aspiring businesspeople. The Southern Christian Leadership Conference (SCLC) criticized the Johnson administration for favoring investment in

business over people. In a document entitled "A Supplemental Appropriation for the Office of Economic Opportunity, Facts, and a Proposal," the SCLC accused Johnson of steering funding toward business efforts at the expense of "urban programs to fight poverty." The White House decided to support a National Alliance of Businessmen (NAB) program, with use of Office of Economic Opportunity funds that ended supplemental funding for a summer jobs programs for youth. The NAB appropriation also stripped $100 million from the Head Start early-education program, the Neighborhood Youth Corps, and the Job Corps. Supporters of the move said it would help reduce unemployment. But, the SCLC said the proposal was foolhardy in that it would imperil 16 Job Corps Centers, would bar 6,800 people from access to job training, and remove 170,000 low-income youths from Neighborhood Youth Corps programs. Head Start also lost 13,000 slots. "A Supplemental Appropriation for the Office of Economic Opportunity, Facts and a Proposal," undated, King Center Online Archive, http://www.thekingcenter.org/archive/document/supplemental-appropriation-office-economic-opportunity.

50. Sturdivant, xv.
51. Sturdivant, xvii.
52. Sturdivant, 130.
53. Urban historians have chronicled the impact of race on shaping and remaking cities: Arnold Hirsch, *Making the Second Ghetto: Race and Housing in Chicago 1940–1960* (Chicago: University of Chicago Press, 1998); Thomas Sugrue, *The Origins of the Urban Crisis: Race and Inequality in Postwar Detroit* (Princeton: Princeton University Press, 2005); Robert Self, *American Babylon: Race and the Struggle for Postwar Oakland* (Princeton: Princeton University Press, 2003); Becky M. Nicolaides, *My Blue Heaven: Life and Politics in the Working-Class Suburbs of Los Angeles, 1920–1965* (Chicago: University of Chicago Press, 2002); and Richard Rothstein, *The Color of Law: A Forgotten History of How Our Federal Government Segregated America* (New York: Liveright, 2017).
54. For more on white real estate interests and the manipulation of markets, see Nathan Connolly, *A World More Concrete: Real Estate and the Remaking of Jim Crow South Florida* (Chicago: University of Chicago Press, 2014).
55. Sturdivant, xvi.
56. James Forman, "Black Manifesto, To the White Christian Churches and the Jewish Synagogues in the United States of America and All other Racist Institutions," Presentation by James Forman Delivered and Adopted by the National Black Economic Development Conference in Detroit, Michigan, on April 26, 1969, Herzog Race Relations Collection, Box 17, Duke University Library, Durham, NC.
57. Frederick Case, *Black Capitalism: Problems in Development, A Case Study of Los Angeles* (New York: Praeger Publishers, 1972), 5.
58. Case, 9.
59. Case, 9.
60. Case, 47.
61. Case, 50.

62. Andrew F. Brimmer, "The Economic Potential of Black Capitalism," a Paper Presented before the 82nd Annual Meeting of the American Economic Association, New York Hilton Hotel, New York, New York, December 29, 1969, Board of Governors of the Federal Reserve System (U.S.), https://fraser.stlouisfed.org/title/463/item/10372. Accessed on January 6, 2019.

63. Robert Dowling, "Negro Business Leaders Charge Brimmer Is out of Touch with Changing Black Climate," *American Banker*, January 7, 1970. "Ownership Favored, Black Businessmen Hit Brimmer View," untitled newspaper, undated, Dempsey Travis Papers, Box 14, Chicago History Museum Archives Center.

64. Eric Wheelwright, director, *The Brady Keys, Jr. Story*, 2014.

65. *The Brady Keys, Jr. Story*.

66. Max Holleran, "How Fast Food Chains Supersized Inequality," *New Republic*, August 2, 2017.

67. Brady Keys Jr., "I Recommend Blacks Go into Business via the Franchise Route," *Black Enterprise*, May 1974, 28.

68. "I Recommend Blacks Go Into Business via the Franchise Route."

69. "I Recommend Blacks Go Into Business via the Franchise Route." By 1988, Keys held the contracts on 13 Burger Kings in Detroit and 11 Kentucky Fried Chickens in Albany, Georgia, and other parts of the state. Keys expanded his business interests into video games, a computer- and telephone-based educational tutoring service, real estate, and energy production.

70. See Meg Jacobs, *Panic at the Pump: The Energy Crisis and the Transformation of American Politics in the 1970s* (New York: Hill & Wang, 2016).

71. Ernest Holsendolph, "Keeping McDonald's Out in Front," *New York Times*, December 30, 1973.

72. Robert Gordon, "Abernathy Advocates 'Black Socialism': Wants Rich Communities, Not People," *Chicago Defender*, January 9, 1969.

73. Caption to photo of Ralph Abernathy, *Chicago Defender*, April 29, 1969.

Chapter Three: The Burger Boycott and the Ballot Box

1. For more on Cleveland's racial demographics, see Kenneth Kusmer, *A Ghetto Takes Shape: Black Cleveland, 1870–1930* (Urbana: University of Illinois Press, 1978), and Bessie House-Soremekun, *Confronting the Odds: African American Entrepreneurship in Cleveland, Ohio* (Kent, OH: Kent State University Press, 2011).

2. Leonard Moore, *Carl B. Stokes and the Rise of Black Political Power* (Urbana: University of Illinois Press, 2003), 45. See also David Stradling, *Where the River Burned: Carl Stokes and the Struggle to Save Cleveland* (Ithaca: Cornell University Press, 2018).

3. "White Withdrawal: Ghetto Merchants Shy Away from Civic Ties in Areas They Serve," *Wall Street Journal*, August 16, 1977, 1.

4. Kyle Swenson, "How a Mayor's Bold Action Helped Save His City from Burning After MLK's Assassination," *Washington Post*, April 4, 2018, and "Cleveland Mayor Takes to Streets: Stokes Praises His City for Avoiding Racial Disorder," *New York Times*, April 12, 1968.

5. James Robenalt, *Ballots and Bullets: Black Power Politics and Urban Guerilla Warfare in 1968 Cleveland* (Chicago: Chicago Review Press, 2018).

6. John Kramer, "The Election of Blacks to City Councils: A 1970 Status Report and Prolegomenon," *Journal of Black Studies* 1, no. 4 (June 1971): 443–76, and Jon C. Teaford, "'King Richard' Hatcher: Mayor of Gary," *Journal of Negro History* 77, no. 3 (Summer 1992): 126–40.

7. For two examples on local control movements in policing and education, see Tera Agyepong, "In the Belly of the Beast: Black Policemen Combat Police Brutality in Chicago, 1968–1983," *Journal of African American History* 98, no. 2 (2013): 253–76, and Heather Lewis, *New York City Public Schools from Brownsville to Bloomberg: Community Control and Its Legacy* (New York: Teachers College Press, 2013).

8. Keeanga-Yamahtta Taylor, *From #BlackLivesMatter to Black Liberation* (Chicago: Haymarket Press, 2016), 85.

9. "White Withdrawal: Ghetto Merchants Shy Away from Civic Ties in Areas They Serve."

10. Frederick Sturdivant, *The Ghetto Marketplace* (New York: Free Press, 1969), 134.

11. "Operation Breadbasket memo, dated December 12, 1967, Statement by Dr. Martin Luther King, Jr.," Alvin Pitcher Papers, Box 1, Folder 4, University of Chicago Special Collections Research Center.

12. "Breadbasket Technique Called Passé in Cleveland," *Chicago Defender*, February 10, 1968.

13. "Restaurant Chain Will Expand Here," *Cleveland Plain Dealer*, June 12, 1961.

14. "Blacks Picket McDonald's, Demand Negro Ownership," *Cleveland Plain Dealer*, July 11, 1969.

15. "A Minister Finds His Work in the Slum," *Wall Street Journal*, April 10, 1967.

16. For more on the Black Israelites movement and other groups that formed to offer black religious alternatives to Christianity, see Jacob S. Dorman, *Chosen People: The Rise of American Black Israelite Religions* (Oxford: Oxford University Press, 2016).

17. Moore, 120.

18. "Rabbi David Hill Plans Black Xmas," *Call & Post*, November 29, 1969.

19. "In McDonald's Boycott, Leaders Plead Innocent," *Daily Kent Stater*, October 9, 1969.

20. Moore, 121.

21. "The Price of Equality," *Call & Post*, March 30, 1989.

22. "Don't Buy at McDonald's Flyer," undated, Operation Black Unity Records, Box 1, Folder 3, Western Reserve Historical Society, Cleveland, Ohio.

23. "Don't Buy at McDonald's" Flyer.

24. Moore, 123.

25. "McDonald's Moves Franchisees as Fast as Hamburgers," undated press clipping, OBU Papers, Box 1, Folder 4, Western Reserve Historical Society.

26. "Blacks Picket McDonald's, Demand Negro Ownership."

27. "Protestors Request Parley with Head of McDonald's," *Cleveland Plain Dealer*, July 20, 1969.

28. "Two McDonald's Outlets Stay Open Despite Protest," *Cleveland Plain Dealer*, July 16, 1969.

29. Anthony Ripley, "Negroes Continue a Boycott in Ohio: Protest All but Closes Four McDonald's," *New York Times*, July 16, 1969, and Toni Berry, "The Afro Set," *Cleveland Historical*, accessed March 7, 2019, https://clevelandhistorical .org/items/show/777.

30. "Negroes Continue a Boycott in Ohio."

31. "Negroes Continue a Boycott in Ohio."

32. "Unity Group, McDonald's to Parley on Picketing," *Cleveland Plain Dealer*, July 26, 1969.

33. "Unity Group, McDonald's to Parley on Picketing," and "Two McDonald's Outlets Stay Open Despite Protests."

34. Nishani Frazier, *Harambee City: The Congress of Racial Equality in Cleveland and the Rise of Black Power Populism* (Fayetteville: University of Arkansas Press, 2017), 160.

35. "Unity Group, McDonald's to Parley on Picketing," and "Two McDonald's Outlets Stay Open Despite Protests."

36. "Memo Regarding OBU Protests," undated, OBU Papers, Western Reserve Historical Society.

37. "Two McDonald's Outlets Stay Open Despite Protests."

38. "McDonald's to Open in Face of Boycott," *Cleveland Press*, July 11, 1969.

39. "Negroes Continue a Boycott in Ohio: Protest All but Closes Four McDonald's."

40. "Search for Blacks Told by McDonald's," *Cleveland Press*, July 14, 1969.

41. "Search for Blacks Told by McDonald's."

42. "NAACP, Urban League Ask McDonald's to Delay Opening," *Cleveland Press*, August 8, 1969.

43. "McDonald's Rejects Plan for Negro Profit Sharing," *Washington Post*, August 23, 1969.

44. "Gift Question Delays Sale of 4 McDonald's," *Cleveland Press*, August 22, 1969.

45. "McDonald's Offers Swim Pool Aid," *Cleveland Press*, August 28, 1969.

46. "Memorandum from Walker Williams to Philip Mason," dated August 12, 1969, Box 23, Folder 440, Hough Area Development Corporation Papers, Western Reserve Historical Collection, Cleveland, Ohio.

47. Carlotta Washington, "500 at Antioch Meet, Black Unity to Expand Boycott of McDonald's," *Call & Post*, August 30, 1969.

48. "A Negro Protest in Cleveland Ends on Primary Eve," *New York Times*, September 30, 1969.

49. "NAACP, Urban League Ask McDonald's to Delay Opening."

50. "Negroes Continue a Boycott in Ohio: Protest All but Closes Four McDonald's."

51. "McDonald's Is Reopening Four Outlets in Inner City," *Cleveland Plain Dealer*, August 8, 1969.

52. "500 Meet at Antioch."

53. "McDonald's Is Reopening Four Outlets in Inner City."

54. "Black Unity Hit by Urban League," *Cleveland Press*, September 2, 1969.

55. "Hill Ousted as Leader of Black Unity Negotiators," *Cleveland Plain Dealer*, September 9, 1969.
56. "Probes by Jury Urged in McDonald's Dispute," *Cleveland Plain Dealer*, August 23, 1969.
57. "Accord Seen in McDonald's Dispute," *Cleveland Plain Dealer*, August 21, 1969.
58. "Racism Charge Stirs Boycott of McDonald's: Hamburger Hassle Imperils Stokes," *Washington Post*, August 25, 1969.
59. "Kelly Rips Boycott of McDonald's," *Cleveland Press*, September 8, 1969.
60. "Kelly Rips Boycott of McDonald's."
61. "Racism Charge Stirs Boycott of McDonald's."
62. "Stokes Nominated for Second Term in Cleveland Vote: Stokes Nominated for 2d Term as Cleveland Mayor," *New York Times*, October 1, 1969.
63. For more on the HADC and the sale of the McDonald's franchises, see Nishani Frazier, "A McDonald's that Reflects the Soul of the People," in Laura Warren Hill and Julia Rabig, eds., *The Business of Black Power: Community Development, Capitalism, and Corporate Responsibility in Postwar America* (Rochester, NY: University of Rochester Press, 2012).
64. Letter from DeForest Brown to James DiGilio, dated October 27, 1969, Hough Area Development Corporation Records, Box 23, Folder 440.
65. The HADC used a sophisticated mix of financing strategies by accessing federal urban development funds to enter franchising. This model was used to transfer ownership of all the East Side McDonald's locations throughout the 1960s and into the early 1970s. These deals also expanded the portfolio of McDonald's in black neighborhoods from four to six. In the winter of 1969, the Office of Economic Opportunity approved the HADC's acquisition of the East 107th Street McDonald's, but made clear that the OEO was not "the guarantor of the total purchase price," and approved their use of $62,500 from the agency's Venture Capital Fund to acquire the franchise. Letter from Geoffrey Faux to DeForest Brown, dated December 10, 1969, Hough Area Development Corporation Records, Box 23, Folder 440. The remaining funds were secured by a loan of $100,000 to the HADC from Union Commerce Bank. See also "Action of Directors Without a Meeting," undated, Hough Area Development Corporation Records, Box 23, Folder 440. HADC later borrowed $225,000 to acquire the 83rd Street store. McDonald's was happy to allow HADC to franchise the two locations but required that each store install a manager who could hold a 25% stake in the business. See Certification, Hough Area Development Corporation Records, Box 23, Folder 440. In the case of the 107th Street location, the HADC proposed loaning $11,000 to Harry Sykes to manage the restaurant. Using a second mortgage on his house as collateral, Sykes had already invested $12,500 in the 107th Street Corporation. Sykes could not secure traditional bank financing because he had too little of his own money and was a credit risk due to his assuming the franchise and the lease, and he could not find a loan at rates "he could reasonably be expected to meet." HADC decided to provide the loan because they deemed Sykes "uniquely qualified to run the new restaurant." Sykes was

from Cleveland and he had worked at McDonald's for years, climbing his way up from a "$1.50 an hour . . . hamburger dispenser," to a manager at the 83rd Street store. He was so successful in the McDonald's System that he was given a salary of $15,000 per year, a considerable wage by the area's standards. Sykes demonstrated his enthusiasm by enrolling in special training courses and was attending a local college part-time to study business administration. Letter from DeForest Brown to James DiGilio. A short-lived Kinsman Development Corporation took over the franchise agreement of a sixth location in 1971. Headed by Wilson Rogers, a die maker at National Screw and Manufacturing Company, Rogers later owned the Kinsman restaurant outright, but the development company probably helped him secure the $232,500 loan for the store, which was guaranteed by General Motors, the SBA, and a local Cleveland community trust. See "Kinsman Businessmen Buy Area McDonald's," *Call & Post*, November 13, 1971.

66. "McDonald's Says It Asked Hough Corp. to Buy In," *Cleveland Press*, April 7, 1970.

67. "3 Franchise Seekers Say They Paid Nothing to Hill," *Cleveland Press*, September 23, 1969.

68. "Jail Boycott Leader on Blackmail; Pickets Gone but McD Biz Slow," *Restaurant News*, October 27, 1969.

69. "Hill Lost Rights as Incompetent, Judge Declares," *Cleveland Press*, August 11, 1969. See Jonathan Metzl, *The Protest Psychosis: How Schizophrenia Became a Black Disease* (Boston: Beacon Press, 2010), which links the development of antipsychotic drugs, the criminalization and medicalization of black anger, and the development of schizophrenia as a diagnosis commonplace among blacks in Detroit.

70. "Cleveland Negro Wins a Franchise," *New York Times*, January 25, 1970.

71. Robert Morris, "Funds Sought to Save HADC," *Call & Post*, July 24, 1982.

72. "Cleveland Negroes Boycott White-Owned Businesses," *Atlanta Daily World*, March 31, 1970.

73. See Gaiutra Bahadur, "The Jonestown We Don't Know," *New York Review of Books*, December 21, 2018.

74. "Black Boycott's Leader Ends Exile," *Cleveland Plain Dealer*, August 14, 1992; "Cult Leader Awaits Word on Old Blackmail Charges," *Cleveland Plain Dealer*, August 7, 1992; and "Cleveland Fugitive to Leave Guyana Prison," *Cleveland Plain Dealer*, February 9, 1992.

75. "Man Who Fled Cleveland in '71 Returning to the U.S.," *Cleveland Plain Dealer*, August 8, 1992.

76. "Cult Ex-Leader Hill in Guyana for Book," *Cleveland Plain Dealer*, November 1, 1992.

77. "Raplin Honored for Boycott Role," *Cleveland Plain Dealer*, September 25, 1993.

78. "Jim Raplin Remembers His Search for a Pot of Gold for Blacks Behind McDonald's Golden Arches," *Call & Post*, August 23, 1975.

79. "Jim Raplin Remembers His Search for a Pot of Gold for Blacks."

80. Patricia Harris Sowell, *None of Us Is as Good as All of Us: How McDonald's Prospers by Embracing Diversity and Inclusion* (Hoboken, NJ: Wiley, 2009), 44.
81. Harris, 50.

Chapter Four: Bending the Golden Arches

1. "Why Black Enterprise?" *Black Enterprise*, August 1970, 4.
2. "Minority Franchising: Boom or Bust?" *Black Enterprise*, August 1970, 51.
3. Peggy Pascoe, *What Comes Naturally: Miscegenation Law and the Making of Race in America* (New York: Oxford University, 2015).
4. DeNeen L. Brown, "When Portland Banned Blacks: Oregon's Shameful History as an All-White State," *Washington Post*, June 7, 2017.
5. Karen J. Gibson, "Bleeding Albina: A History of Community Disinvestment, 1940–2000," *Transforming Anthropology* 15, no. 1: 3–25.
6. Ethan Johnson and Felicia Williams, "Desegregation and Multiculturalism in the Portland Public Schools," *Oregon Historical Quarterly* 11, no. 1 (Spring 2010): 6–37.
7. "Calm Returns to Fire-Raked Albina District," *Oregonian*, June 19, 1969.
8. Lucas N. N. Burke and Judson L. Jeffries, *The Portland Black Panthers: Empowering Albina, Remaking a City* (Seattle: University of Washington Press, 2016), 60–89.
9. Jakobi Williams, *From the Bullet to the Ballot: The Illinois Chapter of the Black Panther Party and Racial Coalition Politics in Chicago* (Chapel Hill: University of North Carolina Press, 2015).
10. Alondra Nelson, *Body and Soul: The Black Panther Party and the Fight Against Medical Discrimination* (Minneapolis: University of Minnesota Press, 2013), 9.
11. Nelson, 111.
12. The Black Panther Party for Self-Defense was founded in Oakland in 1966 by Bobby Seale and Huey Newton. Donna Murch, "The Campus and the Street: Race, Migration, and the Origins of the Black Panther Party in Oakland," *Souls: A Critical Journal of Black Politics, Culture, and Society* 9, no. 4 (2007): 333–45, and Donna Murch, *Living for the City: Migration, Education, and the Rise of the Black Panther Party in Oakland, California* (Chapel Hill: University of North Carolina Press, 2010). For more on the history of school lunches, see Susan Levin, *School Lunch Politics: The Surprising History of America's Favorite Welfare Program* (Princeton: Princeton University Press, 2010), and A. R. Ruis, *Eating to Learn, Learning to Eat: The Origins of School Lunch in the United States* (Newark: Rutgers University Press, 2017).
13. "Breakfast for School Children Programs Flyer," National Committee to Combat Fascism, Folder 3/5, Black Panther Party Police Records, City of Portland Archives.
14. "Breakfast Clinic Programs Belie Militant Panther Image," *Oregonian*, November 12, 1971.
15. As quoted in Burke and Jeffries, 110.
16. As quoted in Burke and Jeffries, 108.
17. "Breakfast Clinic Programs Belie Militant Panther Image."

18. "Breakfast Clinic Programs Belie Militant Panther Image."

19. "Boycott Flyer," Folder 2/5, Black Panther Party Police Records, City of Portland Archives.

20. "Crowd Storms City Hall to Protest Shooting," *Oregonian*, February 20, 1970.

21. "Intelligence Division Report," dated September 13, 1970, Folder 3/5, Black Panther Party Police Records, City of Portland Archives.

22. "Hamburger's Last Stand: Hidden Costs of Fast Food," *East West Journal*, June 1979, 36.

23. Annelise Orelick, *Storming Caesar's Palace: How Black Mothers Fought Their Own War on Poverty* (Boston: Beacon Press, 2006).

24. "McDonald's Field Report," Folder 2/5, Black Panther Party Police Records, City of Portland Archives.

25. "Officers Report, re: McDonald's Hamburger," dated August 12, 1970, Folder 2/5, Black Panther Party Police Records, City of Portland Archives.

26. "Officers Report."

27. "Officers Report."

28. "Officers Report."

29. "Narrative," dated August 8, 22, 1970, Folder 2/5, Black Panther Party Police Records.

30. "Report of Crime Against Property," dated September 14, 1970, Folder 2/5, Black Panther Party Police Records.

31. "Confidential Detective Division Report, Confidential Informant Note," dated August 18, 1970, Folder 2/5, Black Panther Party Police Records, City of Portland Archives.

32. The Counterintelligence Program was an official FBI initiative between 1956 and 1971 with the explicit intention of keeping tabs on and undermining the work of activist groups. Although COINTELPRO has ceased, state surveillance of activists continues. Betty L. Medsger, *The Burglary: The Discovery of J. Edgar Hoover's Secret FBI* (New York: Vintage, 2014), and David J. Garrow, *The FBI and Martin Luther King, Jr.: From "Solo" to Memphis* (New York: W. W. Norton, 1981).

33. Burke and Jeffries, 131.

34. Nelson, 122.

35. Polina Olse, *Portland in the 1960s: Stories from the Counterculture* (Mount Pleasant, SC: History Press and Arcadia Publishing, 2012).

36. Burke and Jeffries, 181–223.

37. C. Gerald Fraser, "Burger Shop in Harlem Shows It Can Cut the Mustard," *New York Times*, November 11, 1972.

38. Joseph B. Treaster, "White Youths Attack Blacks in Washington Square," *New York Times*, September 9, 1976.

39. "Hamburger's Last Stand," 35.

40. "Hamburger's Last Stand," 35.

41. "Ogontz Neighbors Association Flyer," 1969, and "Philly Black Community Battles to Keep Out McDonald's Unit," undated press clipping, Ogontz Area Neigh-

bors Association Records, Box 3, Folder 5, Temple University Special Collections Research Center, Philadelphia, Pennsylvania.

42. Letter from Kelly E. Miller to Edmund N. Bacon, dated June 27, 1969, Ogontz Neighbors Association Records, Box 3, Folder 6.

43. "Hamburgers vs. Education Flyer," 1963, CORE Chicago Chapter, Congress of Racial Equality Papers (CORE), 1941–1967, Wisconsin Historical Society, Madison, Wisconsin.

44. Letter from Robert Smalls to Paul Rand Dixon, dated July 21, 1970, Ogontz Neighbors Association Records, Box 3, Folder 7.

45. "Petition to Councilman Paul D'Ortona," President of City Council, Ogontz Neighbors Association Records, Box 3, Folder 6.

46. "Residents' Outcry: 'Too Many,'" undated article, Ogontz Neighbors Association Records, Box 3, Folder 6.

47. Letter from Edmund Bacon to Kelly Miller, dated June 23, 1969, Ogontz Neighbors Association Records, Box 3, Folder 5.

48. Maurice White, "McDonald's Restaurant Owner Pushing His Way Up Business Ladder," *Philadelphia Tribune*, December 5, 1978, and "McDonald's Cites Financial Reasons for Ouster of Owner," *Philadelphia Tribune*, October 28, 1983.

49. "Soft Ice Cream Sales Soar as Demand Dips for Regular Variety," *Wall Street Journal*, January 8, 1951.

50. For more on the Freedom Rides, see Raymond Arsenault, *Freedom Rides: 1961 and the Struggle for Racial Justice* (Oxford: Oxford University Press, 2007).

51. U.S. Supreme Court, *Bond v. Floyd*, 385 U.S. 116 (1966).

52. For more on Atlanta and the New South, see Maurice J. Hobson, *The Legend of the Black Mecca: Politics and Class in the Making of Modern Atlanta* (Chapel Hill: University of North Carolina Press, 2017); Jessica Ann Levy, "Selling Atlanta: Black Mayoral Politics from Protest to Entrepreneurism, 1973 to 1990," *Journal of Urban History* 41, no. 3 (May 2015): 420–43; and Beverly Hendrix Wright, "Atlanta: Mecca of the Southeast," in Robert D. Bullard, ed., *In Search of the New South: The Black Urban Experience in the 1970s and 1980s* (Tuscaloosa: University of Alabama Press, 1989). "Blacks Played Major Role in City's Economic Development," *Atlanta Daily World*, August 13, 1978. Clark Rozell, "Auburn's 'Sweet' History," *Atlanta Daily World*, June 17, 1979.

53. "Vet Says He'll Make Good in Business," undated, unsourced article, Julian Bond Papers, Box 116, MSS 13346, University of Virginia Albert and Shirley Small Special Collections Library, University of Virginia.

54. "It's Business—Not Charity," undated article, Julian Bond Papers, Box 116, University of Virginia Special Collections Library.

55. Jon Nordheimer, "Black Atlanta Venture Backfires on Liberals," *New York Times*, June 15, 1970.

56. George S. Schuyler, "Atlanta's Sorcerer's Apprentices," *Macon Herald*, news clipping, Julian Bond Papers, University of Virginia Special Collections Library.

57. T. M. Alexander, "Nothing New," undated clipping, Julian Bond Papers, University of Virginia Special Collections Library.

58. "Bond's Fast Food Business Robbed 15 Times," *Jet*, June 4, 1970, and David Halberstam, *The Children* (New York: Fawcett Books, 1999), 690–94.

59. "Minutes of Special Meeting of Directors," dated June 1, 1970, Julian Bond Papers, University of Virginia Special Collections Library.

60. "Minutes of Special Meeting of Directors."

61. "Minutes of Special Meeting of Directors."

62. Letter from Charles M. Kidd to Julian Bond, Julian Bond Papers, University of Virginia Special Collections Library.

63. "Franchise Route Looks Good for Blacks—Thomas," *Atlanta Inquirer*, February 24, 1973.

64. William Reed, "Saluting a Champion—Businessman Henry Thomas," *Smithsonian*, November 29, 2017.

65. "Sisters Chicken and Biscuits a Hot Item in East Cleveland," *Call & Post*, June 6, 1981, and "Sisters Chicken and Biscuits Coming, Controversy Started," *Call & Post*, May 30, 198.

66. "Sisters Chicken and Biscuits Coming, Controversy Started."

67. Garth Bishop, "Repast from the Past," *City Scene*, October 29, 2013, http://www.cityscenecolumbus.com/eat-and-drink/eat/repast-from-the-past/.

68. For more on the politics of schools in the 1970s, especially community control over education, see Matthew Delmont, *Why Busing Failed: Race, Media, and the National Resistance to School Desegregation* (Oakland: University of California Press, 2016), and for more on the community development movement in the 1970s, see Tom Adam Davies, *Mainstreaming Black Power* (Berkeley: University of California Press, 2017).

Chapter Five: Black America, Brought to You by . . .

1. Gerald R. Ford: "Message on the Observance of Black History Month, February 1976," February 10, 1976. Online by Gerhard Peters and John T. Woolley, *The American Presidency Project*, http://www.presidency.ucsb.edu/ws/?pid=6288.

2. For more on the Bicentennial and public history in the 1970s, see M. J. Rymsza-Pawlowska, *History Comes Alive: Public History and Popular Culture in the 1970s* (Chapel Hill: North Carolina University Press, 2017).

3. "Soul of a Nation: An Illustrated Collection of Historical Narratives Reproduced from McDonald's Special Black Bicentennial Radio Series," 1976, booklet, Andrew J. Young Papers, Box 33, Folder 19, Auburn Avenue Research Library, Atlanta, Georgia.

4. "McDonald's Soul of a Nation."

5. Eric Wheelwright, director, *The Brady Keys, Jr. Story*, 2014.

6. For more on Mahalia Jackson's Glori-Fried Chicken, see Bill Carey, "Failed Fortunes," *Nashville Scene*, September 28, 2000, https://www.nashvillescene.com/news/article/13004920/failed-fortunes, and Bill Carey, *Fortunes, Fiddles, and Fried Chicken: A Business History of Nashville* (Franklin, TN: Hillsboro Press, 2000). ChampBurger's short life was chronicled in many African-American newspapers. See also "Sports of the Times: Foodstuffs," *New York Times*, November

21, 1968, 57; "Ali an Owner of New Negro Drive-In Chain," *Washington Post*, November 21, 1968, H10; "Ali Has $1 Million Hamburger-Stand Deal Grilling: Firm Hops to Franchise Drive-Ins for $10,000," *Philadelphia Tribune*, December 28, 1968; and "Muhammad's Ali's ChampBurgers," *Chicago Defender*, December 21, 1968, 1. James Brown's Gold Platter, despite receiving an investment of $1 million, could not survive. "James Brown Announces 'Gold Platter' Chain of Restaurants," *New York Amsterdam News*, January 18, 1969; "Soul Singer Forms Fast Food Restaurant Chain," *New Pittsburgh Courier*, January 15, 1969; "Soul Singer James Brown Opens 2 Restaurants in His Home Town," *Philadelphia Tribune*, September 2, 1969; and "Jim Brown's Chain Fading," *Baltimore Afro-American*, February 21, 1970.

7. Lisa Napoli, *Ray and Joan: The Man Who Made the McDonald's Fortune and the Woman Who Gave it Away* (New York: Dutton Press, 2016), 10. Mrs. Kroc became known for her contributions to a wide array of liberal and left-leaning causes after Ray's death, and it seemed like her donations were done as much in the spirit of actual generosity as they were declarations of independence from her husband's notable conservativism.

8. Napoli, 10.

9. "McDonald's Hosts Tour," *Call & Post*, July 8, 1972.

10. "Wilson Rogers Has Personal Plan for Affirmative Action," *Call & Post*, June 16, 1973, and "Ground Breaking for McDonald's on Miles," *Call & Post* December 27, 1975.

11. "Hamburger's Last Stand: Hidden Costs of Fast Food," *East West Journal*, June 1979, 30.

12. "McDonald's to Sponsor Double Dutch League," *Atlanta Daily World*, June 14, 1983. For more on the Double Dutch and hand game traditions, see Kyra D. Gaunt, *The Games Black Girls Play: Learning Ropes from Double-Dutch to Hip-Hop* (New York: New York University Press, 2006).

13. "102 Youngsters March in McDonald's Band," *Atlanta Daily World*, December 2, 1979.

14. "Area Youngsters Fitted with Fancy Footwear," *Call & Post*, December 16, 1972.

15. Shuara Wilson, "Inner City McDonald's Restaurant Gets Computer Training Terminal," *Call & Post*, September 15, 1979.

16. U.S. Department of Commerce, Census Bureau, Current Population Survey (CPS), October 1967 through October 2006.

17. "Inner City McDonald's Restaurant Gets Computer Training Terminal."

18. "Chemical Peril Eased in Chicago," *New York Times*, April 28, 1974.

19. Jon Van, "Gas Victims Help Each Other; Kept in Dark, They Assert," *Chicago Daily Tribune*, April 28, 1974; Frank Zahour, "Fume Victims Still Feeling Symptoms," *Chicago Daily Tribune*, May 5, 1974, 22; and "$5.4 million Suit Filed in Gas Leak," *Chicago Tribune*, May 24, 1974.

20. David Smallwood, "Gas Peril Continues," and Lorac Lawas, "Gas Fumes Invade Community," *South End Review*, May 2, 1974.

21. "Big Mac Helped Big Leak Victims," *Chicago Daily Defender*, June 1, 1974.

22. Jason P. Chambers, "A Master Strategist: John H. Johnson and the Develop-

ment of Chicago as a Center for Black Business Enterprise," in Robert E. Weems and Jason P. Chambers, eds., *Building the Black Metropolis: African American Entrepreneurship in Chicago* (Urbana: University of Illinois Press), 191.

23. Chambers, 198, in Weems and Chambers, *Building the Black Metropolis*.

24. Chambers, 198, in Weems and Chambers, *Building the Black Metropolis*.

25. Jason Chambers, *Madison Avenue and the Color Line* (Philadelphia: University of Pennsylvania Press, 2008), 246. See also David Green, "How McDonald's Learned Specific Target Marketing; Ads Show 'They Understand Me; They Get It,'" *Advertising Age*, June 3, 1996.

26. D. Parke Gibson, *$70 Billion in the Black: America's Black Consumers* (New York: Macmillan, 1978), 82.

27. "Commercial Evaluation of Racial Integration, 1977," 5-14, ViewPoint, letter dated November 6, 1977, From ViewPoint, Inc. to Sharon Ray, Needham, Harper and Steers Advertising, Inc, ViewPoint, Inc. Archives, Vivian Harsh Collection, Carter G. Woodson Regional Library, Chicago Public Library.

28. Kelvin Wall, "Positioning Your Brand in the Black Market," *Advertising Age*, June 18, 1973.

29. Chambers, 192, in Weems and Chambers, *Building the Black Metropolis*.

30. Chambers, *Madison Avenue and the Color Line*, 246.

31. *The Negro Family: The Case for National Action*, United States Department of Labor Office of Policy Planning and Research, U.S. Department of Labor, 1965.

32. Chambers, 204, in Weems and Chambers, *Building the Black Metropolis*.

33. "Breakfast: We Do It All for You," McDonald's Advertisement, YouTube, 1978. Accessed January 10, 2019.

34. "Commercial Evaluation of Racial Integration, 1977," letter dated November 6, 1977, from ViewPoint, Inc to Sharon Ray, Needham, Harper and Steers Advertising, Inc, ViewPoint, Inc. Archives, Box 5, Folder 14.

35. Lenika Cruz, "'Dinnertimin' and 'No Tipping': How Advertisers Targeted Black Consumers," *The Atlantic*, June 7, 2015, https://www.theatlantic.com/entertainment/archive/2015/06/casual-racism-and-greater-diversity-in-70s-advertising/394958/; Chris Bodenner, "When Do Multicultural Ads Become Offensive? Your Thoughts," *The Atlantic*, June 22, 2015, https://www.theatlantic.com/entertainment/archive/2015/06/advertising-race-1970s-stereotypes-offensive/395624/; and Code Switch, "Black People Are Not Dark-Skinned White People," National Public Radio, September 5, 2017.

36. "Analysis of McDonald's National Baseline Study for 1974 and for 1977 As It Relates to Black Consumers, 1978," Box 62, Folder 3, Project Reports, Other, Burrell Advertising Analysis of McDonald's National Baseline Study for 1974 and for 1977 as it Relates to Black Consumers, 1978, 62-3, ViewPoint, Inc.

37. McDonald's Advertisement, *Ebony*, November 1984.

38. McDonald's Advertisement, *Ebony*, May 1984.

39. "Hamburger's Last Stand: Hidden Costs of Fast Food," *East West Journal*, June 1979, 35.

40. For more on African Americans on television, see David J. Leonard and Lisa A. Guerrero, eds., *African Americans on Television: Race-ing for Ratings* (New

York: Praeger Press, 2013); Darnell Hunt, *Channeling Blackness: Studies on Television and Race in America* (New York: Oxford University Press, 2004); and Donald Bogle, *Primetime Blues: African Americans on Network Television* (New York: Farrar, Straus & Giroux, 2002).

41. "Good Time, Great Taste," McDonald's Advertisement, YouTube. Accessed January 9, 2019.

42. Author interview with Robert Jackson, March 20, 2017.

43. Amitai Etzioni, "The Fast-Food Factories: McJobs Are Bad for Kids," *Washington Post*, August 24, 1986.

44. Robin Kelley, *Race Rebels: Culture, Politics, and the Black Working Class* (New York: Free Press, 1994), 1–3.

45. "McDonald's, National Baseline Study, 1977, Project Reports, Other, Market Facts, Inc., (13) 63-9" Box 29, ViewPoint, Inc. Archives.

46. John F. Love, *McDonald's: Behind the Arches* (New York: Bantam Press), 204.

47. Love, 295–96.

48. Gibson, 63.

49. Fran Zell, "How Women Shop: Why You Buy What You Buy—and What it All Means," *Chicago Tribune*, September 6, 1970.

50. "McDonald's, National Baseline Study, 1977," and "KFC/Brown's Chicken Taste Test, 1981, Project Reports, Other, Market Facts, Inc., (1) 63-7," Box 29, Folder, ViewPoint, Inc. Archives.

51. "Probe on McDonald's Onion Nuggets," Box 15, Folder 12, ViewPoint, Inc. Archives.

52. Love, 204.

53. Love, 226.

54. "Probe on McDonald's Fish Filet," Box 15, Folder 12, ViewPoint, Inc. Archives.

55. Robert Hayes, *The Black American Travel Guide* (San Francisco: Straight Arrow Books, 1971).

56. "Storyboard for McBeefsteak Ad," Box 22, Folder 12, ViewPoint, Inc. Archives.

57. Paul Ingrassia and David Garno, "Burger Battle: After Their Slow Year, Fast-Food Chains Use Ploys to Speed Up Sales," *Wall Street Journal*, April 4, 1980.

58. Frederick Douglass Opie, *Hog and Hominy: Soul Food from Africa to America* (New York: Columbia University Press, 2010), 86–90, and Psyche Forson-Williams, *Building Houses Out of Chicken Legs: Black Women, Food, and Power* (Chapel Hill: University of North Carolina Press, 2006). For more on soul food, see Adrian Miller, *Soul Food: The Surprising Story of an American Cuisine: One Plate at a Time* (Chapel Hill: University of North Carolina Press, 2013).

59. "A Qualitative Exploration of Black Consumer Attitudes Relative to the McDonald's McChicken Sandwich," prepared for Burrell Advertising, by ViewPoint, Inc., August 1979, Box 16, Folder 12, ViewPoint, Inc. Archives.

60. Forson-Williams, *Building Houses Out of Chicken Legs*, 32.

61. Forson-Williams, 64.

62. "A Qualitative Exploration of Black Consumer Attitudes Relative to the McDonald's McChicken Sandwich," prepared for Burrell Advertising. Naming foods was a delicate issue for other ViewPoint clients. Throughout the late 1970s and

early 1980s, ViewPoint consulted with the three chicken chains on the quality of their side dishes, their advertising campaigns, and the quality of the store experience. Church's lackluster French-frying techniques sunk it with blacks. KFC had to work on the size of their chicken pieces, and Popeyes—despite winning high marks on market testing—had to contend with its attempt to mark itself as a Cajun creation. The use of the word Cajun for Popeyes was a lightning rod for consumers in Louisiana, who were protective of the word's rootedness in their experiences in the South. The participants in a ViewPoint study explained that Popeyes was among their favorite fast food outlets, but they got a few things wrong about what it meant to be Cajun. "Chicken doesn't have anything to do with Cajun." "I like Popeyes identifying with New Orleans but not with Cajun." "It's not right. My mother-in-law is Cajun and she makes fried chicken but it's not Cajun fried chicken." In Popeyes' case, founder Al Copeland was an asset to the black consumer base, because of his popular annual Christmas lights display at his home. Copeland's refusal to bend to pressures from neighbors to stop sharing his home with the throngs of viewers made him a hero in the study. "Church's Fried Chicken, Focus Group II, 1986 (1)," Box 5, Folder 18, ViewPoint Inc. Archives, "Focused Group Interviews with Popeyes Users, Prepared for: Fitzgerald Advertising, New Orleans, La., November, 1984," and "A Qualitative Exploration of Black Consumer Attitudes Toward Popeyes Famous Fried Chicken and Biscuits, November 1984," Box 90, Folder 5, View Point, Inc. Archives.

63. David Chappell, *Waking from the Dream: The Struggle for Civil Rights in the Shadow of Martin Luther King, Jr.* (Durham: Duke University Press, 2016), 92. See also Jacquelyn Dowd Hall, "The Long Civil Rights Movement and the Political Uses of the Past," *Journal of American History,* 91, no. 4: 1233–63.

64. Ray Kroc with Robert Anderson, *Grinding It Out: The Making of McDonald's* (New York: St. Martin's Press, 1977).

65. Chappell, 101.

66. Jimmy Carter, "The State of the Union Annual Message to the Congress, January 21, 1980," The American Presidency Project, University of California–Santa Barbara, http://www.presidency.ucsb.edu/ws/index.php?pid=33062. Accessed January 4, 2019.

67. "Atlanta Airport Home for Dr. King Exhibit," *New York Amsterdam News,* January 31, 1987. For more on the battle to equalize opportunities associated with Hartsfield-Jackson Airport, see Maurice J. Hobson, *The Legend of Black Mecca: Politics and Class in the Making of Modern Atlanta* (Chapel Hill: University of North Carolina Press, 2017).

68. Ben Fiber, "McDonald's Corp. Is Still Eating Up Its Fast Food Rivals," *Globe and Mail,* April 27, 1987.

69. Martin Luther King Jr., "The Three Evils of Society, Address at the National Conference for New Politics, August 31, 1967," Martin Luther King, Jr. Research and Education Institute, Stanford University.

70. "Atlanta Airport Home for Dr. King Exhibit."

71. "Martin Luther King Day Advertisement," *Chicago Weekend,* January 10–13, 1985.

72. Kathy Sawyer, "Atlanta Commemoration Limited by Tight Budget: But Enthusiasm Plentiful for Grand Parade," *Washington Post*, January 12, 1986.

73. "Atlanta Commemoration Limited by Tight Budget."

74. "Atlanta Airport Home for Dr. King Exhibit" and "McDonald's Gears Up for King Celebration," *New York Amsterdam News*, November 2, 1985.

75. "McDonald's to Sponsor Lorraine Hansberry Awards," *Atlanta Daily World*, December 8, 1983.

76. In *Double Negative: The Black Image and Popular Culture* (Durham: Duke University Press, 2018), Raquel J. Gates offers a clever read of the cultural politics of *Coming to America*.

Chapter Six: A Fair Share of the Pie

1. "NAACP Boycotts McDonald's on Coast," *New York Times*, April 11, 1984.

2. Advertisement, *Los Angeles Sentinel*, October 9, 1969. Keith Jones was the first black operator in Los Angeles.

3. Advertisement, *Los Angeles Sentinel*.

4. Don't Give Up Your Right to Vote! *Los Angeles Sentinel*, October 5, 1978. In 1987, NBMOA members donated to Jesse Jackson's presidential campaign in recognition of his service to them. Thirty NBMOA members bundled $22,500 for Jackson's presidential campaign after his appearance at their annual meeting, held in Dallas. Jackson's campaign said that this donation was in support of his efforts "through Operation PUSH to promote economic advancement for minorities." "Black Businessmen Donate $22,500 to Jackson," *New York Times*, December 6, 1987.

5. "Business and People," *Los Angeles Sentinel*, July 4, 1974.

6. "NBMOA Annual Conference Program Booklet, 1984," Records of the National Association for the Advancement of Colored People (NAACP), Part VIII, Folder 338, Library of Congress, Washington, D.C.

7. Tom Adam Davies, *Mainstreaming Black Power* (Berkeley: University of California Press, 2017), 172.

8. In Josh Kun and Laura Pulido, eds., *Black and Brown in Los Angeles: Beyond Conflict and Coalition* (Berkeley: University of California Press, 2013), several of the essays in the volume highlight the Los Angeles chapter of the NAACP's advocacy for Mexican-American interests. Shana Bernstein's *Bridges of Reform: Interracial Civil Rights Activism in Twentieth-Century Los Angeles* (Oxford: Oxford University Press, 2011) emphasizes the branch's role in the 1948 *Shelley v. Kramer* case, in which the Supreme Court ruled that restrictive covenants were unconstitutional. For more on Loren Miller, the branch lawyer who was active in the *Shelley* case among other housing cases, see Kenneth W. Mack, *Representing the Race: The Creation of the Civil Rights Lawyer* (Cambridge: Harvard University Press, 2010). For a general view of Los Angeles and the NAACP, see Douglas Flamming, *Bound for Freedom: Black Los Angeles in Jim Crow America* (Berkeley: University of California Press, 2005).

9. Letter from James T. Jones to Los Angeles Chapter of the NAACP, dated February 11, 1975, Part V: Legal Department, Box 2691, Folder 9, NAACP Records.

10. Letter from James T. Jones to Los Angeles Branch of the NAACP regarding "Violation of Civil Rights."

11. Summons in *Jones v. McDonald's System of California*, dated January 2, 1976, Part V: Legal Department, Box 2691, Folder 9, NAACP Records.

12. Summons in *Jones v. McDonald's System of California*.

13. Judgment in *Jones v. McDonald's System of California*, dated September 24, 1975, Part V: Legal Department, Box 2691, Folder 9, NAACP Records.

14. Letter to Nathaniel Jones from Joseph E. Grimmett, dated March 8, 1976, Part V: Legal Department, Box 2691, Folder 9, NAACP Records.

15. Brad Pye, Jr. "Mayor Joins NAACP Miss. Fund Drive—Save the NAACP!" *Los Angeles Sentinel*, September 23, 1976.

16. "Business and People," *Los Angeles Sentinel*, July 4, 1974.

17. "Jesse Jackson Asked McDonald's for Parity," *Los Angeles Sentinel*, January 26, 1984.

18. "Charles Griffis Appointed to Shorter College Board," *Los Angeles Sentinel*, February 25, 1988.

19. Don Forney opened the first black-owned McDonald's in Detroit in 1969. "Black McDonald's Operators' Association Commemorates 25 Years," *Michigan Chronicle*, November 5, 1997.

20. "Discrimination Charge Hurled, Denied: Black Franchise Owner's Relationship with McDonald's Turns Sour," *Los Angeles Times*, August 12, 1984. "Big Mac Attack: Black Franchisee Charges Bias," *ABA Journal* 70, no. 12 (December 1984): 32. The Santa Barbara Avenue store opened in 1969 and advertised to black readers of the *Los Angeles Sentinel*. "Grand Opening Held for New McDonald's," *Los Angeles Sentinel*, January 30, 1969.

21. Al Copeland established Popeyes in 1972 in a New Orleans suburb. The distinctive, spicy chicken and Cajun style offerings distinguished it from competitors Kentucky Fried Chicken and Church's Chicken. Popeyes began contracting franchises in 1976.

22. "Big Mac Attack: Black Franchisee Charges Bias," 32.

23. "McDonald's Is Battling with Black Franchisee," *New York Times*, March 12, 1984.

24. "Minority Operator Sues McDonald's, Former Trainee Joins In," *Los Angeles Sentinel*, January 12, 1984. Around the same time Griffis initiated his countersuit, Herman V. Christopher Jr. also filed a claim that McDonald's misrepresented the terms of the franchise by charging him twice the agreed upon amount for franchising fees.

25. "McDonald's Faces Contract Fight," *Los Angeles Sentinel*, March 8, 1984.

26. "McDonald's Is Battling with Black Franchisee."

27. "Shootout Rocks McDonald's: Gunfire Rocks Area McDonald's Franchise," *Los Angeles Sentinel*, March 15, 1984.

28. "McDonald's Is Battling with Black Franchisee." Black mayors and mayoral candidates in Cleveland, Los Angeles, New York, and Memphis have all been entangled with McDonald's issues, and they have all paid close attention to local BMOA chapters and their demands. For more on black mayors, see J.

Phillip Thompson, *Double Trouble: Black Mayors, Black Communities and the Call for a Deep Democracy* (Oxford: Oxford University Press, 2005).

29. "McDonald's Faces Contract Fight."

30. "McDonald's Faces Contract Fight."

31. For an analysis of the transition from slave labor to free labor and the gendered ramifications of this process see Tera W. Hunter, *To Joy My Freedom: Southern Black Women's Labor and Lives After the Civil War* (Cambridge: Harvard University Press, 1998), and Amy Dru Stanley, *From Bondage to Contract: Wage Labor, Marriage, and the Market in the Age of Slave Emancipation* (Cambridge: Cambridge University Press, 1998).

32. "McDonald's Loses First Round," *Los Angeles Sentinel*, February 16, 1984.

33. Davies, 183.

34. Davies, 210.

35. Max Boas and Steve Chain, *Big Mac: The Unauthorized Story of McDonald's* (New York: E. P. Dutton, 1976), 159–60.

36. Boas and Chain, 161.

37. Boas and Chain, 70.

38. "McDonald's Is Battling with Black Franchisee."

39. Jube Shiver, Jr., "Discrimination Charge Hurled, Denied: Black Franchise Owner's Relationship with McDonald's Turns Sour," *Los Angeles Times*, August 12, 1984, E3.

40. "Black Boycott Unfair, McDonald's Says," *Montreal Gazette*, April 12, 1984.

41. "Discrimination Charge Hurled, Denied."

42. Ange-Marie Hancock, *The Politics of Disgust: The Public Identity of the Welfare Queen* (New York: New York University Press, 2004).

43. "McQueen of the Golden Arches," *Black Enterprise*, September 1987, 64–69.

44. "NAACP Boycotts McDonald's on Coast," *New York Times*, April 11, 1984.

45. "A Crumbling Legacy: The Decline of African American Insurance Companies in Contemporary America," *Review of Black Political Economy* 23, no. 2 (Fall 1994): 25.

46. "3 Firms to Get Major McDonald's Contracts," *New York Amsterdam News*, December 17, 1983.

47. "PUSH Announces Anheuser-Busch Boycott," *Pittsburgh Courier*, October 2, 1982.

48. "Black Promoters Join Bud Boycott," *Chicago Independent Bulletin*, February 17, 1983, Harold Washington Archives and Collections, Development Sub-Cabinet, Box 20, Folder 3, Harold Washington Library Center Special Collections, Chicago Public Library, and "Promoters Join Brewery Boycott," *New York Amsterdam News*, February 26, 1983.

49. "Jackson: Busch Using King's Dream," *Philadelphia Tribune*, February 18, 1982.

50. "Operation PUSH Calls Off Boycott of Anheuser-Busch," *Afro-American*, September 17, 1983.

51. "Turnout Small at King Memorial," *Chicago Sun-Times*, April 15, 1983.

52. David Chappell, *Waking from the Dream: The Struggle for Civil Rights in the Shadow of Martin Luther King, Jr.* (New York: Random House, 2014), 125–27.

53. "NAACP, Coors Set Plan," *Los Angeles Sentinel*, April 10, 1984.
54. "Advertisement," *Los Angeles Sentinel*, May 10, 1984.
55. "NAACP Halts 3-Day McDonald's Boycott," *Los Angeles Times*, April 14, 1984.
56. "Advertisement," May 10, 1984.
57. "Big Mac Attack: Black Franchisee Charges Bias."
58. "McBias Case Over: Burger Chain, Operator Settle," *ABA Journal* 71, no. 1 (January 1985): 25.
59. Tamar Lewin, "McDonald's Dispute on Coast," *New York Times*, November 9, 1984.
60. "Chicken Charlie's Coupon Special, Great Food Bargain," *Los Angeles Sentinel*, January 28, 1988.
61. "NAACP Bids Reagan Meet with its Leaders," *New York Times*, February 17, 1985.
62. "NAACP Works for L.A. Gains at McDonald's," *New York Times*, February 19, 1985.
63. "Black McDonald's Franchisees Address Economic Development," *Los Angeles Sentinel*, October 26, 1989. The Griffis case was not the last claim about racial discrimination and franchisees in the fast food world. Throughout the ensuing decades, McDonald's franchisees of color have continued to call into question how McDonald's manages potential franchise locations. A 2000 case involving Deborah Sonnenschein also involved a local chapter of the NAACP. Sonnenschein, who stated she had worked for McDonald's her entire adult life, claimed that McDonald's opened several competing stores near her four outlets, and that this move was emblematic of discriminatory practices toward black franchisees. The case was originally a lawsuit based on unfair market practices, but evolved into a racial one after Sonneschein's attorneys collected data about similar problems felt by other black franchisees. "Black Owner Spars with McDonald's," *Chicago Tribune*, December 28, 2002.

Chapter Seven: The Miracle of the Golden Arches

1. "The Multiracial Nature of Los Angeles Unrest in 1992," in Kwang Chung Kim, ed., *Koreans in the Hood: Conflict with African Americans* (Baltimore: Johns Hopkins University Press, 1999), 24–26.
2. "McDonald's," *PR Newswire*, May 1, 1992.
3. Patricia Sowell Harris, *None of Us Is as Good as All of Us: How McDonald's Prospers by Embracing Diversity and Inclusion* (Hoboken, NJ: Wiley, 2009), 72.
4. Brenda Stevenson, *The Contested Murder of Latasha Harlins: Justice, Gender, and the Origins of the LA Riots* (Oxford: Oxford University Press, 2013), 299.
5. Carol Byrne, untitled article, *Star Tribune*, March 21, 1993.
6. James V. Grimaldi, "Cleanup, Outsiders Turn Out to Pitch in," *Orange County Register*, May 3, 1992, and Jenna Chandler, Adrian Glick Kudler, and Bianca Barragan, "Mapping the 1992 L.A. Uprising," April 30, 2018, LaCurbed.com, https://la.curbed.com/maps/1992-los-angeles-riots-rodney-king-map.
7. "Rainbow of Anger, Decades of Rage at the Root of Tumult in South-Central Los Angeles," *Fort Lauderdale Sun Sentinel*, May 3, 1992.

8. David Leon Moore and Maria Goodavage, "Crisis in L.A," *USA Today*, May 1, 1992.

9. Susan Campbell, "Untitled," *Hartford Courant*, July 7, 1992.

10. National Black McDonald's Operators Association, "NBMOA Video," Larry Tripplett interview transcript, 15–16.

11. Jacques Kelly, "Theodore Holmes, Founder of Chicken George Restaurant Chain," *Washington Post*, December 8, 2011.

12. "Guts, Spice, and Integration: A Recipe for One Man's Success," *Washington Post*, April 3, 1983.

13. For more on *Roots*, see Matthew F. Delmont, *Making Roots: A Nation Captivated* (Oakland: University of California Press, 2016), and Erica L. Ball and Kellie Carter Jackson, eds., *Reconsidering Roots: Race, Politics, and Memory* (University of Georgia Press, 2017).

14. "Chicken George: Triumph and Disappointment," *Baltimore Sun*, March 1, 1987.

15. "Guts, Spice, and Integration: A Recipe for One Man's Success."

16. Sam Fulwood III, "Running off Power of One Man's Charisma, Food Empire Falters," *Baltimore Sun*, March 2, 1987.

17. Eric Harrison, "Once-Radical Group Now Is the System," *Philadelphia Inquirer*, June 23, 1985.

18. "Chicken George's D.C. Roots," *Black Enterprise*, February 1982, 28.

19. "Advertising Accounts," *Daily Oklahoman*, March 5, 1984.

20. Tim Chavez, "Chicken George Picks Oklahoma to Expand Chain," *Daily Oklahoman*, January 4, 1983.

21. "Chicken George's D.C. Roots." See also "Theodore Holmes," *Ebony*, August 1983, 162.

22. "Running off Power of One Man's Charisma, Food Empire Falters."

23. "Running off Power of One Man's Charisma, Food Empire Falters."

24. "Kentucky Fried Chicken Launches Hip New Restaurants in D.C. and Baltimore," *PR Newswire*, April 8, 1993.

25. Jennifer Lin, "Pecking Order—Fried Chicken Outlets Staking Out Turf," *Philadelphia Inquirer*, April 19, 1984; and "Chicken George: Triumph and Disappointment."

26. "Theodore Holmes, Founder of Chicken George Restaurant Chain."

27. Pizza Hut Commercial, undated, YouTube. Accessed January 11, 2019.

28. Trudy Gallant-Stokes, "Franchisee of the Year: Brady Keys Does Franchising Right," *Black Enterprise*, September 1988, 56.

29. Marc Rice, "A Taste of Life Outside the Ghetto," *Chicago Sun-Times*, September 6, 1994.

30. "La-Van Hawkins' Future Plans Will Still Involve Lots of Food: The Checkers Man," *Afro-American Red Star*, February 17, 1997.

31. Robert A. Mofitt, "From Welfare to Work: What the Evidence Shows" (Washington, D.C.: Brookings Institution), January 2, 2002. See also Barbara Ehrenreich, *Nickel and Dimed: On (Not) Getting By in America* (New York: Picador, 2011); Katherine Newman, *No Shame in My Game: The Working Poor in the Inner City* (New York: Vintage, 2000); and Joseph Shapiro and Barbara Murray,

"Fast Food and Welfare Reform: Success of the Effort May Hinge on 'Dead-End Burger' Flipping-Jobs," *U.S. News & World Report*, August 18–25, 1997.

32. For more on the War on Drugs, see Michelle Alexander, *The New Jim Crow: Mass Incarceration in the Age of Colorblindness* (New York: New Press, 2010), and Elizabeth Hinton, *From the War on Poverty to the War on Crime: The Making of Mass Incarceration in America* (Cambridge: Harvard University Press, 2016).

33. Larry Copeland, "Foes: Checkers Should Check Out: The Chain Disrespected the Girard Avenue District, Critics Say," *Philadelphia Inquirer*, December 31, 1993.

34. United States Department of Housing and Urban Development, "List of Current Empowerment Zones and Updated Contact Information," 2013.

35. William J. Clinton: "Remarks to the White House Conference on Empowerment Zones," *Public Papers of the Presidents of the United States*, January 1 to June 30, 1996.

36. Chin Jou, *Supersizing Urban America: How the Federal Government Created the Obesity Crisis* (Chicago: University of Chicago Press, 2017), 139.

37. "Clinton: $3.5 for Empowerment Zones," *Time*, December 21, 1994.

38. United States Department of Housing and Urban Development, *Spotlight on Results: Capturing Successes in Renewal Communities and Empowerment Zones* (U.S. Department of Housing and Urban Development, 2015), 40, 68.

39. T. Trent Gegax, "Burger King Plans Inner-City Venture," *Washington Post*, February 22, 1996, and Peter Behr, "Fast Food Tracker," *Newsweek*, May 25, 1997.

40. "Fast Food Tracker."

41. "Keeping the Faith," *Christian Science Monitor*, November 2, 1998.

42. Donna DeMarco, "Hawkins Leaving Town," *Baltimore Business Journal*, November 23, 1998.

43. "Black Agents Sue Denny's," *New York Times*, May 25, 1993.

44. "KFC About to Be Skinned?" *Michigan Chronicle*, July 16, 1997.

45. Alexei Barrionuevo, "Franchising Hope: Chain Outlets Offer Promise as Seeds for Inner-City Development," *Los Angeles Times*, February 3, 1993.

46. Staci Bush, "Bias in the Chicken? Former Kentucky Fried Chicken (KFC) African American Employees Along with Franchise Holders," *Sacramento Observer*, November 23, 1994.

47. "Burger King Corporation Announces Update on Legal Proceedings with La-Van Hawkins, Urban City Foods," *PR Newswire*, May 2000.

48. "Restaurateur on Way to Prison Is Sued by Franchiser," *Chicago Tribune*, December 22, 2007.

49. "Ex-BK Franchisee Gets 'Sweet New Start,'" *Nation's Restaurant News*, July 8, 2002.

50. Nichole M. Christian, "A Model Partnership for Inner-City Renewal, Derailed," *New York Times*, May 14, 2000.

51. Adrian Sanz, "Sharpton Calls for Burger King Boycott," *Philadelphia Tribune*, September 12, 2000.

52. Jack Newfield, "Rev. vs. Rev.," *New York Magazine*, January 7, 2002.

53. "Franchise Acceptance Corporation, $8.4 Million," *PR Newswire*, New York, December 2000.

54. "Burger King Loses Round One in $1.9 Billion Lawsuit, Announces Attorney Willie Gray," *PR Newswire*, New York, September 27, 2000.

55. "Ex-BK Franchisee Gets 'Sweet New Start.'"

56. "La-Van Hawkins Linked to Philadelphia Corruption Probe," *Black Enterprise*, September 1, 2004.

57. "Local Restaurateur Serving Time for Fraud Accused of Fraud," *Chicagoist*, January 8, 2008, http://chicagoist.com/2008/01/08/local_restaurat.php.

58. Susan Saluny, "Detroit Mayor Pleads Guilty and Resigns," *New York Times*, September 4, 2008.

59. "Convictions of Corey Kemp, Four Others Upheld," *Bond Buyer*, August 29, 2007.

60. La-Van Hawkins, "LaVan Hawkins on *American Entrepreneur*," interview by Ed Foxworth, *American Entrepreneur*, YouTube video, at 4:03–5:02, https://youtu.be/xcH0z7tLJ94.

61. "Chicago Chicken and Waffles Owners Sue Former Partner," *Austin Weekly News*, December 14, 2011.

62. In the late 2010s, Hawkins produced another local advertisement for his new venture, a Krispy Krunchy Chicken in Detroit. The ad reminded viewers that they were probably familiar with Hawkins from his "hundreds" of Burger Kings and Pizza Huts, "as well as Georgia Brown's." In 2017, Hawkins was part of a new effort, the Boaz Group, and tried to make a move toward purchasing the Ruby Tuesday restaurant, which chose a private equity group instead. "Ruby Tuesday Publicly Rejects, Criticizes New Offer for Company," *USA Today*, December 18, 2017.

63. Annalise Frank, "Onetime Metro Detroit Fast Food Mogul, Restaurateur La-Van Hawkins Dies," *Crain's Detroit Business*, April 10, 2019.

64. Margaret K. Webb, "'Magic Johnson' to Buy Stakes in Pepsi's D.C.-Area Bottler," *Washington Post*, July 21, 1990.

65. "Our History," Magic Johnson Enterprises, http://www.magicjohnson.com/company.

66. Bryant Simon, "'A Down Brother': Earvin 'Magic' Johnson and the Quest for Retail Justice in Los Angeles," *Boom: A Journal of California* 1, no. 2 (Summer 2011): 43–58.

67. United States Public Health Service, *Surgeon General's Health and Nutrition Report*, 1988.

68. Nancy Luna, "McDonald's and NLRB Reach Settlement in Joint-Employer Case," *Nation's Restaurant News*, March 20, 2018. Michelle Chen, "Trump's Labor Board Is Making It Even More Difficult to Unionize Fast-Food Workers," *The Nation*, February 9, 2018.

69. Bethany Moreton, *To Serve God and Wal-Mart: The Making of Christian Free Enterprise* (Cambridge: Harvard University Press, 2009), 99.

70. "Commercial Real Estate: Seeking Customers in a Blighted Area," *New York Times*, February 12, 2013.

71. William Booth and Jeff Adler, "Los Angeles Looks Back at Riots," *Washington Post*, April 28, 2002.

72. "In Wake of LA Riots, Industry Must Do Its Part for Inner Cities," *Nation's Restaurant News*, May 25, 1992.

73. Dean E. Murphy, "Former Gang Members, Minister Call for Jobs to Keep Post-Riot Truce," *Los Angeles Times*, August 9, 1995.

74. "Franchising Hope: Chain Outlets Offer Promise as Seeds for Inner-City Development."

75. Melissa Chadburn, "The Destructive Force of Rebuild LA," *Curbed Los Angeles*, April 27, 2018, https://la.curbed.com/2017/4/27/15442350/1992-los-angeles-riots-rebuild-la.

76. Andrea Maier, "Black-Owned Beauty Salons Hurt by Riots," *Los Angeles Times*, July 2, 1992.

77. Daniel Wood, "Diet-Conscious Los Angeles Eyes Moratorium on Fast-Food Outlets," *Christian Science Monitor*, September 13, 2007.

78. Timothy Weaver, "Elite Empowerment," *Jacobin* 29 (Spring 2018).

79. William Yardley, "Peter Hall, Who Devised the Enterprise Zone, Dies at 82," *New York Times*, August 6, 2014.

80. "Black Banks Can't Fix Racial Capitalism," *Public Books*, June 8, 2018. For more on racial capitalism, see Donna Murch, ed., *Racial Capitalism in the Age of Trump* (Cambridge: Massachusetts Institute of Technology Press, 2019), and Cedric Robinson, *Black Marxism: The Making of the Black Radical Tradition* (Chapel Hill: University of North Carolina Press, 1983).

81. Chris Ying, "The Los Angeles Fast Food Revolution," *The Guardian*, February 21, 2016.

82. "The Los Angeles Fast Food Revolution."

83. Justin Phillips, "LocoL Closes Uptown Oakland Location," *San Francisco Chronicle*, June 25, 2017.

84. Monica Burton, "LocoL Isn't Making a Lot of Money—but Roy Choi Says That's Okay," Eater.com, September 29, 2017, https://www.eater.com/2017/9/29/16384706/locol-business-model-roy-choi.

85. "The Los Angeles Fast Food Revolution," and Hillary Dixler Canavan, "The LocoL Revolution Is on Hold," Eater.com, August 24, 2018, https://www.eater.com/2018/8/24/17770792/locol-roy-choi-daniel-patterson-closing-watts-san-jose-rip.

Conclusion: Bigger than a Hamburger

1. Tracy Jan, "Four Years After Michael Brown Was Shot by Police, the Neighborhood Where He Was Killed Still Feels Left Behind," *Washington Post*, June 21, 2018.

2. Carol Anderson, *White Rage: The Unspoken Truth of Our Racial Divide* (New York: Bloomsbury, 2015), 3.

3. Naomi Klein, *The Shock Doctrine: The Rise of Disaster Capitalism* (New York: Metropolitan Books, 2007), 14–15.

4. Food studies scholar Kyla Tompkins makes the point: "No matter how many kale salads Starbucks puts in their case, Starbucks is a fast-food purveyor." The

latte, she argued, "is a high-calorie food that's being pushed in an industrialized way largely to working-class people." And, she added, "it's important to think about the explosion of all of these industrialized lattes, all these frozen lattes, all the Frappuccinos, as links to a larger problem of creating cheap, high-calorie, low-nutrition food for working-class people." She continued, "How does the symbolism of a thing get dislodged from the ways in which it's actually used and actually consumed? What is that except another way in which we're stopped from really looking at what problems actually exist?" Anna North, "If You Read This, You Might Never Drink a Latte Again," *New York Times*, July 10, 2014. Jonathan Metzl's research on whites and health argues that despite imperiling white health and life expectancy, some white voters still support detrimental policies in order to maintain their sense of racial superiority and power. Jonathan Metzl, *Dying of Whiteness: How the Politics of Racial Resentment Is Killing America's Heartland* (New York: Basic Books, 2019).

5. Michael Pollan, *The Omnivore's Dilemma: A Natural History of Four Meals* (New York: Penguin, 2007), 113.

6. Alison Alkon and Julie Guthman, eds., *The New Food Activism: Opposition, Cooperation, and Collective Action* (Oakland: University of California Press, 2017).

7. Ella J. Baker, "Bigger than a Hamburger," *Southern Patriot* 18 (1960).

INDEX

Page numbers in *italics* indicate photographs. Page numbers followed by *n* indicate notes.